The Privatisation of Higher Education in Postcolonial Bangladesh

This book problematises contemporary realities of the political dimension of the privatisation of higher education in Bangladesh. By exploring the complexities of neoliberalism as an economic and ideological doctrine, a mode of governance, and as a policy package, it considers the 'post' attached to and hyphenated with 'colonialism' as more aspirational than achieved. Based on an interdisciplinary study involving contemporary theories from political and social sciences, economics, and the socio-economics of education, this book explores the unique ways in which Bangladeshi higher education has evolved over the past four decades, and the complex politics behind its privatisation. Through an empirically based account of how neoliberalism has worked its way through the higher education sector in the fastest growing economy in the South Asian context, it discusses how changes have been characterised by policy reforms, massification, and a sustained friction between control and autonomy in the university sector.

The authors take a nuanced approach to their geo-political and onto-epistemological positionalities as diasporic and hybridised scholars by rejecting epistemological exclusion inherent in the colonial present and research conducted in such contexts. This position allows the reinforcement of a colonial present, theorising from within Global South *de*colonial and postcolonial research literature.

This book contributes to discourses of 'globalisation from above' and 'globalisation from below' and sheds light on the often-idiosyncratic ways in which higher education reform has unfolded in South Asia. It will be of interest to comparative educators and those researching higher education policy and education developments in Global South nations.

Ariful H. Kabir teaches sociology of education and teacher education in the Institute of Education and Research at the University of Dhaka. He has Masters degrees in Sociology and in Education and a PhD in Education, and researches into micro-politics, network governance and education policy formulation, critical pedagogy, teacher education, higher education and international education.

Raqib Chowdhury teaches TESOL, bilingualism and sociolinguistics in the Faculty of Education at Monash University. He has Masters degrees in English Literature and in TESOL, a PhD in Education, and researches into culture and pedagogy, teacher education, TESOL, international education, identity and critical ethnography.

Routledge Critical Studies in Asian Education
Series Editors: S. Gopinathan, Wing On Lee and Jason Eng Thye Tan

Building Teacher Capacity in Vietnamese English Language Teaching
Research, Policy and Practice
Edited by Van Canh Le, Hoa Thi Mai Nguyen, Thi Thuy Minh Nguyen, Roger Barnard

Is it Time to Let Meritocracy Go?
Examining the Case of Singapore
Nadira Talib

Localizing Global English
Asian Perspectives and Practices
Edited by Hikyoung Lee and Bernard Spolsky

Internationalization of Teacher Education and the Nation State
Rethinking Nationalization in Singapore and Beyond
Rita Z. Nazeer-Ikeda

Education and Social Justice in Japan
Kaori H. Okano

The Privatisation of Higher Education in Postcolonial Bangladesh
The Politics of Intervention and Control
Ariful H. Kabir and Raqib Chowdhury

Tamils, Social Capital and Educational Marginalization in Singapore
Labouring to Learn
Lavanya Balachandran

For more information about this series, please visit: www.routledge.com/Routledge-Critical-Studies-in-Asian-Education/book-series/RCSAE

The Privatisation of Higher Education in Postcolonial Bangladesh

The Politics of Intervention and Control

Ariful H. Kabir and Raqib Chowdhury

Routledge
Taylor & Francis Group
LONDON AND NEW YORK

The HEAD Foundation

First published 2021
by Routledge
2 Park Square, Milton Park, Abingdon, Oxon OX14 4RN

and by Routledge
605 Third Avenue, New York, NY 10158

Routledge is an imprint of the Taylor & Francis Group, an informa business

British Library Cataloguing-in-Publication Data
A catalogue record for this book is available from the British Library

Library of Congress Cataloging-in-Publication Data
A catalog record has been requested for this book

ISBN: 978-0-367-21871-3 (hbk)
ISBN: 978-1-032-00072-5 (pbk)
ISBN: 978-0-429-26660-7 (ebk)

Typeset in Galliard
by Taylor & Francis Books

Dedicated to my father – Md Dabir Uddin
and my daughter – Shiesta A. Kabir
– first author

Dedicated to my mother – Dr Jahanara Chowdhury
– second author

Contents

Tables

Preface

Positioning ourselves in the study

> Neoliberalism … is not just a question of economy but a new form of civilization. The impossibility or lack of credibility of universal or world histories today is not advanced by some influential postmodern theory, but by the economic and social forces generally referred to as globalization and by the emergence of forms of knowledge that have been subalternized under … modern colonialisms and colonial modernities.
>
> (Mignolo, 2012, p. 22)

When a study situates itself within a postcolonial framework of understanding, it becomes important to explain how authors position themselves within the study (Lingard, 2009). Positionality of the researcher in this context refers to the "spatial location of the researcher, specifically national location, and the positioning of that nation in respect of global geopolitics, including location within the Global North/Global South divide" (Lingard, 2009, p. 229). In this preface, we therefore briefly explain how our onto-epistemological as well as geo-political positions originated from and have been influenced by both Global South and Global North contexts within which we are both situated. While these positions can facilitate unique critical insights, we acknowledge that they can also be problematic in some ways. The brief biographical notes in this preface intend to humanise our positioning as diasporic scholars with Bangladeshi origins yet those who are currently working within the conceptual confines of what is known as the Global North.

First, we both share a common journey of having had the privileged opportunity to have studied and taught in Bangladesh and Australia. In particular, along with our schooling and education in different institutes in Bangladesh, both of us earned our first degrees from the University of Dhaka, Bangladesh, and our doctorates from Monash University, Australia. Along with sharing such educational experiences from the same universities in the two socioeconomically different countries, the first author has studied and worked intensively with scholars in New Zealand and Australia, and is currently involved in teaching sociology of education and teacher education at the Institute of Education and Research at the University of Dhaka, Bangladesh. Likewise, the second author taught literature, including postcolonial literature (in the 90s, at a time – notably – when it was labelled "third world literature" – see Spivak, 1990) in the Department of English at the

University of Dhaka, as well as in countries such as Vietnam, Indonesia and Brunei, and is currently teaching in the Faculty of Education, Monash University. Our individual and collective educational and professional experiences thus mean that as intellectual beings, we have travelled, spatiotemporally and intellectually, across different times and spaces and have absorbed, contested and negotiated with myriad discourses from both the Global South and North contexts over a period of more than two decades. This has inevitably imbibed in us certain discursive positions which we speak from, discourses that have influenced, consciously or unconsciously, our understanding of the processes under this study.

Second, we acknowledge and keep in mind that we are both socioeconomically and culturally privileged, Western-educated, male, Bangladeshi-Australians of a certain age, living and working in the first quarter of the twenty-first century. Given the topic of the politics of privatisation of higher education, our ontological and epistemological location as researchers in the Global South, undertaking this study on their country of origin in the Global South, yet perhaps in many ways economically and culturally aligned with the Global North, is therefore an important critical dimension for the reader to keep in mind. This study is a reflection of the critical sensitivities that we both embody as residents, citizens, educators and researchers who are located in all the aforementioned contextual particulars.

To overcome the complex tensions of thus representing both the Global South and in the Global North, we have integrated our divergent identities to construct what Bhabha (1994) calls 'hybridity' in fine-tuning our analysis as we attempt to understand the politics of the privatisation of higher education in Bangladesh. More specifically, being researchers from the Global South, we understood the historical and political processes of introducing the British education system in Bangladesh and its potential effects on the current higher education policy formation process from the first-hand experiences of growing up in Bangladesh. We therefore, for example, understand nation states as "firmly established in the horizon of coloniality" (Mignolo, 2012, p. 16), as we explain below. Our lived experiences of historical and political antecedents help us frame our understanding of the power relations between the coloniser and colonised, and the complexities of the power relations between the Global North and the Global South, and the influence of various interest groups in the development of privatisation policies in Bangladesh.

Then again, the reference to postcolonialism in the title of the book is problematic. Such as term is not just connotatively loaded and inconclusively contestable but understood differently through different critical lenses. We have therefore kept in mind that not only is the geopolitics of knowledge (Mignolo, 2002) important, but that colonialism has morphed in various ways into current times and has changed social relations in major ways. For example, although the British colonisers left the Subcontinent in 1947 and Bangladesh became independent from Pakistan in 1971, for the indigenous minorities of Bangladesh, the country today continues to be colonialised by majority Bengali Muslims. As we unpack the 'postcoloniality' of current day Bangladesh in relation to power politics in private sector higher education, we keep this frame in mind.

Rather than understanding colonialism in a purely linear-historical sense, we adopt what Mignolo (2007) calls the "coloniality of power", and "de-colonial thinking" that allow us to capture and explain the "simultaneous histories" which are "inter-connected by imperial and colonial powers, by imperial and colonial differences" (pp. 155–156). Mignolo (2007) argues that modernity cannot be understood without coloniality, because coloniality is *constitutive* of modernity. In fact, modernity (in our case, the various manifestations of globalisation and neo-liberal practices) tends to hide coloniality because the latter can symbolise oppression and exploitation, although both have embedded instruments of control such as capitalism: "the rhetoric of modernity and the logic of coloniality … relate to the control of economy and control of authority" (p. 163).

Mignolo (2012, p. 6) also talks about the "border thinking" and "border gnoseology" of colonial knowledge which explain the forms of knowledges that originate from the discourses of modern forms of colonialisms (in our case, pro-globalisation doctrines and neoliberal rationales), as much as from the discourses that originate from the histories of former colonies. For Mignolo, this is how "hegemonic forms of knowledge" (such as policies from international financial institutes and government machineries) can be appropriated by subaltern discourses. By exposing the knowledges and discourses that have been subalternised through the processes of colonisation, this book, then, provides counter-discourses to what Mignolo calls the "colonial subalternization of knowledge" (p. 12) which legitimises the colonial difference.

Finally, in explaining the colonial matrix of power, Peruvian sociologist Quijano (2000) describes four interrelated domains: control of economy through appropriation of land, exploitation of labour and control of natural resources; control of authority through state institutions and the armed forces; control of gender and sexuality through education and family structures; and finally the control of knowledge and subjectivity, through formal education structures and the curriculum. The duality of the neoliberal mindset in Bangladesh which we describe in the first chapter can be explained through this last domain, the "coloniality of knowledge" (p. 533), which is *re*produced through residual coloniality (Chowdhury & Kabir, 2014, p. 4) in the current education system that has outlived the historical colonial power structures since the 1947 British exit.

In keeping this sensitivity in mind, therefore, during interviewing and documents analysis, we emphasised the importance of understanding whether policy actors identified privatisation as a 'taken-for-granted' feature of modernity and modern times, or as Appadurai (2000, p. 3) says, privatisation from "below". We found that a significant number of policy actors had conceptualised privatisation and neoliberalism as somewhat 'natural' ways of understanding policy problems in the contemporary higher education sector; but they also considered the socio-political and economic factors in neoliberal policy development. For instance, one policy actor stated that although the idea of a 'cost-sharing' approach was being used in the financing of universities in many Western countries, in Bangladesh it was necessary to adapt it by considering the local socio-political and economic contexts in which the government needed to reduce costs. The ways in which participants engaged in the interviews also indicated that our 'hybrid' identities were not becoming predominant positions and influenced the interview processes of the participants. Rather, it was a privilege for us to be able to use our hybridised identities to critically understand whether policy actors were 'politicking' their perceptions or went through the 'authentic' processes in their involvements during the privatisation of higher education in Bangladesh.

To conclude, we are aware that theories we have adopted in this study might still represent the predominance of white, Anglo, male voices. However, our analysis attempts to look beyond such privileged positions by bringing in alternative voices from the Global South. This would include contemporary Southern scholars such as Ong, Naidoo, Sindhu, Mignolo and Quijano. Throughout the analysis in this book we have kept in mind this sensitivity and it is our intention and hope that readers will keep in mind an awareness of our positioning while engaging with the book.

Foreword

Researching postcolonial higher education

Arif H. Kabir and Raqib Chowdhury's *The Privatisation of Higher Education in Postcolonial Bangladesh* is a very welcome addition to the research literature on higher education in nations of the Global South, specifically here, Bangladesh. This is the first study of its kind focused on the privatisation of Bangladeshi higher education. Amongst may other things, this book provides an exemplary account of the ways the positioning of researchers frames the collection and analysis of data in the social sciences. While the authors suggest such articulation of researcher positionality is necessary in research framed by a postcolonial disposition, I would argue that all social science research must reject epistemological innocence, and thus needs to make public researcher positionality to strengthen the confirmability and trustworthiness of research-based understandings.

The authors of *The Privatisation of Higher Education in Postcolonial Bangladesh* articulate in an exemplary Preface their geo-political and onto-epistemological positionalities in respect of their research study of privatisation of higher education in Bangladesh. This is very sophisticated theorising and is an example of scholars with both Global South and Global North residential, citizenship and educational experiences making transparent in a theoretically informed way their stances in relation to the topic of their research. Furthermore, they demonstrate the theorising of diasporic, travelling, hybridised, creolised scholars who have taken the opportunity to move beyond a common approach to researching nations and social institutions of the Global South, that is, simply seeing them as empirical mines, as it were, for data collection, to be analysed by Global North theorising. Instead, rejecting such an approach that reinforces a colonial present, they take the opportunity to work with a stronger concept of internationalisation of social science research by theorising from within Global South de-colonial and postcolonial research literatures, including the work of Mignolo, Bhabha, Quijano, Appadurai, Spivak, Ong and others. Their stance is central to rejecting epistemological exclusion inherent in the colonial present and research conducted in that context.

Kabir and Chowdhury demonstrate, *à la* Edward Said and Stuart Hall, how multiple displacements of various kinds (e.g. spatial, epistemological, existential), being out of place, as it were, for some, not all, can be productive intellectually for high quality social science research that functions in a de-colonising way against epistemological exclusion. Their approach is an excellent example of what Appadurai refers to as the necessity of deparochialising research towards a stronger internationalisation of the research imaginary in the social sciences. I congratulate Kabir and Chowdhury on this achievement and suggest that their Preface provides a very commendable intellectual and pedagogical resource for those who teach social science research methods in comparative education, and indeed for educational and social science researchers more broadly.

The Privatisation of Higher Education in Postcolonial Bangladesh, of course, does much more than this. The analysis of privatisation of higher education in Bangladesh over the last 30 years or so provides an empirically-based account of the way neoliberalism has worked its way through the higher education sector in Bangladesh. Three aspects have been important here, namely, neoliberalism as economic and ideological doctrine, as a mode of governance, and as a policy package.

Bangladesh has witnessed the huge expansion of participation (mass higher education) since the 1990s, growth of private universities, both for and not-for profit, the quasi-privatisation and corporatisation of public universities (e.g. VCs as CEOs rather than academic leaders), and the achievement of expansion through transfer of costs to students (fees in public and private universities). This analysis demonstrates the links between neoliberalism and postcoloniality and the ways the former works in a path-dependent manner in the Bangladeshi context. Their analysis demonstrates how the past is prelude, with the framing of the first universities in what became Bangladesh by British colonisation and then subsequently after 1947 by Pakistani colonisation. It is here that we see that 'post' attached to/hyphenated with colonialism is more aspiration than achievement and why Kabir and Chowdhury argue the necessity of de-colonisation, both as theory and practice. Following Bangladeshi independence in 1971, they also demonstrate how the initial *raison d'etre* for higher education was nation-building, but subsequently with expansion and privatisation of higher education from the 1990s the *raison d'etre* shifted from nation-building to human capital production within a market logic. It is also here they show in a granular way how a path-dependent manifestation of neoliberalism played out in higher education policy and practice in Bangladesh.

The introductory chapter that deals with these historical, dominant and emergent policies and practices in Bangladeshi higher education is then followed by a number of very insightful chapters. Neoliberalism and trends in higher education policy are outlined in a global context with a focus on vernacular globalisation from below. The privatisation of higher education in a number of Asian reference societies is then dealt with and informative comparative analyses provided of privatisation developments in the higher education systems of China, India, Malaysia, Sri Lanka and Vietnam. This is exemplary comparative education research. The financing of higher education is next considered, including the role of international financial organisations such as the World Bank and aid agencies, and followed by an account of the new modes of governance in and of universities, covering consideration of the impact of a vernacular expression of new public management on such governance. The *Strategic Plan for Higher Education in*

Bangladesh: 2006–2026, which underpinned many of the developments analysed in the book, was a response to World Bank funding and related policy exhortation. Quality control and auditing of higher education are subsequently addressed. The nature of the new private universities is canvassed next with a focus on both for- and not-for profit universities analysed. The ambivalence of the government in relation to for-profit universities is also documented. The analysis proffered throughout shows how privatisation has also affected public universities. This is illustrated through a case study of Jagannath University, a new university established at the time of the production of the *Strategic Plan for Higher Education in Bangladesh: 2006–2026*. The book draws to a close in a summative way and also speculates on possible future trajectories regarding the privatisation of Bangladeshi higher education and suggests such an approach has now been sedimented.

Arif H. Kabir and Raqib Chowdhury's *The Privatisation of Higher Education in Postcolonial Bangladesh* will be essential reading for those researchers interested in higher education policy, education developments in nations of the Global South, and for comparative educators. The analysis provided also offers an important methodological provocation regarding research and theorising in a Global South nation and the necessity to reject epistemological innocence and utilise instead articulation of researcher positionality to enhance the trustworthiness of our research-derived understandings.

Emeritus Professor Bob Lingard
Emeritus Professor, The University of Queensland
Professorial Fellow, Australian Catholic University

Acknowledgements

At the outset we would like to express our earnest gratitude to Emeritus Professor Bob Lingard from the University of Queensland, Australia for his thoughtfulness in writing the Foreword for this book. We also acknowledge Emeritus Professor Janinka Greenwood (University of Canterbury, New Zealand), Professor Syed Manzoorul Islam (University of Dhaka, Bangladesh), and Associate Professor Riyad A Shahjahan (Michigan State University, USA) for endorsing this book. We are in particular grateful to Associate Professor Riyad A Shahjahan for his insightful feedback on the manuscript which helped us fine-tune some of the arguments we have engaged in.

The core idea of this book originates from the PhD thesis of first author and therefore it is our privilege to acknowledge Professor Susan Webb, the supervisor of first author's PhD thesis, and her support in developing critical insights into the policy formulation processes in the context of developing countries.

Our profound gratitude also goes to all the policy actor participants who were interviewed for this study despite their busy schedules. This project would have been impossible without the generosity and patience of every participant.

We also acknowledge our colleagues from both Monash University and the University of Dhaka, and across the globe for their intellectual support and affirmation in writing this book. In particular, we acknowledge Dr Omar Faruque, SSHRC Postdoctoral Fellow in the Department of Global Development Studies at Queen's University, Canada, for his encouragement and critical insights into some of the themes of the book.

We are grateful for the thorough and meticulous review we received from the Series Editor and our Editorial team from Routledge, as well as the three blind reviewers who provided invaluable feedback on the book proposal and on the manuscript.

Finally, we express our deep gratitude to our foremost sources of inspiration – our families – and the sacrifices they made to their time and inspired us to get involved in the production of this book.

1 Privatisation of higher education in Bangladesh

Humble beginnings

Scope of the book

In its myriad interpretations and manifestations, the development and spread of privatisation – based on neoliberal policy doctrines – have become a predominant world phenomenon since the 1970s. Higher education is not an exception; in fact, as Slaughter and Rhodes (2004, p. 1) argue, the way in which higher education has been transformed, shaped and used in recent decades could be identified as "academic capitalism". We could say that the rise of new global economy has changed the relationship between university and society in fundamental ways. However, the way privatisation is enacted in different countries does not look similar; rather, local contexts almost always determine local privatisation processes, which Appadurai (1996, p. 10) calls "vernacular" forms of privatisation.

This book addresses the complexities of and challenges in the privatisation of higher education and the intricate politics behind it in the context of modern-day, postcolonial Bangladesh. While presenting a chronology of the evolution of higher education as its broad canvas, it focuses on a number of key aspects of the privatisation of higher education in Bangladesh from a distinctly postcolonial[1] perspective. It includes a consideration of financial modes of higher education, quality assurance and its governance and administration, as well as the notions of and debate surrounding the private university as a 'not-for-profit' or 'for-profit' institution. The book explores these issues in relation to the desires of stakeholders in developing a distinctly 'Bangladeshi form' of privatisation model and its practices in higher education. Against this backdrop, the book also critically examines the roles local and global forces have been playing in shaping such a Bangladeshi form of privatisation. The critical discussion adds complexity to existing discourses of 'globalisation from above' and situates the often-idiosyncratic ways in which higher education reform has been shaped in this part of the world.

The study showcased in the book is developed based on a five-year empirical research that has employed contemporary theories from political and social sciences, economics and education to problematise current debates on monetary approaches into the higher education sector in Bangladesh. To our knowledge, a book of this scope and intention has not been published offering both public and private sector higher education of Bangladesh as the primary focus.

Well into this relatively new century already, the purposes of higher education continue to be determined by market discourses that have aggressively regulated global higher education systems in past decades. Since the 1980s, it has been a worldwide trend for universities to adopt privatisation models of knowledge, skills, curriculum, finance, accounting and management organisation. This book sees the need to respond to these phenomena by offering frameworks of understanding offered through the chapters of this book, as a way of analysing, making sense of, and then appropriating these discourses. In doing so we also attempt to locate the trajectory of future *épistémès* (Foucault, 1977) that are likely to shape the evolution of private provision of higher education in the country.

In particular, in the backdrop of market forces having usurped the centre stage in shaping the nature of higher education over the last three decades (Chowdhury & Le Ha, 2014; Sidhu, 2005), this book discusses the nature and degree to which neoliberalism has become a prominent feature and the *raison d'être* of private higher education in postcolonial Bangladesh. More specifically, the book focuses on how historical, political and socio-economic processes have influenced contemporary higher education policy affairs and shaped privatisation processes in the Bangladeshi higher education sector in ways sometimes conspicuously different from what is experienced elsewhere in the global context.

In this sense, the book offers new ways to reconstruct our relationship with higher education, which allow the negotiation of sociocultural and socio-political frictions, individual, institutional and national tensions, and the various ways in which we seek legitimation of our educational practices through engaging with our peers in the wider discourse community of teachers and researchers. In order to commence the discussion, it is first important to understand the historical context which provides important perspectives, especially given the postcolonial framework we have adopted in our analysis.

Historical context of higher education in Bangladesh

Higher education development in Bangladesh has always been part of a political process (Chowdhury & Kabir, 2014). Therefore, it is useful to briefly trace the political processes and the historical roots of the introduction of a Western higher education in Bangladesh and the importance of identifying these political processes and historical antecedents for understanding the nature of the contemporary higher education system and the present-day educational cultures and values in Bangladesh.

The beginning of a Western education system in the Indian subcontinent might be traced back to 1835 (Aggarwal, 2007). The now infamous 'Macaulay's Minute' of 1835 triggered the rapid reformation aligned with British-based education system in the Indian Subcontinent (Zastoupil & Moir, 1999). Based on Macaulay's Minute of 1835 the British colonial rulers formulated the English Education Act 1835 in which they set up the aim, content and medium of instruction of Education in British-India. In time, universities as institutions adopted the Westernised model with English as the medium of instruction and the introduction of new areas of studies. Modelled on the London University, the first three modern universities in the Indian Subcontinent were set up in three metropolitan cities of Calcutta (now Kolkata), Bombay (now Mumbai) and Madras (now Chennai) in 1857 (Vats, 2008), with another university in Lahore later in 1869 (Aggarwal, 2007). During this period, British education policies, such as Wood's Despatch in 1854, also promoted the growth of higher education through the establishment of Colleges at the private level across British-India (Aggarwal, 2007).

Although within the territorial boundaries now comprising Bangladesh there was no university until 1921, some first-grade affiliated colleges of East Bengal, for example, Rajshahi College (1873), Dhaka College (1881) and Jagannath College (1884), were entitled to offer higher studies under the University of Kolkata at that time (University Grants Commission, 2009a). Therefore, we could say that the origin of modern higher education in Bangladesh could only be traced back to when the British colonial regime established the first university – University of Dhaka – in 1921.

Historians broadly view the decision to establish a university in Bangladesh as compensation for the annulment of the partition of Bengal in 1905. The Partition provided a hope to the majority Muslim community in East Bengal, and Assam (now one of the provinces of India) for socioeconomic and political development. However, the Bengal partition was lifted in 1911 in the wake of massive protests by West Bengal-based intelligentsia groups and powerful Hindu leaders in India. Such a decision left deep anger and dissatisfaction among the Muslim community of East Bengal (University Grants Commission, 2009a). Subsequently, the Muslim community led by the Muslim leaders met the British Viceroy Lord Hardinge and expressed their fear that the annulment could impede the educational progress of Muslims in these regions. To assuage the feelings of the Muslim community and to ensure the progression of the 'backward' Muslim community in these regions, the British Raj promised to establish a university in the capital of East Bengal (now Bangladesh) – Dhaka (University Grants Commission, 2009a).

It was expected that the socio-economic, political and cultural conditions of the majority Muslim populace in the then East Bengal would be uplifted by ensuring modern higher education (Rahman, 2009). However, the British rulers had created the University of Dhaka (DU) in East Bengal as a way of dealing with social unrest and political difficulties within the country they ruled (Chowdhury & Kabir, 2014). Indeed, they had intended to achieve political reconciliation between Muslims and Hindus in Bengal through the establishment of DU. The view of the British rulers was in fact expressed by the then DU Chancellor and the Governor of Bengal, Lord Lytton, in the course of the Convocation address in the University of Dhaka in 1922. He commented that the University of Dhaka was "an imperial compensation to the Muslims for the annulment of the partition of Bengal" (University Grants Commission, 2009a, p. xviii).

The entire process of the evolution of this university in East Bengal could be described using the words of the first Vice Chancellor of the University of Dhaka, Dr. P. J. Hartog, as the "political origin" of the institution (cited in Majumdar, Ghose, Chatterjee, Bandyopadhyay, & Chatterjee, 1994, p. 31). The espoused political agenda of British education in the Indian Subcontinent was to create a class that would be Indian in blood and colour, but English in taste (Macaulay, 1835, cited in McLeod, 2000). In particular, once India came under the direct rule of the British Royalty and Parliament in 1857, the British ruler designed and provided higher education "to a class of people whose sympathy it was necessary to win in the political interests of the Britishers" (Singh, 1989, p. 2).

The British eventually left the Indian Subcontinent in 1947 by splitting it into two countries – India and Pakistan – based on a predominantly religious Two-Nation theory. Since then, Bangladesh (then East Bengal) became East Pakistan as part of the newly formed colonial state of Pakistan. The state under Pakistani rulers (1947–1971) formulated several policy documents, for example, the 1957 Educational Reforms Commission for East Pakistan, the Commission on National Education in 1958 (Government of Pakistan, 1958), the New Education Policy in 1970; and set up five more universities in East Pakistan (University Grants Commission, 2009a). In its first National Educational Conference held in Karachi in 1947, the Pakistani rulers reassessed the British Education System in Pakistan and designated Islamic religious ideology as a vision across the entire education system. The Commission on National Education in 1959 asserted that the fundamental value of education is "to preserve the Islamic way of life.... The moral and spiritual values of Islam combined with the freedom, integrity, and strength of Pakistan should be the ideology which inspires our educational system" (Government of Pakistan, 1958, p. 11). The Pakistani rulers positioned religion, tradition and the past British traditions in the education system for building up Pakistani nationalism by ignoring the diverse socio-political and economic factors existing in different regions in Pakistan. As a new state, Pakistan designed its education system from its colonial past to construct the 'citizens' "in the same image – obedient, loyal, hardworking and able to subordinate themselves to authority" (Saigol, 2003, p. 12).

Although the British rulers introduced the English education system as a means to gaining political and economic interests, the Indian leaders as well as the English-educated class saw in English "the key to the West" (Basu, 1974, p. 73). As the new language, English arrived with a new world view for Indians. The following decades saw the Indian English-educated class gradually become the driving force in Indian politics who shaped English education to generate new political life and ideas. They recognised English as the medium of expression that would eventually forge the unity of all Indians (Basu, 1974).

Indeed, the establishment of University of Dhaka by the British in East Bengal in 1921 helped an East Bengal-based intelligentsia to emerge for the first time, which produced the politically unintended consequence at the end of the British regime and around the turn of the Pakistani regime (1947–1971). Once the British departed, East Bengal became part of Pakistan, but the political leaders and educated class felt no differences between the British and Pakistani rulers. The political leaders and educated class of then East Pakistan saw higher education as a catalyst to achieve their political goals during the Pakistani regime (Kabir, 2010). Consequently, the role of higher education in the society changed, turning against the Pakistani rulers. Similar to what education did for India, the development of the East Bengal-based intelligentsia created the climate and the actors for a social movement to push forward the establishment of a new country – Bangladesh – in 1971 (Basu, 1974). Under the Pakistani regime from 1947 to 1971, both students and academics contributed toward the establishment of democracy and liberty of the country (Quddus & Rashid, 2000) through the mobilisation of anti-government rhetoric and active protests.

Undoubtedly, the British colonial legacy has left indelible marks on the texture of contemporary higher education system in Bangladesh. For example, like in many other countries with a colonial history, the university structure, academic hierarchy, curricula and examination system of the university, have all been influenced (and to a large extent remains influenced) by the British higher education system (Altbach, 1989). These political processes and historical ascendances have influenced the ideologies and cultures of the post-independence Bangladeshi society (Alavi, 1972). In effect, the Western-based higher education in Bangladesh became a political project by the British to develop an elite class to do the bidding of the colonisers once they had left. Once Bangladesh became independent in 1971, this elite class assumed the position of the nouveau elite class in post-independence Bangladesh. They wanted power for themselves and used the colonial organisational context to do their politicking to develop ideas to lead the country (Kochanek, 2000), as we will see later in this book. Perhaps more crucially, the system left deep traces of the colonial mindset which reconfigured into new forms of power play in post-independence Bangladesh, including the duality of governance which we discuss in Chapter 5.

Since Bangladesh's independence in 1971, the state under successive governments formulated various policies to shape and recontextualise the education system from a broader nationalistic view (Chowdhury & Kabir, 2014). In its first education commission in 1974 – Bangladesh Education Commission – the government emphasised the importance of nation building through higher education (Ministry of Education, 1974). In this post-independence period, the new government set up two interwoven goals for higher education: to contribute to the newly born country's overall development, and to contribute to creating an equitable society (Ministry of Education, 1974). Since independence from Pakistan in 1971 and until 1990 the country had six public universities and some affiliated colleges. All of these universities and affiliated colleges in Bangladesh adopted the same role in the higher education system until 1990 (University Grants Commission, 2009a), when neoliberalist ideologies took over which saw the establishment and expansion of private sector higher education in Bangladesh.

Neoliberal shifts in higher education in the post-1990s periods

Since the 1970s, several powerful countries including USA, UK and China have adopted neoliberal policy doctrines in various national development sectors. In the next chapter, we discuss the historical, political and theoretical development of neoliberalism, the role of International Financial Institutions (IFIs) in adopting neoliberalism in different sectors across the world and how higher education has been influenced and shaped by these doctrines. Similar to other countries, a new phase of higher education began in the 1990s in which a remarkable transformation took place in the higher education system in Bangladesh, largely based on market-driven economic forces (Kabir, 2010, 2011, 2012, 2013a, 2013b, 2020a, 2020b; Kabir & Greenwood, 2017). Human resources development was identified in key education policies as the main objective to be achieved by higher education for the nation's overall development (University Grants Commission, 2009a; World Bank, 2009). Consequently, creating a knowledge-based society become the key driver of the current higher education system (Kabir, 2011). This transformation underpins and characterises all subsequent neoliberal changes in the higher education sector.

In a broader sense, neoliberalism refers to an economic model or paradigm (Steger & Roy, 2010). However, three intertwined dimensions need to be understood in order to conceptualise neoliberalism fully: neoliberalism as an *ideology*, a *mode of governance*, and a *policy package* (Steger & Roy, 2010). "Ideologies organize their core ideas into fairly simple truth-claims that encourage people to act in certain ways … legitimize certain political interests and to defend or challenge dominant power structures" (Steger & Roy, 2010, p. 11). The second dimension encompassing the idea of neoliberalism as a mode of governance refers to what Foucault (1991) called "governmentalities" (cited in Steger & Roy, 2010, p. 14), which are deep rooted in entrepreneurial values; for example, competitiveness, self-interest and decentralisation. This emphasises individual empowerment and decentralisation of the power to local units; and thus neoliberalism promotes a self-regulating free market in order to ensure proper governance. The final dimension, a policy package, refers to the deregulation of the economy, liberalisation of trade and industry, and privatisation of state-owned enterprises. It also includes "massive tax cuts; reduction of social services and welfare programmes; replacing welfare with 'workface'" (Steger & Roy, 2010, p. 14). This last feature is not discussed in this book as it lies beyond the scope of the book's critical interests.

Since the 1980s, neoliberal policies of the IFIs have played a crucial role in reshaping socio-economic policies in many developing countries (Torres, 2009). One of the key agendas of neoliberalism is the conviction that human welfare is best served by the withdrawal of the state from welfare policies (Harvey, 2007).

The state is presumed to create a congenial atmosphere for the economy by reforming laws, policies and institutions necessary for the market (Olssen & Peters, 2005). The economic reformation that later came to be known broadly as 'privatisation' emerged in the West and later spread around the world with help of a host of international financial institutes, such as the World Bank. In Bangladesh, privatisation initiatives in higher education started in the early 1990s. As a developing country Bangladesh began introducing a pro-market economic policy in 1975 when the military junta came into power by overthrowing the post-independence socialist government (Kabir, 2013b; Nuruzzaman, 2004). Since the early 1980s, neoliberalist projects shaped various sectors of the economy; for example, development in agriculture, industry and finance and banking was accelerated as a result of enormous pressures from the IFIs, as well as by the economic and political interests of the ruling military-civil elites (Kabir, 2013b). By accelerating these neoliberal reforms through structural adjustment policies, the successive military rulers (1975–1990) attempted to build up a coalition between dominant socio-political forces – military-civil bureaucrats, businessmen and industrialists (Quadir, 2000). These new initiatives also aimed to reform public policies and *re*defined the role of the state in serving its citizens (Nuruzzaman, 2004), a narrative that was sustained in subsequent regimes for decades to come, as we will see in the later chapters of this book.

In keeping with this trend, democratic regimes since the 1990s continued to introduce neoliberal reforms such as privatisation in service-related sectors (Kabir, 2013b). More recently, the higher education sector in Bangladesh has also experienced significant changes (Table 1.1). The first move was to promulgate the

Table 1.1 Major neoliberal policy shifts in the higher education sector

Year	*Name of the key policies*	*Targeted university sector*
1992	Private University Act	Private university sector
1998	Private University Act 1992 (Amendment)	Private university sector
2006	Strategic Plan for Higher Education 2006–2026	Both public and private university sectors
2008	Private University Ordinance 2008	Private university sector
2009	Higher Education Quality Enhancement Project (HEQEP) 2009–2018	Both public and private sector
2010	Private University Act 2010	Private university sector
2014	'Guiding Rules for Regulating the Branch Campuses' or 'the Study Centre of Foreign University or Institute 2014'	Private university sector
2017	Strategic Plan 2017–2030[2]	Both public and private university sectors
2017	The Bangladesh Accreditation Council Act 2017	Both public and private university sectors

first Private University Act 1992 on 9 August, 1992 (Government of Bangladesh, 1992). In April 1998, the government amended the Private University Act 1992 (Government of Bangladesh, 1998), while in 2008 the army-backed Caretaker government repealed all private university Acts and promulgated the Private University Ordinance 2008 (Government of Bangladesh, 2008). However, the state under the following democratic government did not ratify the Ordinance 2008. Rather, the government repealed all previous Acts and enacted the new Private University Act 2010 (Government of Bangladesh, 2010b), superseding all previous statutes. The previous government also initiated a number of reform programmes in the higher education sector under the supervision and guidance of the World Bank. One of these reform policies is the introduction of a 20-year *Strategic Plan for Higher Education in Bangladesh: 2006–2026* (University Grants Commission, 2006). The government and the World Bank identified this plan as a ground-breaking initiative to address current problems and issues in Bangladeshi higher education. Based on the Strategic Plan 2006–2026, the government developed a long-term project named Higher Education Quality Enhancement Project (HEQEP) for the higher education sector with financial support from the World Bank in 2007 that was implemented between 2009 and 2018 spending about US$238.1 million (University Grants Commission, 2017).

Notably, the SPHE adopted a set of neoliberal solutions to the problems (University Grants Commission, 2009b; World Bank, 2009). Along with these neoliberal policies, the government also adopted the *Guiding Rules for Regulating the Branch Campuses* and the *Study Centre of Foreign University or Institute 2014* (Ministry of Education, 2014). More recently, two other major policies – the Bangladesh Accreditation Council Act 2017 and the Strategic Plan 2017–2030 (as of now, awaiting endorsement) – have also been adopted for expanding and improving the standard of higher education in Bangladesh (University Grants Commission, 2017). The recent Strategic Plan 2017–2030 was developed in order to update the first Strategic Plan 2006–2026 in the light of the higher education objectives of the government and in keeping with the Sustainable Development Goals (SDGs) (University Grants Commission, 2017).

In terms of the relationships between these neoliberal policies, some of them are for private universities while some are sector-wide for both public and private universities – the private university Acts focus on the development and establishment of private higher education, whereas the Strategic Plans cover the entire higher education sector in Bangladesh. In addition, unlike private universities, each public university was set up by an individual Act, unlike the one Act that applies to the entire range of public universities. Consequently, unlike the private universities, all public universities have an independent one-to-one relationship between themselves and the state.

Although some of these policies were developed to reform particular university sectors – either public or private or both, there is are significant relationships between these in terms of what Holford and McKenzie (2013) call 'policy tracing' or 'policy trail'. By policy tracing, Holford and McKenzie refer to understand how certain characteristics of policy in terms of ideas, people and both ideational and material resources, have travelled through over time, "either intentionally or accidentally, as well as its physicality and imaginary potentials" (Milana, 2015, p. 517). Significantly, it can be observed that some of these ideas were pulled together into the public sector as part of 'policy tracing' or 'policy trail' from the private sector (see, for example, the case of Jagannath University, Chapter 8), and vice-versa.

Massive growth of higher education in the post-1990s periods

The post-1990s neoliberal policy shifts in higher education escalated the massive growth of universities in both public and private sectors in Bangladesh (Table 1.2). In particular, numbers of both public and private universities, as well as number of students and other academic activities dramatically increased during this period.

The number of students also saw a corresponding increase in across both sectors over the last three decades. On 1 July, 1921, the first university – University of Dhaka – started with only 12 departments under three faculties, namely Arts, Science and Law with 877 students; whereas this premier university, the first in the country, is currently operating with 83 departments under 13 faculties, 12 institutes and 56 research bureaus and centres, with about 37,000 students (University of Dhaka, 2020). Forty-five out of 49 public universities and 95 out of 103 private universities are currently operating across Bangladesh offering degrees in various areas. According to 2018 statistics, student numbers in public universities and their affiliated colleges have increased by tenfold, from 1,382,286 to 3,606,137 in the last decade from 2009 to 2018 (Table 1.3) (University Grants Commission, 2018a). The student numbers include National University (NU), Bangladesh Open University (BOU) and Islamic Arabic University (IAU). These three universities are the largest in terms of student population, operating and offering degrees in different ways. NU is catering to general and professional degrees in 34 disciplines through its 2,269 graduate and postgraduate affiliated colleges and institutions with 2,528,689 students spread all over Bangladesh (University Grants Commission, 2018b). Similar to NU, IAU also offers degrees through its 1,336 Madrasha Colleges with 87,143 students across Bangladesh; while BOU is offering various degrees through distance mode with 318,526 students as of 2018 (University Grants Commission, 2018b).

With the exception from NU, BOU and IAU, the rate of enrolment in private universities is higher than in public universities. In fact, in 2018 private universities enrolled more than 100,000 students than the number of students enrolled in the remaining 34 universities offering degrees directly. In particular, 354,333 students were enrolled in 85 private universities in 2018, whereas 238,866 students were enrolled in 34 public universities at that time (University Grants Commission, 2018b).

Such massive growth of the university sector in the post-1990s periods seemed to push higher education from what Trow (1973) calls 'elite' to mass education in Bangladesh. However, the question remains as to how far these universities are

Table 1.2 Growth of public and private universities in Bangladesh over the decades

Year(s)	*Number of public universities established*	*Year(s)*	*Number of private universities established*
1921–1952	Only one University – University of Dhaka		
1953–1971	Five public universities added – University of Rajshahi, Bangladesh Agricultural University, Bangladesh University of Engineering and Technology (BUET), University of Chittagong, and Jahangirnagar University		
1971–1985	No University added, although the Act of Islamic University was passed in 1980		
1986–1990	Three universities added – Islamic University, Shahjalal Science and Technology University and Khulna University	1990–1995	13 private universities added
1990–1999	Four universities added, including National University and Bangladesh Open University	1996–2001	Four private universities added
2000–2009	18 public universities added including 10 science and technology universities, three agricultural universities and five general universities	2002–2007 2007–2008	37 private universities added No private university added
2010–2018	18 public universities added, including six science and technology related universities, and two general universities. Of them, five public universities are yet to commence operation.	2009–2013 2014–2018	26 private universities added 25 private university added
Totals	49 public universities (of them, five yet to be operated)		105 (of them, eight private universities are yet to be operated and two private universities chartered have been cancelled)

different from those established by the British during the colonial times. The British colonial rulers brought a Western higher education system to the Indian Subcontinent which, as we see above, was tightly connected to colonial interests (Altbach, 2004, 2005). Although in post-independence Bangladesh higher education transformed into taking up a major role in shaping the national identity and playing a significant part in informing the political system – if not broadening the

Table 1.3 Growth of students in higher education sectors

	*Universities operated in public sector**			*Universities operated in private sector*		
Year	*Number of universities*	*Total students*	*Rate of increase/ decrease compared to previous year (%)*	*Number of universities*	*Total students*	*Rate of increase/ decrease compared to previous year (%)*
2008	29	1,176,969	-15.92	51	182,641	+7
2009	31	1,382,216	+17.44	51	200,939	+10
2010	31	1,736,887	+25.65	51	220,752	+9.86
2011	34	2,170,472	+24.96	52	280,822	+27.21
2012	34	1,890,543	-12.90	60	314,640	+12.04
2013	34	2,020,549	+6.87	78	328,736	+4.48
2014	35	2,849,865	+41.04	80	330,730	+0.61
2015	37	3,206,435	+12.51	85**	350,130	+5.87
2016	37	3,150,409	-1.75	95***	337,157	-3.70
2017	37	3,606,137	+14.13	95****	354,333	+5.09

* This includes all affiliated Colleges and Institutions under different universities
** Although 85 private universities were approved in 2015, three of them did not begin academic activities at that time
*** Although 95 private universities were approved in 2016, nine of them did not begin academic activities at that time
**** Although 95 private universities were approved in 2017, five of them did not begin academic activities at that time
(Source: University Grants Commission, 2018b)

social base and serving as a driver of the economic system – in the post-1990s periods, a new role gradually emerged, and that was to serve the market. The government's introduction of the private university Acts and the Strategic Plans focused on shaping the entire higher education system in line with global trends, much more so than looking into national interests alone. All these changes are indicative of wide scale neoliberal reformation in the higher education sector implemented by various governments, regardless of their local political agendas and national interests of the current time.

This book attempts to understand the dynamic and ever-shifting interface of the political processes that have informed and shaped the privatisation of higher education in Bangladesh. In so doing, this book critically analyses a wide range of documents and engages in face to face conversations with a wide range of policy actors who were first-hand involved in developing dominant narratives that have shaped this privatisation process. Our central position in this book is that this can only be done in a sensitive and holistic manner when we engage with the postcolonial history of Bangladesh in understanding how the current character and temperament of the privatisation of higher education system have been the result of the historically situated attitudes of these policy actors and other vested interest groups and the inherent purposes they have espoused either deliberately or in a less tangible manner. The tracing of the political processes and the history in this book thus pay attention to the inconsistencies and ruptures in the discourses that have defined the shifting *épistémès* over a period of more than a century.

How materials have been sourced for this book

The methodology we have adopted for this study is broadly a qualitative one, using case study as a strategy of inquiry (Stake, 2008), and within that, approaches that facilitate an institutional ethnography. According to Smith (1990), institutes are "textually-mediated social organizations" and within them policy documents, legislatures and official reports – including those related to planning and funding – are replicable texts which act as standardising tools. These tools then can be a visible representation of the structure and operational ethos of an institution. An institutional ethnography approach thus allows us to understand how institutes operate through texts and the discourses and organisational cultures produced by such texts. This approach also allows us to also understand how local (institutional) discourses are linked to translocal discourses – such as those in the broader society, and globally. Wright and Rocco (2016, p. 27) explain that these discourses "set the parameters for a person's ability or inability to navigate the structural and political subsystems that impact ... work". They further point out that the role of power as an analytic focus is critically important in allowing us to view the organisation of institutes.

We identified 'privatisation of higher education in Bangladesh' as a case and within this case we look at how and why privatisation has evolved in the higher education sector in the way it has. An instrumental case study approach meant that the focus included privatisation patterns in both public and private universities and a consideration of why the state has used certain controlling and intervention measures in this process to obtain what Murphy (2020, p. 492) calls the "securitization of higher education". The case study has its own research design (Yin, 2009) in which various data collection tools including interviews with key persons or informants, document analysis and observation can be employed to collect data (Swanborn, 2010).

In collecting data, we used a variety of empirical materials, such personal experiences and interviews, cultural texts, artefacts and productions, and media documents (Table 1.4). Document analysis involved two key government documents that accelerated the privatisation process across both public and private universities since the 1990s. These two key documents include the Private University Acts – the Private University Act 1992, 1998 (amendment), the Private University Ordinance 2008 and the Private University Act 2010, and the Strategic Plan for Higher Education with the technical and financial support of the World

Table 1.4 Methods of analysis into data

Methods of analysis	*Sources of data*
Document analysis	– A 20-year Strategic Plan for Higher Education 2006–2026 – Strategic Plan for Higher Education 2017–2030 – 'Guiding Rules for Regulating the Branch Campuses' or 'the Study Centre of Foreign University or Institute 2014' – Private University Acts 1992, 1998 (amended), 2010 – Cabinet Approved Private University Act 2010 – Private University Ordinance 2008 – Public University Acts – UGC reports – University reports – Media reports
Interview analysis	– Five policy administrators from UGC and Ministry of Education – Eleven academics – Three politicians – Four journalists – Five private sector representatives

Bank in 2006. To understand the politics of intervention and control in this privatisation process we also conducted face to face in-depth interviews with 28 policy elites who were involved in these policy formulation processes in various capacities. Along with these two key policy documents – the Private University Acts and the Strategic Plan for Higher Education 2006–2026 – we also analysed some other documents including a range of public university Acts and media reports.

Some parts of document analysis and the interviews with policy actors were conducted by the first author of this book as part of a doctoral study where he attempted to understand the processes in the formation of neoliberal ideas in the Bangladeshi higher education sector (see Kabir, 2016). From the reviews of the Acts (1992, 1998, 2008 and 2010) and the Strategic Plan, we found that some of these policies were developed almost 25 years ago while others were relatively recent policy processes. For example, the first Private University Act was formulated in 1992 and the government introduced an amendment of this Act in 1998. However, some of these policies – the Private University Ordinance 2008, the latest Act 2010 as well as the Strategic Plan – were relatively new neoliberal policies in higher education. We found out that the formation of all of these neoliberal policies was influenced by the involvement of a range of 'elite' policy actors. Consequently, the first author employed "retrospective elite interviewing" as it seemed to offer a better understanding of past events and processes (see for reference, Selwyn, 2013, p. 343). We use pseudonyms to ensure anonymity for the participants when we use their information in this book.

To examine this case, we first used global literature to theorise the concept of neoliberalism and postcolonialism on a global scale. We then focused on the specific issue of privatisation of higher education in Bangladesh based on data drawn from the aforementioned documents and interviews analysis.

Disclaimer – what this book is not about

In theory, this book is not about judging whether market fundamentalism (Sidhu, 2006) or excessive government intervention is 'bad' – or good. Rather this book uses a critical lens to understand how a complex web of power relations embedded in and originating from Bangladesh's colonial history has seeped into current day constructions of higher education in certain distinctive and locally-sensitive ways. This book, therefore, seeks to problematise power and politics in the current day development of higher education using postcolonial perspectives.

In Bangladesh, higher education is offered through a range of academic institutions including full-fledged public and private universities, as well as their affiliated colleges. As stated above, affiliated colleges under the National University (NU) and the Islamic Arabic University (IAU) cover about 77% of all higher education institutes nationwide (University Grants Commission, 2017, 2018a). Apart from these affiliated colleges under NU and IAU, there is also a large number of colleges and institutes including medical, agricultural and engineering colleges that offer higher education under different universities. For example, under the University of Dhaka, there are more than 100 affiliated colleges including general and medical and technical colleges offering degrees in various areas (University of Dhaka, 2020). There are also about 3,885 affiliated Colleges and Madrashas (Islamic religious schools) under public universities offering various higher education degrees spread over the country (University Grants Commission, 2018b).

Although these affiliated colleges and institutes offer degrees under different universities, their governance systems are significantly different from those operating as full-fledged universities. The relationship between these affiliated colleges and the full-fledged universities are confined in terms of curriculum and academic development. This means that academic matters, including the curriculum, examination and degree awards of affiliated colleges are controlled and managed by the respective university under which it operates; however administrative and governance systems, including teacher and staff recruitments and their promotion and transfer are controlled, managed and administered by the government as well as non-government bodies powered by different Acts and Laws promulgated by the government.

This book does not address how these affiliated colleges and institutions operate and are governed by the state. Rather, the scope of the book is confined to looking into how full-fledged universities adopt and have adopted various models of privatisation into their systems and the micro-politics of state control and intervention through which the privatisation processes are enacted in the higher education sector. Inevitably, although the focus of the book is on private universities, we will discuss the case of public universities too, which have also seen forms of neoliberalist ideologies that have positioned them somewhat in the continuum of what we consider to be characteristic of privatisation (see, for example, the case of Jagannath University in Chapter 8). Therefore, the analysis will cover both public and private universities, including NU and IAU.

Nor does this book address how the three international universities – Islamic University of Technology, run and funded by the Organisation of Islamic Cooperation (OIC) (Islamic University of Technology, 2020), Asian University of Women, established by the international philanthropic organisations including the Goldman Sachs Foundation and the Bill & Melinda Gates Foundation and the Government of Bangladesh (Asian University of Women, 2020) and South Asian University, located in India, established with the technical and financial support of the South Asian Association for Regional Cooperation (SAARC) member states – operate in Bangladesh (South Asian University, 2020). These three universities are different in terms of governance and financing systems from the universities and study centres approved by the government under the Private University Act 2010 and the 'Guiding Rules for Regulating the Branch Campuses' or 'the Study Centre of Foreign University or Institute 2014'. Unlike private universities and international study centres, all of these three international universities are operated by their own Acts. Similar to the case of affiliated colleges, this book does not expand on the analysis of the governance systems of these international universities. However, overall, analyses into the trends of privatisation certainly covers how the overall university sector operates, as well as the wider economic context of privatisation in Bangladesh.

Chapter summaries

This book comprises eight chapters in addition to this introductory chapter. These chapters reflect how privatisation processes have been adopted and reinforced in both public and public universities in Bangladesh, each critically considering a different aspect of the processes. In so doing, these chapters focus on key aspects of privatisation including financial modes of higher education, quality assurance mechanisms, the governance system of higher education, debate about whether private university should be operated in a not-for-profit or 'for-profit' manner, and how public universities are expected to be operated in Bangladesh. The summaries of these chapters are presented next.

Chapter 2 constructs the conceptual framework employed in this book to understand the concept of neoliberalism and postcolonialism, generally, and in the context of the study. In so doing, it first discusses both the philosophical and ideological aspects of the origin of neoliberalism and then looks at how these political ideologies have been incorporated in the national and global policy domains including the higher education sector. The discussion further covers how International Financial Institutions (IFIs) became key promoters of neoliberal policy doctrines across the globe. Such discussion helps to conceptualise how global actors influence local forces (in this case, in Bangladesh) from post-colonial perspectives. The final part of the chapter critically explores how power relations between the coloniser and the colonised and the residual influences of such power relationships have impacted on current policy affairs in the postcolonial space. Interspersed in this discussion, this chapter also identifies the key trends of global higher education across the world today.

Chapter 3 explores contemporary trends and issues of privatisation of higher education in a number of selected Asian countries. This analysis traces how certain persisting trends have characterised the planning and provision of private higher education in these countries in order to situate contemporary trends of higher education privatisation in Bangladesh. These countries include China, India, Malaysia, Sri Lanka and Vietnam. In selecting the countries, rather than considering their geographical locations, we have considered a cross-section that features substantial diversity as well as similarities in their historical, economic, political and cultural profiles, as well as a wide-spectrum of policy rhetoric as significant markers in understanding the trends of privatisation of higher education Bangladesh. This chapter closely looks at how policies have not only travelled unidirectionally from the West to the East, but also from region to region.

Chapter 4 explores how a diverse range of financial strategies adopted in both public and private universities helped mitigate the financial burden of higher education in Bangladesh. It argues that the government has developed a 'cost-sharing' approach in a way that not only ensures that the government has little or no financial responsibility for private universities, but also offloads *public* higher education costs to its end users. It also explores the micro-politics of adopting these different financial approaches across the entire higher education sector and the ways in which different and successive governments have justified and legitimised higher education as an end-users-pay system in both private and public universities.

Chapter 5 discusses the governance system of higher education by considering the key feature of the New Public Management (NPM) approach in Bangladesh. This approach takes the form of the retention of the centrality of government control and the application of this control across both public and private universities. The chapter argues that although NPM as a governance system originally emerged from the private management model and has been applied to public sector in order to ensure public accountability of state-run universities in the West, arguably in Bangladesh a distinctly *localised* form of NPM has developed over the last three decades. It explores how state involvement in the governance of the private universities has been justified and extended significantly in the noughties, so that to date private universities in Bangladesh are significantly different organisations from their original manifestation.

Chapter 6 discusses forms of quality controlling mechanisms, and how far some of these 'deviate' from market norms and expectations. It addresses the causes and effects of the discursive forces of marketisation and the political motives and interests embedded in shaping how 'quality' is understood in higher education. The chapter argues that although the idea of external audits was introduced in line with global trends, the government's involvement was also ensured in the quality assurance process through its conveniently placed 'arm's-length' bodies – such as the University Grants Commission (UGC) and the Accreditation Council.

Chapter 7 discusses the complexities surrounding the government's sustained tentativeness in situating higher education in Bangladesh as neither 'for-profit' nor 'not for-profit', or both. It explores how the government of Bangladesh has developed a distinctive form of the private university model by remaining non-committal to either position. To identify this unique position, this chapter first looks at how the idea of the 'private university' has been shaped across the globe over the last few decades and then discusses how far some of the features of global private universities align with the idea of the private university in Bangladesh. The chapter concludes with the assertion that the concept of the private university in Bangladesh was done through reference to the understanding that an academic institution could be set up by a person or a group of people in a way that is neither 'for-profit' nor 'not for-profit', or both, although the government might *still* control its existence through regulations and state-sanctioned power of quality assurance bodies, such as the UGC.

Chapter 8 discusses the politics of neoliberal planning in *public* higher education. Through the case study of one public university, this chapter looks at journalistic, media and scholarly discourses about various issues in the higher education sector as a whole, and explores how the government has succeeded in pulling various neoliberal ideas together into the operationalisation of public higher education in Bangladesh. To explore neoliberal planning in the public higher education, this chapter identifies the establishment of the Jagannath University during the time of formation of the Strategic Plan for Higher Education (SPHE) as a case. We take the SPHE as a departure point to analyse the micro-politics of neoliberal planning in public higher education sector and pay attention to the relationship between local and global policy actors. This chapter shows that although the Jagannath movement succeeded in achieving its desired changes, there has been no meaningful change in the overall direction of neoliberal transformation in public higher education sector. Public universities have creatively adopted various measures to offload financial pressure onto students.

Chapter 9 concludes by drawing on the analysis and discussion of the preceding chapters. This chapter moves on to discussing the implications of the arguments set forth in the book and elucidates possible future trajectories of privatisation in postcolonial Bangladesh. While the past quarter of a century has in some ways been a period of trial-and-error for the government, more recent years have seen the sedimentation of policies which continue to shape neoliberal agendas, albeit at a slower, if steadier pace. The chapter discusses if this is a symptom of policy change overload, or if the current trends of globalisation have somehow sedimented into a *newer* form of privatisation.

Notes

1 Please see Preface for our understanding of the concept of 'postcolonial' as used in this book.
2 Awaiting final approval at the time of writing

2 Neoliberalism, postcolonialism and global higher education trends

> Neoliberalism … is reconfiguring relationships between governing and the governed, power and knowledge, and sovereignty and territoriality. (It) … can also be conceptualized as a new relationship between government and knowledge through which governing activities are recast as nonpolitical and nonideological problems that need technical solutions. It … is a profoundly active way of rationalizing governing and self-governing in order to "optimize" … a historical process that unevenly articulates situated political constellations.
>
> (Ong, 2006, p. 4)

Introduction

To understand how neoliberal interests often provide the *raison d'être* for higher education in general, and how they shape higher education directives, this chapter critically reviews relevant scholarly literature to construct a conceptual framework grounded in an understanding of the concepts of monetary approaches and the contextual variables of the postcolonial space. It first discusses the philosophical and political rationales for the origins of neoliberalism, and how these are manifested in national and global economies, and in particular, how they have developed within and have shaped higher education in the past two decades. The discussion then focuses on the role of international financial institutions (IFIs) in promoting neoliberalism worldwide. Finally, it critically considers global influences on local forces (in this case, in Bangladesh) from a post-colonial perspective. The final part of the chapter critically explores how power relations between the coloniser and the colonised, and the residual influences of such power relationships continue to impact current policy affairs within the postcolonial space. Interspersed in this discussion, this chapter also identifies the key trends of global higher education across the world today.

Problematising the concept of 'neoliberalism'

The term 'neoliberalism' broadly refers to economic and social transformation agenda under the discourses of free market economy (Connell, 2010). Within neoliberal discourses, it is believed that human well-being could be advanced by "the maximization of entrepreneurial freedoms within an institutional framework characterized by private property rights, individual liberty, unencumbered markets, and free trade" (Harvey, 2007, p. 22). It is in this sense that neoliberalism, as a set of principles for economic policy reform, is concerned with "privatization, financialization, the management and manipulation of crisis, and state redistributions" (Harvey, 2006, p. 44).

In relation to economic reform, Martinez and Garcia (2000) further describe four key points of neoliberalism. First, *the rule of market* refers to liberating free/private enterprise from any restriction imposed by the state (government), no matter what attendant social damage results. Second, *cutting public expenditure for social services* refers to the reduction of government support from education and healthcare. Third, *deregulation* refers to the reduction of government regulation on business activities (including, in our case, in higher education). Fourth, *privatisation* means to sell state-owned enterprises, goods and services to private investors (including public education services). Finally, *elimination of the concept of "public goods" or "community"* means the individual has the core responsibility to manage his or her own life (cited in Ross & Gibson, 2007, p. 3). Together these economic principles of neoliberalism impact the everyday life of the individual in a number of ways, for example – changing public health or childcare or education provisions not only increases the cost of individual, but also affects individual wellbeing and social relationships (Braedley & Luxton, 2010).

At its core neoliberalism embraces market fundamentalism (Sidhu, 2005) i.e. it not only seeks to expand current markets, but also looks to create new markets (Connell, 2013), because it perceives that state interference in the market mechanism contributes to poor economic performance. It therefore influences a number of changes in the relationships between state and society where the role of the state is shifted to create an appropriate institutional framework for the market to operate effectively (Harvey, 2007). Prechel and Harms (2007, p. 5) identify five stages in this process:

> *expand markets* by eliminating government policies interfering with markets, *cut taxes* to simultaneously reduce the resources of inefficient government and channel them to private investors for capital formation, *privatize* by selling public properties to private economic actors, *commodify* things that were not originally produced to be exchanged in the market (e.g. health, education, pollution), and *eliminate* social programs to establish personal responsibility.

However, in the contemporary global context, neoliberalism needs to be understood as having influence *beyond* the expanse of market, money and commodity (Bockman, 2013; McCarthy & Prudham, 2004). In his book *Firing Back: Against the Tyranny of the Market 2,* consisting of a series of public lectures, Pierre Bourdieu (2003), discusses the relationship between globalisation and neoliberalism. He argues that globalisation is often treated as a form of neoliberal economic policy, yet the practices of globalisation also have another meaning beyond such economic reform. Lingard, Rawolle and Taylor (2005, p. 765) argue, "in emphasizing the 'performative' sense of globalization as a term or concept with particular economic and political connotations, Bourdieu noted how economic globalization is the effect of a particular politics articulated by powerful agents of neo-liberalism". We discuss this in more detail below, in relation to postcoloniality.

Although globalisation has thus become an intrinsic feature of neoliberalism, and the terms 'globalisation' and 'neoliberalism' are, almost epistemologically interrelated, they refer to quite different sets of mechanisms. The economic, political and cultural aspects of society are directly affected by the complex values, ideologies and practices of neoliberalism (Ross & Gibson, 2007). Steger and Roy (2010) perceive neoliberalism to be an intertwined manifestation of an ideology, a mode of governance, as well as a policy package. The mode of ideology refers to an understanding of how to "legitimize certain political interests and to defend or challenge dominant power structures"; whereas the mode of governance embraces the idea of a self-regulating 'free' market to promote entrepreneurial values (Steger & Roy, 2010, p. 11). Klijn and Koppenjan (2000) explain that initially the notion of governance emerged from the idea of reducing state power through employing new public management (NPM) techniques and distinguishing between regulation and control directly by the government and governance of the self and organisations through self-organising networks. In turn, the idea of governance through self-organising networks has shifted the hierarchical mode of governance to network governance (Fawcett, Manwaring & Marsh, 2011).

However, models of NPM or network governance that ensure state control through what King (2004, cited in De Boer, Enders & Schimank, 2007, p. 141) calls "arm's-length" government bodies (as will be discussed in Chapter 5) and self-regulation, have provided a regulatory framework to ensure public accountability of public institutions (Ranson, 2003). Therefore, both NPM and network governance facilitate neoliberalism as an ideology because they legitimise, enforce and ensure that the ideas of the state are accepted. From this perspective, England and Ward (2011) outline its four main features: neoliberalism as an ideological hegemonic project, neoliberalism as policy and programme, neoliberalism as a state form, and neoliberalism as a form of governmentality. In the following chapters will look at the case of higher education in Bangladesh considering and utilising all of these four perspectives and how they have shaped understandings of welfare and entitlements, public and private good, profit and the commercialisation of higher education.

Although scholars have often discussed the concept of neoliberalism against the broader perspective, marketisation – which has been redefined in the global context – remains a key point of neoliberalism. Consequently, the market becomes the key principle of political, social and economic decisions (Chowdhury & Le Ha, 2014; Giroux, 2005; Sindu, 2005) in a setting where corporate power seizes individual freedom, public goods, democracy and citizenship (Giroux, 2005). Olssen and Peters (2005, p. 314) argue that "neoliberalism must be seen as a specific economic discourse or philosophy which has become dominant and effective in world economic relations as a consequence of super power sponsorship". By emphasising super power sponsorship, Olssen and Peters in fact highlight the *political* dimension of neoliberalism, which has become an ideology that affects political processes and legitimises the policies used to accumulate capital for the dominant power block of the world (Prechel & Harms, 2007) as well as vested interest groups, both nationally and internationally.

This section has provided a brief understanding of neoliberalism. At this point, the discussion is still not linked to higher education, but offers a broader understanding of the relationships among the economy, politics and culture in a society. Such a theoretical underpinning of neoliberalism helps us understand the relationships between the state and neoliberal shifts in higher education policies. In the next section, we look at the philosophical and political dimensions of neoliberal understandings.

The theoretical origins of neoliberalism

As a theoretical paradigm, the concept of neoliberalism has been successively developed by scholars representing a wide range of epistemologies and academic fields (Peck, 2008). Prechel and Harms (2007, p. 3) noted that the classical liberal tradition expressed in *The Wealth of Nations* by Adam Smith in 1776 provided the theoretical ground for neoliberal ideology. While all the early scholarly writings provided insights valuable for the development of the neoliberal theoretical paradigm as we understand it today, the systematic formation of neoliberalism was grounded in the collective works of Fredrich August von Hayek, and theorists associated with the Chicago School. These scholars worked with the theory of monetarism by Milton Friedman, public choice theory by James Buchanan as well as human capital theory by Theodore Schultz and Gary Becker (see Olssen & Peters, 2005; Roberts, 2007).

In the book *The Road to Serfdom*, Hayek (1944) discussed the problems of the planned socialist economy and suggested that "the absence of a pricing system would prevent producers from knowing true production possibilities and costs" (cited in Roberts & Peters, 2008, p. 12). In his paper in 1949, *The Intellectual and Socialism,* Hayek critiqued the role of intellectuals, academic institutions and their ideas for the rise of socialism. He argued that any movement in the direction of socialism leads to totalitarianism, and that economic freedom should be treated as the political and moral force that shapes all aspects of a free and open society. He argued that "the increasing of economic freedom led not only to rapid economic growth and the development of science and technology but also to the 'undesigned and unforeseen by-product of political freedom'" (Hayek, 1944, cited in Kohl & Farthing, 2006, p. 16).

For Hayek, individual freedom from society was a key aspect in the development of modern European history and industrial freedom created spaces for using new knowledge to change the world rapidly in the last 150 years. Hayek argued that money is the most important tool of freedom because it gives people choice in society, and that economic control means the control of all sorts of things in life. However economic freedom in central planning means that planning is led by collectivism rather than individualism and it makes one accept that collective efforts can solve our combined economic problems. In a similar manner, and more recently, Ong proposed that, as a "political philosophy", the principal elements of neoliberalism are a claim that the market is better than the state at distributing public resources; and that it is a return to a "primitive form of individualism: an individualism which is 'competitive,' 'possessive,' and construed often in terms of the doctrine of 'consumer sovereignty'" (2006, p. 11).

In another continent, Milton Friedman played a significant role in the formation of the American strands of neoliberalism (Peters, 2001). In his theory of monetarism, Friedman developed the idea of 'freedom to choose' where he argued for economic freedom, contending that two broad principles needed to be addressed to create maximum opportunity for economic growth. First, "the scope of government must be limited", and second, "government power must be dispersed" (Friedman, 1962, p. 2). In line with this, liberals contributed to establishing and patronising state intervention in the name of welfare and social equity in the twentieth century. For Friedman, economic freedom is an indispensable condition for social development, while political freedom is a *result* of economic freedom:

> There is an intimate connection between economics and politics, that only certain combinations of political and economic arrangements are possible, and that, in particular, a society which is socialist cannot also be democratic, in the sense of guaranteeing individual freedom.
>
> (Friedman, 1962, p. 8)

Economic freedom is also an indispensable part of total freedom and a particular style of economic organisation in ensuring economic freedom. Theoretically at least, capitalism is necessary for political freedom since it contributes to the separation of economic power from political (or state) power.

Similarly, James Buchanan introduced a major shift from liberal to neoliberal government processes of reform in which state mechanisms set out to work for economic growth (Olssen, 2002; Olssen & Peters, 2005). "Public choice", as a set of ideas about politics, emerged during the post-revolutionary and post-socialist periods of intense ideological conflict and had matured with the decline of Marxist views of socialist and collectivist ideals (Buchanan, 1993, p. 67). Buchanan argued that public choice provides an explanation of the failure of political processes of the socialist system:

> The consequences of public choice will presumably be reflected in the increased difficulty that collectivist-control advocates will face in restoring the status quo ante in non-Western regimes and in expanding the range of politicization in Western settings.
>
> (Buchanan, 1993, p. 67)

In Buchanan's view, "public choice theorists were concerned with the marketization of the public sector through the deliberate actions of the state" (Olssen & Peters, 2005, p. 319). Markets were seen as a useful technology to be used by the state. Buchanan relied on *conscious action* instead of faith in the concept of the 'spontaneous' ordering of market that was also emphasised by Hayek (Reisman, 1990, cited in Olssen & Peters, 2005). He distinguished between the 'protective state' and the 'productive state'. The protective state is one that develops a strong set of constitutional rules, whereas the productive state allows relatively free participation where the state acts merely as a 'policeman' to regulate market flow positively (Reisman, 1990, cited in Olssen & Peters, 2005, p. 319).

The marketability of higher education was serendipitous. While Hayek, Freedman and Buchanan argued for individual freedom, freedom of choice and neoliberal government in the public sector respectively for market expansion (Olssen & Peters, 2005), it was Theodore Schultz and Gary Becker who looked at how education could be used as a *tool* in the economy of a country. They formulated the human capital theory through which they argued for the economic value of investing in education. Schultz (1961) identified education as an investment in people to form human capital:

> Since it [education] becomes an integral part of a person, it cannot be bought or sold or treated as property under our institutions. Nevertheless, it is a form of capital if it renders a productive service of value to the economy.
>
> (Schultz, 1960, p. 571)

Similarly, Becker (1993) developed a theoretical model in which he developed an argument about why people should invest in education. He critiqued the traditional form of capital, such as that held in bank accounts and in the share market, because of its fragility. Instead, Becker (1993, p. 16) argued, investing in education produced human capital "because you cannot separate a person from his or her knowledge, skills, health, or values the way it is possible to move financial and physical assets while the owner stays put".

All these theorists provided the philosophical and political bases of neoliberalism as it is known and enacted today. In particular, Hayek's political and economic philosophy provided the basis for restructuring state bureaucracy, and prompted the notions of 'deregulation', 'internationalisation', 'corporatisation' and 'privatisation'; while Friedman's ideas of 'freedom to choose' and Buchanan's idea of 'public choice' provided the theoretical underpinnings of New Public Management (NPM); and Schultz and Becker's idea of human capital theory provided the theoretical basis for what we now call the 'knowledge economy'. By now, these concepts of privatisation, NPM, internationalisation and the knowledge economy have become essential components of the dominant neoliberal discourses in higher education policies across the world, which we discuss later in this chapter. An understanding of these theoretical and philosophical underpinnings of neoliberalism provides us a solid grounding into the conceptual foundation of the various neoliberal ideas in higher education policies.

International financial institutions (IFIs) and neoliberal policies

Based on the neoliberal philosophies of the late 1970s, the then US President Ronald Reagan and British Prime Minister Margaret Thatcher formulated and implemented what Peters (2001, p. 19) calls "a policy mixer based on free trade and open economy". At the same time the Chinese government also took momentous steps towards the liberalisation of its communist economic system (Harvey, 2005). Since then, International Financial Institutions (IFIs) including the World Bank, the International Monetary Fund (IMF), as well as some agencies of the United Nations, including the United Nations Educational, Scientific and Cultural Organisation (UNESCO) and the Organisation for Economic Cooperation and Development (OECD), became involved in promoting neoliberal activities around the World (Torres, 2009).

Since then, the IFIs, particularly the IMF, the World Bank, as well as regional development banks, have provided significant amounts of money to the developing world in the name of aid for policy reformation. Rizvi and Lingard (2010) argue that along with the IMF and the World Bank, some other international agencies, for example the OECD, have assumed positions as the leading organisations in social policy over the last few decades. The roles of the OECD include providing technical support to prepare educational indicators and the measurement of educational performance globally. Like other international organisations, the OECD influences national politics through neoliberal discourses that are required to be accepted in their changes in policy (Rizvi, 2014; Lingard & Rawolle, 2011).

International agencies have built up networks with global civil societies to construct a global policy model and to promote policies in different parts of the world (Schriewer, 2000; Steiner-Khamsi, 2004). The key aim of such global policy models is to shape national policy into "economisation" by adopting the idea of human capital (Lingard & Rawolle, 2011, p. 492). As discussed in the previous section, the idea of the economisation of education to promote human development was originally proposed by Schultz (1960) and Becker (1993). Based on their premise, transnational corporations consider human resource management (HRM) and human resource development (HRD) as significant policy practices.

The idea of human development however was broadly exported into the developing world without considering the socio-cultural consequences of the transfer of such HRM and HRD practices (Turbin, 2001) in such settings. This means developing countries were forced to adopt global policy models through continuous pressure from the international community, international agents and agencies in the form of donations and other economic incentives (Kabir & Chowdhury, 2017). Policies are also taken from the 'global North' and applied inconsiderably to the 'global South' under international agreements – for example, the Education For All (EFA) or Millennium Development Goals (MDGs) (Steiner-Khamsi, 2006).

In policy studies, neoliberalism is often clustered synonymously with the term 'Washington Consensus'. The latter was coined by John Williamson in 1990 and refers to the "lowest common dominator of policy advice directed at mostly Latin American countries by the International Monetary Fund, the World Bank, and other Washington-based international institutions and think tanks" (Steger & Roy, 2010, p. 19). The Washington Consensus is viewed as an 'international convergence', where it is believed that economic reform is needed for greater achievement to occur (Rizvi & Lingard, 2010). The Washington Consensus has a ten-point programme which includes a list of factors and ideas that are required for the 'global South' to achieve economic development. The 10 points include fiscal discipline and control of budget deficit, reduction of public expenditure, tax reform, financial liberalisation, competitive exchange rates, trade liberalisation, promotion of foreign direct investment, privatisation of state enterprises, deregulation of the economy and protection of property rights (Steger & Roy, 2010). Through this ten-point programme, "market-fundamentalism" is given priority in policy processes and practices by IFIs throughout the world.

Neoliberal economic reforms were introduced and operated worldwide by the General Agreement on Tariffs and Trade (GATT) agreement imposed by the World Trade Organisation (WTO) starting in 1995 (Lang, 2011). The WTO functions as a judicialised trading system used to reach consensus between power blocks and remove obstacles to the deregulation of markets. A set of international rules has been adopted by the powerful countries in order to create space for multilateral economic organisations in the world trading system (Munck, 2005).

Although certain revisions have been made to the neoliberal Washington Consensus since the 1990s, free trade remains a core issue of this policy agenda. The Washington Consensus addresses not only tariff reduction, but also the coordination by the WTO of institutional, legal and political reforms. Deraniyagala (2005, p. 100) argues that the WTO "seeks to bring about international harmonisation of institutional, regulatory and legal standards through a variety of agreements and standards". Based on the Washington Consensus, various countries have introduced reforms into their education sectors such as reducing state funds for higher education, privatisation and deregulation of education (Rizvi & Lingard, 2010). In addition, the notions of intellectual and property rights have been explicitly introduced in education policy in accordance with WTO. Under neoliberalism, knowledge is treated as a raw material to be protected from all sorts of sites, to preserve its patent, copyright and trademark, and to sell it at a profit on the market. For example, Slaughter & Rhoades (2004) show how universities in the West use a wide range of mechanisms to protect its intellectual property.

This section has provided a focused understanding of the nature of neoliberal policy transfer in the global context and its relationship with the various activities, priorities and agenda of IFIs. The discussion has shown how IFIs have influenced developing countries and have used various strategies to formulate and disperse neoliberal polices at the national level in these countries. In the introductory chapter we critically discussed how the government of Bangladesh initiated a range of neoliberal policy reforms, such as the Strategic Plan for Higher Education as part of its higher education overhaul, with financial and technical support of the World Bank. The understanding of IFIs' activities around the world and the relation of these to the promotion of neoliberal ideas at the state level help to extend our understandings of some of the central concepts explored in this book.

Neoliberalism and global higher education trends

As discussed, since the late 1970s neoliberalism has consolidated into a key policy doctrine in nearly every sector around the world (Giddens, 1999; Harvey, 2005). Among these, education is yet another sector where a neoliberal policy agenda has been conspicuously incorporated over the last three decades. Initially, the attempt to incorporate the neoliberal policy agenda was conceived for and activated in the primary and secondary education sectors (Levidow, 2007). In universities, on the other hand, overt privatisation had mainly targeted non-educational and logistic or infrastructural aspects – such as catering and security, rather than the provision of education, the designing of the curriculum and aspects of teaching and learning. However, from the 1980s, it has been a worldwide trend for universities to adopt commercial models of knowledge, skills, curriculum, finance, accounting and management organisation (Levidow, 2007). For example, universities in the US have adopted 'business models', aiming at cutting costs, reducing academic activities, increasing faculty teaching responsibilities and privatising various institutional functions (Johnstone, 1997; Slaughter & Rhoades, 2004).

Similarly, higher education institutions in the UK are treated as 'borderless business' (Levidow, 2007). Indeed, government funds for universities were reduced substantially while Thatcher was the Prime Minister of the UK in the 1980s. At the same time, the first research assessment exercise was carried out in all universities in 1986 (Edwards, 1997), while in the late 1990s, the UK government abolished students' maintenance grants and introduced tuition fees (Levidow, 2007) for the first time.

Similar to the US and the UK, in 1989 the government of Australia first introduced tuition fees along with the Higher Education Contribution Scheme (HECS) (Naidoo & Williams, 2015). This meant that domestic postgraduate students in non-research degrees were now charged with commercial fees for the first time, while all doctoral programmes were designed to recruit more 'foreign' students in a now cross-border market (Marginson, 2006). In the same way, based on the 'Third Way' approach, the government of New Zealand, a country once known as the laboratory of welfare of the world, adopted neoliberal policy agendas more than two decades ago (Roberts, 2009). The idea of the Third Way approach refers to the idea of mixing policies taken from the right and left of economic policy reforms. Third Way policies involve the government supporting citizens to generate human capital so that they can become self-supporting and the state can eventually reduce its role, "rather than the direct provision of economic maintenance" by the state to its citizens (Giddens, 1998, p. 117) – an approach sometimes referred to as nudge theory (Leggett, 2014).

The 'entrepreneurial' model of the university (Marginson & Considine, 2000) has since become entrenched in many developing countries around the world (Bensimon & Ordorika, 2006). For many Asian countries, along with the IFIs

(Torres, 2009), the US has also provided ideas and fostered academic development (Altbach, 2004). Altbach (2004) explains that many Asian countries such as Japan, Korea, Singapore and Taiwan adopted the idea of a knowledge-based economy in the higher education sector as a key factor in their national economic development. Other Asian countries, such as China and India, as regional giants, have also moved towards transforming their higher education systems into those of "'post-industrial information societies'" – as have South Korea, Taiwan and Malaysia (Altbach, 2004, p. 21). China began adopting market-related approaches in its higher education institutions in the post-Mao period (from 1978 up to the present) (Mok, 2005); while India had begun shifting to a neoliberal economic model from state regulation in the early 1990s (Kamat, 2011a). Kamat (2011b) argues that rather than being the *result* of a state-level initiative, the high-tech society network in the Indian city of Hyderabad played a key role in spreading the neoliberal model in higher education across the nation. In 2005, the Indian government formed a National Knowledge Commission to outline a new vision for higher education (Kamat, 2011a). In China, the key reforms related to higher education were aimed at deregulation and marketisation (Mok, 2003). The Chinese government opened up higher education to the private sector with many foreign universities offering higher education in China (Mok, 2009). Additional details of these countries are presented in the next chapter.

Ross and Gibson (2007) explain three key processes in integrating neoliberalism in the education sector. First, the educational services market is opened up to profit-based educational management through international trade and investment agreements – such as the General Agreement on Trade in Services (GATS). This New Public Management (NPM) became recognised as one of the most striking trends in the public management sector around the world (Hood, 1991; Lorenz, 2012). The central trend of this change in public management is a shift toward accountability and administration (Hood, 1995). Ward (2012) points out four major changes that have been brought into higher education institutions following the adoption of NPM. The first was the introduction of private sector management practices in the public sector with a particular focus on ongoing development in productivity and efficiency. The second involved offering market-style incentives to wipe out government bureaucracies. The third was the development of customer-oriented behaviour where "consumer choice", "client services" and "customer satisfaction" are established as key principles of the university (Kettl, 2000, cited in Ward, 2012, p. 53).

Universities use many strategies and techniques to advertise certain programmes as 'unique' and as the best available, and in order to appeal to customers (in this case, prospective students). They develop "glossy promotional materials and sophisticated websites filled with air brushed photos of happy students, proud parents and distinguished faculty" (Ward, 2012, p. 54; see also, Chowdhury & Le Ha, 2014). Fourth, within public institutions, a "user pays" system (Arshad-Ayaz, 2007) and "responsibility center management" (Zemsky et al., 2008) are introduced (cited in Ward, 2012). Thus, the various departments within a university are required to become self-dependent by paying their own expenditure and costs, and managing their own tasks as defined by the service provider – in this case, the university.

Second, educational costs are reduced (Ross & Gibson, 2007). This reduction often happens through infrastructural downsizing, such as closing school libraries, reducing the number of special needs teachers and increasing class sizes. In effect, universities around the world have adopted diverse sources of funding strategies to mitigate their financial needs (Amaral, Meek, & Larsen, 2003) that have come to be often labelled, euphemistically, as *cost-sharing* (Johnstone & Marcucci, 2010). Cost-sharing refers "to a shift of at least some of the higher educational cost burden from governments, or taxpayers, to parents and students" (Johnstone & Marcucci, 2010, p. 2). In accordance with the cost-sharing approach, parents and or students are increasingly responsible to pay tuition and other fees for higher education (Altbach et al., 2010).

Third, curriculum standards and "accountability" are created (Ross & Gibson, 2007, p. 4). Torres (2009) points out that the main agendas of neoliberalism in education are to privatise and decentralise public education, set narrow educational standards, develop purely quantitative testing of academic achievement, and call for accountability on the basis of a narrow range of outcomes. A range of quality assurance mechanisms are developed and implemented to assess quality of institutions and the quality of programmes universities offer (Altbach et al., 2010; El-Khawas, DePietro-Jurand, & Holm-Nielsen, 1998). Two types of quality assurance processes have been developed in higher education. While the *Internal quality assurance* emphasises developing policies and mechanisms for the institution and programmes to meet its own objectives and standards, *external quality assurance* involves the operations of the institutions and its programmes to be assessed by an external body to determine whether it meets agreed-upon or predetermined standards (Sanyal & Martin, 2007).

Quality assurance mechanisms have been developed in different forms, including 'quality audit', 'quality assessment' and 'accreditation'. 'Quality audit' is treated as the first step in the quality assurance process in which audits are performed by individuals not involved in the subject examined. They examine an institute or one of its sub-units using a system of quality assurance procedures and determine its adequacy. Such a 'self-study' process in an institution evaluates the effectiveness of the internal quality system (Altbach et al., 2010). On the other hand, the 'accreditation' approach involves external agencies in the quality assurance processes. The accreditation council "evaluates the quality of a higher education institution as a whole, or a specific higher education programme/course, in order to formally recognize it as having met certain predetermined criteria or standards and award a quality label" (Sanyal & Martin, 2007, p. 6). Both the ideas of internal and external quality assurances are developed from the neoliberal orientation of NPM. Through introducing quality assurance mechanisms, the public accountability of higher education institutions is ensured (see for example, Westerheijden, Stensaker, & Rosa, 2007).

Although the governments of non-Western countries developed neoliberal models in higher education in line with global developments, they formulated their own forms of governance and administration in their higher education systems to accommodate the needs of their different market conditions. This is one of the central interests of this book. Arguably, the cost-sharing approach of financing in the higher education sector takes many different forms worldwide. However, the extent to which cost-sharing can be implemented depends on the particular countries and the status of their economic development, their relative wealth and level of industrialisation, as well as, of course, the historical development of higher education and level of participation, the prevailing political ideologies, and the overall size and maturity of privatisation of higher education (Johnstone & Marcucci, 2010).

Often governments of middle and low-income countries throughout the world are influenced by IFIs in adopting a cost-sharing approach in the higher education sector. For example, in 1998, the World Bank proposed ten recommendations for universities in Mexico to manage their own finances. These included introducing a large amount of registration fees, charging full fees for room and board, introducing a mechanism to investigate economic resources for student loans and grants, introducing student loans based on the market interest, introducing private companies to collect student loans, imposing graduation fees and implementing them, promoting philanthropy, ensuring entrepreneurial training for improving quality education, offering for-sale research project findings and training courses, and increasing the number of private institutions with a corresponding decrease in public education (Delgado-Ramos & Saxe-Fernández, 2009). The neoliberal measurements the Mexican government adopted during the 1980s and 1990s with such prescriptions from IFIs eventually changed the relationships between the state and its higher education institutions. In particular, as reported in Alcántara, Llomovatte and Romão's (2013) study, public universities' governance, evaluation of funding systems and its overall directions were directly affected by the government's intervention based on the aforementioned neoliberalist principles.

Mok (2008) argues that the key trend of such neoliberal models in Asian countries opens up the higher education sector to foreign entrants and can provide only limited improvement to the universities' autonomy. For him, for example, despite the different approaches of private universities in Asian countries, their key characteristic is to develop a hybrid form of private university through the blending of a neoliberal model and the (pre-existing) state-model of public universities. These hybrid-forms of private universities are a result of the way in which domestic socio-political and economic factors mediate the global pressure for adopting neoliberal ideas in local contexts (Rosser, 2016) as we will see in the next chapter.

Consequently, while universities in USA and UK are expanding as elite/semi-elite or demand absorbing institutions by attracting a large number of revenue generating students, universities in developing countries, such as China and India, have shaped this kind of revenue generating interaction in the private sector by imposing policies and regulations in order to control 'low quality' universities (Naidoo, 2011). In many cases, such distinctive hybrid forms of the neoliberal model have been transferred between regional countries – for example, instead of adopting a Western model, Indonesia has developed a "centralist and predatory model" of higher education derived from other East-Asian countries such as China, Singapore, Malaysia and Hong Kong (Rosser, 2016, p. 123). Rosser (2016) reports that the key features of this model are limited autonomy for higher education institutes, restricted competition and poor quality control.

Similarly, although the internationalisation of higher education has been a common phenomenon in many Asian countries, the governments of these countries would have different interests in this process and thus, different governments have adopted different kinds of policies and regulatory measurements to regulate their international universities. For example, while the government of Hong Kong has adopted the free market approach for transnational higher education, the rise of transnational education in Malaysia was connected with the financial crisis in Asia in 1997 (Mok, 2008). The financial crisis affected the Malaysian economy, particularly with the falling of local currency, and thus the government prioritised the internationalisation of local higher education, thereby allowing private higher education provision through international universities operating locally, as a way of tackling financial crisis in the higher education system (Mok, 2008).

It would appear from the above discussion that such forms of neoliberalism have been the key feature of contemporary global higher education systems. However many countries have been translating various neoliberal ideas in sometimes significantly different ways into their higher education systems. Hall and Soskice (2001, p. 2), for example, argue that "varieties of capitalism" is a feature of world economies, and therefore, the *style* of democracy and socio-political contexts would vary among countries. Appadurai (1996, p. 10) terms the way in which the development of local policies is mediated through both global policy discourses and local socio-cultural contexts "vernacular globalization". Such discussion by scholars like Appadurai (1996) indicates the shifting of the balance of power especially in the field of education policy making between the West and developing nations, including 'postcolonial' countries such as Bangladesh. Appadurai (2000, p. 3) argues that "a series of social forms has emerged to contest, interrogate, and reverse these developments and to create forms of knowledge transfer and social mobilisation that proceed independently of the actions of corporate capital and the nation-state system". Considering local social phenomenon and its relationship with the market, this way of thinking about "grassroots globalisation" can be identified as "globalisation from below" (Appadurai, 2000, p. 3). Consequently, Carney (2009) argues that globalisation must be understood as a phenomenon in the sense of it being *both* an object and a process.

In addition, Sellar and Lingard (2013) have discussed the growing complexity of the role of global governance in education. They argue that international global agencies are playing an increasingly significant role in introducing popular ideas within national contexts. Ball (2008) argues that this kind of change in the field of education policy has fostered new relationships between the education sector and other organisations and interests based on the development of network governance in the policy communities where new policy actors and agencies are brought together and are then able to influence education policies. By identifying the significance of global factors, Ball rescales the context of policy and emphasises the importance of "both international organizations and global edu-business in the education policy cycle and the implications for doing policy analysis" (Lingard & Sellar, 2013, 265).

"Postcoloniality" and neoliberalism

More importantly, an understanding of the colonial histories of the postcolonial space is important when analysing the education policy effects of globalisation (Lingard, 2009). As discussed in the Preface and in Chapter 1, we acknowledged the importance of the colonial political and historical processes of adopting the British Education system in Bangladesh and identified how these processes have been influential in shaping current day higher education policies in a number of ways. Scholars that adopt a postcolonial theoretical strand have discussed the power relations between the coloniser and the colonised and the effects and influences of residual power relationships on current policy affairs of the post-colonial space (Bhabha, 1994; Spivak, 1990; see also, Kabir & Chowdhury, 2017).

It is important to note here, once again, that as we outlined in the Preface, we understand that the notion of 'postcolonial' is problematic and relative; not just in the context of formerly colonised countries like Bangladesh, but even when used in a broader, more absolutist sense. Colonialism or postcolonialism is more about the both historical *and* ahistorical configurations and reconfigurations of power and hegemonic structures (both material and symbolic) that are legitimised through privileged discourses at any given time. In fact, critics like Shohat (1992) and Dirlik (1994) warn about the inadequacy of postcolonial theories, arguing that in considering colonialism as a mere event of the past, the canon of post-colonial scholarship has essentially failed to address the continuing legacy of colonialism through various forms of 'neocolonial' economic globalisation in contemporary times. In fact, Shohat (1992) saw the hegemonic expansion of free trade and trade liberalisation as nothing but "new forms of colonialism" (p. 107) or neo-colonialism. Dirlik (1994, p. 353) similarly argued that postcolonialism has been a "theoretical endeavour" to camouflage the crisis of global capitalism:

> to put it bluntly, postcoloniality is designed to *avoid* making sense of the current crisis and, in the process, to cover up the origins of postcolonial intellectuals in a global capitalism of which they are not so much victims as beneficiaries.
>
> (p. 353)

Bhabha (1994) uses the term 'ambivalence' to understand how stereotypes and identities are constructed to reinforce the cultural supremacy between the colonised and the coloniser, or between the subjugator and the subjugated. In order to understand how such ambivalence works, Bhabha (1994) argues that colonial discourses produce a subordinate subject (the colonised) that *re*produces colonial habits, attitudes and values (cited in Andreotti, 2006) – one who cannot fully realise how they are downplaying the imposition of power by the coloniser. The way in which colonial attitudes, habits, assumptions and values are copied by the colonised are referred to by Bhabha as 'mimicry' (Bhabha, 1994). Similarly, in her critique of imperialism, Spivak (1990) emphasises the importance of understanding the cultural dimension of imperialism and its relation in the creation of a 'Third World'. For Spivak (1999), through cultural imperialism the colonial changes the 'Subaltern's' perception to neutralise and legitimise the cultural supremacy of the First World and reinforce the adoption of Western ideas as global ideas into colonised countries (Andreotti, 2006).

It is in this sense that Nandi (2016) insists that hybridity is a quintessential condition of globalisation. The turn of the new century has seen what Nandi (2016, n.p.) calls a "materialist turn" in postcolonial studies, with emphasis shifted to the "material realities of the postcolonial world in the context of neoliberal globalization". This book considers the case of Bangladeshi higher education within the macro context of current day power dynamics – between local, national and international institutes and corporations, nation states and global markets, as well as the instruments and mechanisms of international trade and policy, including the aforementioned IFIs. To that extent, it is difficult to ignore the persistence of networks of power and hegemony distributed across these various actors, and the power hierarchies espoused within such understandings. A colonial mindset and the networks of power dispersed through such established structure, vis-à-vis the agentive role of individuals as education consumers – and in this case, students seeking education in private universities – allow neoliberal structures and mechanisms to be seen as ideological artefacts that embed both symbolic and material forms of hegemonic control.

Postcolonial theorists such as Stuart Hall and Ania Loomba both believed that all of the recent phenomena of the modern world could be understood through the framework of colonialism. Similarly, Mignolo (2007) explains the futility of understanding modernity without understanding coloniality because of their mutually constitutive nature. He goes on to argue that modernity often disguises coloniality due to the latter's connotative associations with control, oppression and exploitation. He therefore proposes the use of the terms "coloniality of power", and "de-colonial thinking" to explore "simultaneous histories … inter-connected by imperial and colonial powers" (pp. 155–6). These terms provide a strong lens for utilising postcolonial theories and frameworks in understanding neoliberal rationales and principles for higher education, especially in a country like Bangladesh which has a history of 200 years of colonial rule.

Postcolonial theories also provide a powerful basis to understand how knowledge is produced, justified, circulated, consumed and serve the interest of the Global North, which continues to enjoy a position of power over the Global South (Lingard, 2009). It follows from this theorisation that 'ethnocentrism', centred on the West, has become a universal psychological process through which people tend to continue to believe in the superiority of the Western view as the best way to change the world (Dasen & Akkari, 2009). In this sense, Eurocentric views 'colonise' indigenous and local knowledge and belief systems by imposing Western policies and systems on indigenous people. Colonial and neo-colonial models characterise indigenous knowledge systems as primitive resulting in the destruction of indigenous people's self-esteem and self-confidence (Battiste, 2008). A postcolonial perspective, then, allows one to view globalisation as a continuous and ongoing process of colonialism (Spivak, 1999) and one that "continues to be used in the interest of global consumerist culture anchored in the West and to interrupt the totalizing effects of a neo- imperial globalization" (Lunga, 2008, p. 198).

More importantly, the postcolonial consideration facilitates a nuanced understanding of the growing complexity of new geographies and geopolitics of power and knowledge in the policy borrowing process (Beech & Artopoulos 2016). It is important to look at the original and operationalisations of neoliberal ideas where both the forms of democracy and the varieties of capitalism are 'different', such as in Bangladesh. Therefore, any critical and scholarly discussion on neoliberal theories has only left unexplained the roles of what Hall and Soskice (2001, p. 2) call "varieties of capitalism" in incorporating neoliberal policies in the higher education sector in Bangladesh.

Conclusion

By laying out the conceptual framework for this study, this chapter has problematised neoliberalism and postcolonialism against the backdrop of contemporary global higher education trends. We have seen that the complex historical processes through which ideologies have been mixed and matched to suit local contexts – even as being influenced at the global level – have resulted in distinct and amorphous features of neoliberal practices around the world. In the next chapter we look at some of these international contexts in greater depth.

We have seen that while the British colonisers left the Subcontinent, state machineries in the form of policies, institutes and bodies of power assumed the role of the coloniser by imbibing their epistemic residues. This has made it possible for current practices in higher education to rely on the logic of neoliberalist principles to assume the position of authority and dictate changes, alongside the IFIs who have disseminated the same principles in the guise of their agenda for so-called national development.

3 Privatisation of higher education

Contemporary trends and issues in Asian countries

Introduction

The previous chapter outlined how the higher education sector has been reformed based on neoliberalist privatisation practices across the world. In order to situate the contemporary trends of neoliberal practices in higher education in current day Bangladesh in the backdrop of this global and regional phenomenon, in this chapter we consider some of the persisting trends that have characterised private higher education in some of these countries in Asia. In order to trace some of the distinct features in the privatisation of higher education we look at five countries in Asia – China, India, Malaysia, Sri Lanka and Vietnam.

Ong (2006), who works on the anthropology of emerging global situations, sees neoliberalism as having developed differently in Asian countries from the West. To her, as a "a new mode of political optimization" (p. 4) and a "technology of governing" (p. 13), neoliberalism is used for "transformation where market-driven calculations are bring introduced in the management of populations and the administration of special spaces" (p. 4–5). Referring to Foucault, Ong posits that neoliberalism is essentially a "technology of governing relies on calculative choices and techniques in the domains of citizenship and of governing" (p. 5). In relation to Asian contexts, Ong (2006, p. 5) argues that neoliberal "exceptions" have manifested differently in Asian settings to "recalculate social criteria of citizenship, to remoralize economic action, and to redefine spaces in relation to market-driven choices" resulting in "a range of contingent and ambiguous outcomes that cannot be predicted beforehand". She continues that such practices have also "created new forms of inclusion, setting apart some citizen-subjects, and creating new spaces that enjoy extraordinary political benefits and economic gain".

An important acknowledgement here is that rather than debating loosely defined geographical regions such as 'South Asia', 'South East Asia', 'Australasia' or the 'Far East', we have adopted the broader term 'Asia', and have included in this chapter countries that may or may not fall in any of these categories. Instead, the selection represents a cross-section that features historical, economic, political and cultural diversity and a wide spectrum of policy rhetoric yet are geographically significant in understanding trends happening in Bangladesh.

Policy studies in the past three decades have shown that neoliberal ideas do not just travel unidirectionally from the West to developing countries, but also from region to region (Kabir, 2016). Often such borrowings and transfers first occur at the abstract and ideological level, before it manifests in concrete policy directives. While taking shape, these practices absorb and integrate local value systems and rationales espoused by the ruling elite, including political parties, businesses and other vested interest groups. Such local context shapes neoliberalism in a way which Appadurai (2000, p. 3) identifies as "grassroot globalisation". Ong (2006) in her idea of neoliberalism as exception argues that a contradictory form of neoliberal feature could be experienced in Southeast Asian countries where neoliberal ethos encounters and re-articulates different ethical regimes. For example, neoliberal exception in the Islamic sphere escalates the debate over the "female virtue" in Southeast Asia where economic rationality, religious norms and citizenship values can co-exist with each other (Ong, 2006, p. 9).

In the context of Bangladesh, policymakers often refer to what Kabir (2016) calls 'semi-peripheral references' as an authority and *raison d'etre* to justify the adaptation of neoliberal ideas in the higher education sector. Although the purpose of exploring the features of privatisation of higher education in the selected Asian countries in this chapter is not to make a straightforward comparative analysis, it provides better understanding of how patterns of neoliberalism have shifted in each of these regions and to what extent the Bangladeshi higher education sector has adopted such trends into its system. The ensuing discussion also helps trace some of the discursive mechanisms that have been historically shaped in the region and have contested with Western ideologies in shaping up distinct neoliberal practices in each of these countries.

A substantial part of this chapter is based on facts and figures that were sourced from the available sources of national and international bodies. Significant methodological constraints were experienced in collecting such data, especially in the form of statistics. We realised that it was not always easy to access information such as official or national statistics, policy documents, including successive reform attempts from government and official websites such as the national bureaux of statistics. Even empirical data from interviews had limitations – snowballing often resulted in referrals to entities and players who had a similar stake to referrers in the micropolitics of the neoliberal agenda in private sector higher education, and those whose ideological positions matched with their own. Our realisation was that it was impossible to get a comprehensive picture without a detailed consideration of the local context and how these micropolitics played out. However, the discussion in this chapter is based on recent facts and figures from various local sources in these countries and while not the main aim of this chapter, comparisons are inevitable and have been made to give an integrated image of global and local trends as they play out in this part of the globe.

China

Until 1978 in the People's Republic of China – under the state of Mao Zedong – socioeconomic policies were developed in line with a socialist and centralised ideological doctrine. Higher education policies were no exception, and as a communist state China exercised and adopted high and tight controlling measures over the higher education sector, especially in terms of financing and its governance system (Mok, 2005). Mok (2005) reports that under the state of Mao Zedong, the Chinese Communist Party (CCP) abolished provisions of all kind of non-state-run educational facilities, including Missionaries-run religious education.

In the post-Mao period (from 1978 to present), however, the Chinese Communist Party began introducing economic reforms that were broadly based on neoliberal policy doctrines. Following a period of economic reform, the CCP started adopting market-related approaches in its higher education institutions. During the 1980s, China achieved high literacy rates and impressive economic growth that prompted the Chinese government to adopt neoliberal-based policy doctrines in their higher education system to serve the needs of a high-tech economy (Altbach, 2004). At this stage, the key reforms related to higher education in China were mainly aimed at deregulation, privatisation and marketisation (Mok, 2003) and these initiatives opened up higher education to the private sector, with many foreign universities now offering higher education in the country.

The idea of *minban* (non-state run, but through people, or community-run] university was developed based on a mix-private and public consumption in the higher education sector in the mid-1985. Mok (2009) explains that there were three waves of *minban* higher education in China. The first wave of *minban* began in the early 1980s when a group of experienced professors, school principals and educationists focused on three key reformations: insufficient educational investment, insufficient teachers and poor school infrastructure. The first wave of *minban* put forward reopening the higher education institute into the private sector after 36 years of the closure of private universities in mainland China in 1982 (Mok, 2009). In the early 1990s, the second wave of *minban* began when reformists focused on the status of students studying in private universities compared to state-run public universities. Following this, the Chinese government adopted the 'Provisional Provisions on Setting up Private Higher Education Institutions' through which the Government recognised private higher education institutions as an integral part of country's economy. This ensured the legitimate rights and interests of private higher education institutions and improved the governance system of these institutions. The law also ensured that private higher education institutions and their academic teaching staff and students will enjoy equal status with those enjoyed by state-run universities and their teachers and students (Ministry of Education of the People's Republic of China, 1993). The third wave of *minban* began from the late 1990s and onwards and accelerated the massive growth of private higher education across China (Mok, 2009), a trend that continues today.

Although private universities receive no government funding, they are to be operated in a non-profit manner and are managed by local provincial education administrative departments (Ministry of Education of the People's Republic of China, 2004). As of 2019, there are a total of 2,688 higher education institutions in China, of which 757 are *minban* higher education (Ministry of Education of the People's Republic of China, 2020). Along with these officially recognised *minban* private higher education institutes, there is a large number of unofficial and unrecognised *minban* private higher education operating (Mok, 2009). Students enrolment in recognised *minban* general undergraduate and college programmes have increased to 19.43% over the previous year (Ministry of Education of the People's Republic of China, 2020).

In early 2000, China transitioned into the process of enhancing cross-border education to ensure global research and international training capacity building of its top universities (Altbach, 2004). Currently, China is not only the provider of the largest number of international students all over the world, but also one of the top host countries for international students. Since 2000, the number of Chinese students has increased by around 1,600%, with over 660,000 studying overseas in 2018 (Esaki-Smith, 2020). Similarly, just as the number of outbound Chinese students has increased, the number of international students in universities in China has also increased, following the introduction of the Study in China programme launched by the Chinese Ministry of Education in 2010. As part of this plan, the Chinese government has set up the goal to be the host for 500,000 international students by 2020 (Cai, 2020). Interestingly, the Chinese government reached this goal in 2018, with 492,185 international students enrolled in different Chinese higher education institutions today (Cai, 2020). China is now the second largest host country for international students by overtaking the UK, after the US.

Since 2003, China has also encouraged local higher education institutes – particularly regional universities – to establish collaborative programmes with foreign universities in internationalising these local universities. In order to achieve this goal, in 2010 the Chinese government adopted a 10-year plan named *the National Medium and Long-term Plan for Education Reform and Development (2010–2020)* through which it outlined strategies for improving the quality of higher education by allowing internationally reputed universities to establish their branch campuses with local universities (Hou, Hill, Chen & Tsai, 2018).

Under the Chinese education system, there are currently three types of educational programmes – joint institutions established as independent legal entities; institutions without legal status within or attached to an existing Chinese institution; and joint education programmes – under the Sino-Foreign programmes (Department of Education, Skills and Employment, 2020a). Regardless of the type, all foreign branches/campuses need to operate their programmes in partnership with local institutes. China is currently hosting 32 International Branch Campuses (IBCs) and has become the top host country by edging out UAE in 2015 (ICEF, 2016). In fact, from 2011 to 2015 the growth of IBCs has risen by 26% in China (ICEF, 2016).

Under joint institutions established as independent legal entities programme, there are currently six international universities operating in China (Hou et al., 2018). Among them, the University of Nottingham, which was the first Sino-foreign university was established in 2004 and operated with the full approval of the Ministry of Education in partnership with the Zhejiang Wanli Education Group

(University of Nottingham Ningbo China, 2020). On the other hand, a large number of foreign branch campuses has been operating under local institutions without legal status within or attached to existing Chinese institution programmes. Under this second type of programme, there are three Australian universities – Monash University, Victoria University and the University of Technology Sydney (UTS) that have been operating in China (Department of Education, Skills and Employment, 2020a). This rapid growth of IBCs shows how the Chinese government has been promoting local universities to be connected with foreign universities not only to meet local demands, but also to realise their ambitions in terms of competing in the global higher education sector.

Under the Sino-foreign cooperation programme, the Chinese government has also allowed Chinese private higher education institutes to operate their programmes overseas. An interim policy guideline that was adopted in 2003 in this regard showed that any Chinese private university that intended to operate education programmes overseas must receive approval from the Ministry of Education of the People's Republic of China. However, in 2015, this interim policy measure lapsed and therefore at the moment no Chinese private university is required to get permission from the Chinese Government to run their programme in foreign countries. Under this programme, there are currently six Chinese higher education institutions that are operating overseas (Department of Education, Skills and Employment, 2020b).

India

After gaining independence in 1947 and until the 1990s, the Government of India developed socio-political and economic policies broadly based on the principles of socialism (Misra & Sirguroh, 2014). However, under the guise of the New Economic Policy in 1991, the Indian Government implemented a series of deregulation policies in both economic and social sectors with support from IFIs such as the World Bank and the International Monetary Fund (Mathur, 2018; Kamat, 2011a) which allowed the adoption of a more market-driven approach in higher education. The same year the first Structural Adjustment Programme was adopted by the Indian government under the neoliberal doctrine in 1991 to reform older socioeconomic policies (Mathur, 2017).

Until the 1990s, public universities dominated the Indian higher education sector and the roles of these universities were to facilitate social development and nation-building (Raina, 2019). However, the introduction of widespread laissez-faireism at the beginning of 1990s in higher education policies accelerated not only the emergence of the massification of higher education, but also the rapid growth of private universities (Tilak, 2014). In terms of massification, from only 20 universities and a few hundred thousand students in the 90s, India is now home to nearly a thousand universities, 40,000 colleges and about 10,000 standalone providers of education, with about 37 million students and about 1.5 million teachers (Tilak, 2020, p. 55).

Such rapid massification has placed the Indian higher education system as the second largest in the world after China, and larger than that of the United States

(Tilak, 2020). Among other modes, open and distance education have become one of the largest platforms of offering higher education across the country. Currently there are 15 open universities in India, with the Indira Gandhi National Open University, which claims to be the world's largest university, accommodating more than 4 million students. In fact, Tilak (2019) reports that one-tenth of all students in higher education in Indian today are enrolled in open and distance mode systems.

Although there was just a small handful of private universities before the 1990s, similar to public universities the stated role of these private institutes was one of nation-building, rather than the accumulation of profit (Raina, 2019). In the post-1990s period, both state governments and the central government approved many higher education institutions to operate in the private sector as full-fledged private universities (Hegde, 2016). By 2018 there were more than 380 private universities, in addition to almost 100 private universities. In addition, 65% of colleges were private and self-financed, offering various higher education degrees across the nation (Tilak, 2020). Currently these private institutes account for about two-thirds of the total enrolment in general higher education and four-fifths of enrolments in professional and technical education (Tilak, 2020). In addition, in 2010, the Indian government approved a plan to allow foreign universities to set up their branches in collaboration with local universities, which has further increased the number of universities nationwide, and with that, further competition in attracting students.

In its efforts to drive the knowledge economy, the Indian government developed its own version of the NPM to govern universities in the private sector. Although the University Grants Commission of India is the sole state agency to approve licenses for private universities, they are owned and controlled by either groups or families with their own internal governance systems set up through the establishment of boards of trustees (Raina, 2019). Similar to the UGC of India, both Bangladesh and Sri Lanka established University Grants Commissions to govern their higher education systems. Later in the chapter we look at the case of Sri Lankan higher education and this gives us a clearer picture of the role of the UGC as an 'arm's-length' body as it operates in these countries, and how they differ from each other in terms of their roles in higher education.

Also, similar to some other countries, typically academics at private universities in India have little autonomy and are largely controlled and managed by the institutes. In fact, the increasing trend of de-professionalisation in these private universities (Raina, 2019) has become more conspicuous in recent years. Also, although private universities are supposed to operate in a 'not for-profit' manner, Kumar (2012) notes that often they aim to make profit through overly selling so-called soft skills. Therefore, in offering degrees these private providers of education have almost always chosen market-friendly disciplines, such as business and engineering (Raina, 2019).

In 2004 the National Knowledge Commission (NKC) was formed to outline a new vision for the nation's higher education (Kamat, 2011a). The NKC emphasised the need for creating a central university and a science and technology-related university for each state (Hegde, 2016). As indicated in Chapter 2, Kamat (2011b) argues that rather than being the result of a central, state-level initiative, the strong presence of the high-tech society network in Hyderabad played the key role in spreading the neoliberal model in higher education and pushing for it to happen. As a result the Indian government set up one central university in each state and science and technology related universities including the network of Indian Institutes of Technologies (IITs), Indian Institutes of Management (IIMs), National Institutes of Science Education and Research (NISER), the Indian Institutes of Science Education and Research (IISER), and the All India Institutes of Medical Sciences (AIIMS) across many states in order to promote higher education (Hegde, 2016).

As a result of this, just as students' enrolments in higher education dramatically increased at the national level, international student migrations from India to other countries also increased over the next decade. In 2012 the British Council estimated that India will be among the top five source countries for international outbound students by 2020 (The British Council, 2012). As of 2019, there were about 753,000 Indian students studying abroad (International Education Consultancy, 2020).

In recent years, more than 100,000 Indian students have enrolled annually across universities in the US (Khandekar, 2013), while countries like Canada, Australia and UK have developed plans to attract Indian students to their universities. International enrolments in Australia have gradually shifted from East Asia to South Asia, with India now the second largest source for international students for Australian universities. International enrolments from India have risen to 32% in Australian universities in 2019 over 2018 (Department of Education, Employment and Workplace Relations, 2019). In addition, migration of Indian students is not only confined to Western, primarily Anglophone countries, but also other Asian countries including UAE, Bahrain, Singapore, Japan, South Korea and China. In 2019, there were about 100,000 Indian students studying in the UAE, Bahrain and China (International Education Consultancy, 2020). Not surprisingly, as Khondekar (2013) notes, the key trend of these outbound Indian students' enrolment is in the areas of business and engineering.

Such push towards privatisation is not only to allow and expand higher education in the private sector, but also to influence the state-funded public universities to adopt market-oriented policies in their systems. In fact, many state-run universities are now facing challenges thrown by local private universities, which we will also see in the case of Malaysian state-run public universities where they have adopted various privatisation policies to compete with private universities. Similar to private universities, state-funded public universities have been offering degrees in professional areas (Hegde, 2016). In addition, state-funded universities too have privatised and commercialised their non-teaching activities and have introduced the idea of recruiting academics on contractual basis to reduce costs (Kumar, 2012) and thereby further maximise profit.

Malaysia

On gaining independence in 1957 Malaysia had no full-fledged university. The first fully operational university – the University of Malaya – was established in 1962. At the time of establishing the second university – the Science University of Malaya – in 1969, there was a push from the minority Chinese to set a private university for the Chinese community but this was outright denied by the Malay-led government (Sivalingam, 2006; Lee, Wan & Sirat, 2017). Throughout the period from independence to 1995, the number of public universities gradually increased across the nation. In its early stage the indigenous and majority Malay, widely known as the Bumiputera – or the 'sons of the soil' – had wide access to public higher education system. In particular, the Malay community led government adopted the ethnic quota policy to ensure access for the majority Malay community into higher education that was thought to help reduce the economic gap between different communities, especially between the Malays and the Chinese-Malaysian community (Lee, Wan & Sirat, 2017).

During the 1990s, along with certain internal factors, several external factors created the conditions for private sector stakeholders to be involved in higher education in Malaysia. Among them, the consequence of economic recession in Asia in 1985–1986, demand for higher education among the growing number of people eligible for higher education, and increasing higher costs of overseas higher education financed by the Malaysian government scholarships and self-finance created pressure on foreign reserves and forced the Malaysian government to create alternative sources of higher education at home (Sivalingam, 2006).

Throughout the 1990s, the government adopted two key policy initiatives that helped introduce private higher education provision in Malaysia. The first policy initiative was that of encouraging the private sector to establish training and educational institutions to organise 'twining' programmes and preparatory courses in order to reduce pressure on foreign currency (Sivalingam, 2006). Second, in the middle of 1990s, the Malaysian Government enacted a number of Acts including the Private Higher Educational Institutions Act 1996, the National Council on Higher Education Act 1996 and the National Accreditation Board 1996 to expand private higher education institutions in Malaysia (Anis, Islam & Abdullah, 2018). Since then, two forms of privatisation processes – privatisation of public universities and the rapid growth of private higher education institutions – have taken place in the country (Jamshidi et al., 2012).

Until 2015, there were 20 public universities, 70 private universities, 34 private university colleges and 410 private colleges operating across Malaysia. The key feature of this kind of privatisation was what Lee, Wan and Sirat (2017) call hybridisation. Specifically, many of these higher education institutions were not only developed based on community-based needs, but the adoption of other local sociocultural factors. For example, 17 Islamic and five Chinese community-based higher education institutions have been offering degrees in non-profit manner where the curriculum of these two kinds private universities were infused with the Islamic and traditional Confucian values respectively. Three out of these five

Chinese community-based universities were funded by three influential Chinese groups in Malaysia, including the Chinese Political Party, the Chinese Educationalist Group and groups from the Chinese business community. The key agenda of these groups was not only to provide educational opportunities for Chinese communities, but also to transmit Chinese culture through higher education (Lee, Wan & Sirat, 2017). Along with these non-profit and community-based private universities, there was also a large number of for-profit private universities owned by various businesses in Malaysia. Naidoo (2011, p. 47) argued that:

> while developing countries are influenced by global templates of higher education, at the same time particular aspects of such templates are also transformed, excluded and adapted in line with each country's own historical trajectories, cultural influences and social political milieus.

Following this, as a regional hub of higher education, Malaysia has imposed more regulatory measures in the private university system than would be typical of the private system in more developed economies (Mok, 2008) – a tendency we also see in some other countries discussed in this chapter.

As mentioned in Chapter 2, Malaysia, like many other governments in Asia – including Hong Kong – adopted a free market approach for transnational higher education, the rise of which was connected to the financial crisis in Asia in 1997 (Mok, 2008). Before the financial crisis, Malaysian parents who could afford tuition fees preferred to send children overseas to pursue higher education. However, the financial crisis hit the Malaysian economy hard, resulting in rapid plummeting of the local currency, and prompting the government to quickly internationalise higher education. This meant the provision of private higher education through international universities in Malaysia (Mok, 2008), which saw the opening up of several universities in quick succession in the late 1990s and early 2000s.

Currently there are branch campuses of ten foreign universities from Australia, the UK, Ireland and China operating in Malaysia. Along with these independent foreign branch campuses, there are also local University Colleges and Accredited Training Centres offering a range of degrees and qualifications in collaboration with internationally reputed universities and professional bodies. Students who enrol in these University Colleges spend at least a year abroad at the awarding foreign university's home campus. In addition, a range of international accredited training centres – for example, TAFE Australia – have been registered and are operating under the Department of Skills Development offering TAFE qualifications in Malaysia (Education Malaysia, 2020).

Similar to private higher education institutions, the privatisation of public universities has also escalated through various initiatives including the corporatisation of public universities introduced in 1998, and the promotion of twining arrangements between public and private universities (Jamshidi et al., 2012). The corporatisation of public universities is mainly related to "insufficient state funding in meeting the pressing demands for higher education" (Mok, 2010, p. 426). Under the revised Universities and University Colleges Act 1995, around half of the public universities have been corporatised. The key idea of corporatisation is that of a 'corporate' public university which is typically given more institutional autonomy and is expected to raise funds through all sorts of channels including "charging students tuition fees, increasing the number of students, branching out to work closely with the business and industrial sectors, and offering professional courses, consultancy and community services" (Mok, 2010, p. 426). Many corporatised public universities in turn also began to franchise programmes onto local private colleges, creating a vast network of new providers. Under such franchise arrangements, students spend at least three quarters or entire degrees in a certain college and become awarded with degree qualifications from the affiliating corporatised public university within the curriculum provided by this public university (Mok, 2010). The way in which such corporatisation takes place rationalises public universities to operate like fully fledged business corporations (Lee, Wan & Sirat, 2017).

Sri Lanka

Although Ceylon (current day Sri Lanka) became independent from the British in 1948, the country was still under the domination of British Commonwealth Nations until 1972. In 1972, the country became a republic and was renamed as the Democratic Socialist Republic of Sri Lanka (Wickramasinghe, 2018). The first university – the University of Ceylon – was established in 1942 through the amalgamation of two existing institutes – the Ceylon University College and the Ceylon Medical College. At that time only a few English-speaking affluent families could afford the costs of higher education (Gamage, 1983). However, the higher education system rapidly expanded after independence when the government introduced a free education system up to higher education in the 1950s and 1960s. During this phase, the state had the sole responsibility of providing higher education with no tuition fees (Jayawardena, 2017).

In its early stage, universities enjoyed enormous freedom and could afford to ignore government intervention, although the enactment of the Higher Education Act of 1966 helped the government to establish a solid controlling mechanism over all higher education institutes (Gamage, 1983). Once the Higher Education Act of 1966 came into effect, the Ministry of Education of Sri Lanka appointed former and current civil servants in the top positions of universities. This not only reduced the executive power of university staff, including academics, but also shifted the task of determining tuition fees and matters relating to academic affairs including the development of curriculum and examination systems to the government (Gamage, 1983).

In 1977, Sri Lanka became the first South Asian country to introduce economic liberalisation policy which eventually reshaped its higher education landscape (Jayawardena, 2017). Soon after the introduction of the economic liberalisation policy, the government enacted the University Act 1978 to shape the university as independent and autonomous higher education institutions. In similar fashion as Bangladesh and India, the government also established the University Grants Commission of Sri Lanka as an arms-length body to govern state-funded public higher education institutions of the country (Gamage, 1983).

In the early 1980s, widespread economic liberalisation attracted private investors to be involved in higher education. The first of this kind of private investment was the establishment of a private medical college – the North Colombo Medical College (NCMC) – as a fee-levying institute in 1981. During 1980s as local and foreign degree providing institutes emerged, the government emphasised the need for the marketisation of higher education. Since then Sri Lankan higher education institutions have been developed in three distinct areas – government higher education institutions, market-driven private higher education institutes, and transnational higher education institutes (Jayawardena, 2017).

The government higher education institutes could be categorised into two groups – 15 state-funded public universities and 18 post-graduate institutes under the UGC and the Ministry of Higher Education, as well as six government recognised universities under different ministries or government bodies (University Grants Commission of Sri Lanka, 2020). Unlike in Bangladesh, however, the UGC of Sri Lanka not only oversees the governance system of the state-funded universities, but also controls the admission system of *all* state-funded universities and post-graduate institutes (Jayawardena, 2017). In addition, qualifications offered by other government recognised universities under different ministries or bodies are also recognised by the UGC of Sri Lanka.

However, it needs to be noted that a distinctive feature of these market-driven private and transnational higher education institutes are that in Sri Lanka these institutes are set up under the Company Law and they are therefore not referred to as universities in the country (Wickramasinghe, 2018). Degrees offered by these market-driven private higher education institutes are required to be recognised by the Ministry of Education. At present there are 11 such non-state private institutions with degree-status and six non-state private institutions with recognised programmes operated in Sri Lanka, with 69,000 enrolled students (World Education Service, 2020).

Along with recognised private higher education institutions, there is also a large number of unregistered private providers offering business-related qualifications. These unregistered private higher education providers use loopholes in the Higher Education Acts and operate their programmes in collaboration with foreign providers (World Education Service, 2020). In 2012, there were around 46 such for-fee higher education institutions offering more than 200 degrees in collaboration with their foreign partners. Over the years, these figures have rapidly changed, and although degrees offered by unregistered fee-levying higher education institution are still not recognised by the UGC of Sri Lanka, academics from public universities are getting involved in these institutions on part-time basis. This process has made these academics "dual-career freelancers" in non-state universities (Jayawardena, 2017), a practice that is getting increasingly common and normalised in current day Bangladesh.

More recently, the government initiated the promotion of transnational education by establishing a university – the NSBM Green University Town – in partnership with some international universities. The NSBM was set up in 2016 under the Ministry of Industry and Commerce offering nationally and internationally recognised degree programmes. The key feature of the NSBM is that while it is a state-owned university, it is operated at the international level in partnership with various international universities to attract students at both local and international levels. Along with local degree programmes recognised by the UGC of Sri Lanka, a range of exclusive international degree programmes are offered in collaboration with partner international universities from Ireland, UK and Australia. Students who enrol in these international degree programmes spend their first two or three years in NSBM and the final one or two years in a partner foreign university and are awarded degrees from the international partner university. These international degree programmes attract both local and international students because of the relatively low costs and also because of the involvement of both local and overseas academics from the partner university. Through this government-led transnational higher education initiative the government intends to shape the NSBM as the best education hub in Asia (NSBM Green University Town, 2020).

Vietnam

Until the early 1980s, a centralised planning system dominated the socioeconomic policies of the Socialist Republic of Vietnam. Since the mid-1980s, however, the Communist Party of Vietnam (CPV) began the process of mass reform, largely known as policy of *doi moi* (*Đổi Mới*) or renovation, in its socio-economic policies (St. George, 2010). Following the introduction of *doi moi*, the higher education system in Vietnam has made significant progress in terms of its expansion and diversification (Nghi & London, 2010). There were a number of key implications of the *doi moi* policy reformation for higher education institutions and their graduates. Among them, higher education institutions were meant to create a skilled workforce for non-state sector jobs, obtain income from outside the state sector, and develop their institutional plans and learning programmes to meet the needs of society as well as the state. In addition, the responsibility of searching and matching for suitable employment shifted from the state to the graduates themselves upon completion of their degrees (St. George, 2010).

Although adoption of the *doi moi* policy doctrine created a new environment for higher education institutions and promoted the privatisation of higher education sector, the notion of privatisation can be traced back well before *doi moi*. In fact, the element of privatisation of public higher education was embedded within the government's socialisation policies where families, schools, businesses and the society were encouraged to participate in the process of education development (Hoang, 2019). Encouraging these stakeholders in education development helped the government to reduce the state budget allocation and facilitated the privatisation processes.

In 1986, the government approved the University of Ho Chi Minh City to introduce a form of experimental fee-paying student provision to address teachers' low and under-employment issues and the perceived low quality of degrees. This fee-paying option for students was recognised as a great success and was made public in the following year. Under this fee-paying provision, open student enrolment rose exponentially from one university in 1986 to 30 universities in 1988 across the country (St. George, 2010). Following this, in 1988, the government approved the establishment of a new kind of experimental university – the Thang Long Non-State University Centre, initiated by a group of highly renowned mathematicians trained from Russia and France and started offering courses in mathematics and computers sciences. Initially however, to avoid ideological conflicts with socialist values, the government did not recognise Thang Long Non-State University Centre as either a private or full-fledged university. Eventually in 1994 through tight political scrutiny and guidance on its operations, the Vietnamese Ministry of Education and Training approved the Thang Long University Centre as a 'people-founded' full-fledged university (Thang Long University, 2020; St. George, 2010).

In 1993, the government issued the first regulation of private higher education – the Private University Charter – where private universities could be set up by private organisations or individuals using private resources and contributions. Under this Private University Charter there are three kinds of private higher education institutions – 'people-founded', semi-public and fully private. The key idea of 'people-founded' institutes was that of a collective initiative by a community group such as trade unions, professional associations, youth organisations, women organisations, investors, faculties and staff, strictly following government rules and operating in a not-for-profit manner (Hoang, 2019; St. George, 2010; Hayden & Khanh, 2010). The idea of such semi-public' higher education institute was developed based on the idea of a public-private partnership where the government supported in establishing it, but one that eventually needed to be finically viable through generating revenue from students' tuitions fees and other educational services. In contrast, the fully private university is owned by private investors (Hayden & Khanh, 2010). However, the 2005 Education Law allowed the 'people-founded' and 'semi-public' institutions to be converted into the private category, although they were still required to be operated on a non-commercial basis.

Although the 2012's Higher Education Law eventually recognised private universities as for-profit institutions (Hoang, 2019), the government first allowed direct foreign investment in the higher education sector in the early 2000s. The first of this was the Royal Melbourne Institute of Technology-Vietnam (RMIT) which was established in 2001 as direct foreign investment (Hayden & Khanh, 2010). However, in 2005 the government recognised RMIT as foreign-based fully private university and since then various other fully private universities have been approved to operate in Vietnam. Interestingly, in 2006, the government allowed 19 public sector higher education institutions to become fully private (Hayden & Khanh, 2010). The idea of such conversion from public to private came from the 'socialising' policy where the Vietnamese Government encouraged the private sector to be involved in the delivery of higher education believing that private sector institutes should have public responsibility in sharing the costs of higher education (Hayden & Khanh, 2010). Currently there are at least 23 such self-financed public universities approved by the government to set their own rate of tuition fees (Salmi & Pham, 2019). The government also allowed academics of public universities to hold concurrent part-time positions in these private universities to support their income (Salmi, 2019).

In the latest decree which came into effect in 2018, the Vietnamese Government approved the idea of 'twining programmes' where joint-training with foreign partners in higher education can be approved for a five-year period offering degrees in all areas except the ones related to military and national security, religion and politics. The mode of delivery of the twining programmes could be face-to-face, online or blended (Department of Education and Training, 2018). Currently, a total of 237 higher education institutions including 172 public, 60 private and five schools with 100% foreign capital are operating in the higher education sector across Vietnam (Linh, 2019). The growth of private higher education institutions has increased about fourfold in the period of 2000–2013 from 22 in 2000 to 83 in 2013. The share of student enrolments in these private institutions was around 14.4% in 2013 (Hoang, 2019).

In 2006, the Vietnamese government promulgated a 14-year plan – the Fundamental and Comprehensive Reform of Higher Education in Vietnam 2006–2020 (widely known as Higher Education Reformation Agenda or HERA) – to set up a long-term and extensive reform of higher education (Nghi & London, 2010). This is similar the Bangladeshi government's adoption of the 20-year Strategic Plan for Higher Education (SPHE) in 2006 which we discuss in the following chapters. HERA came up with a range of reform agendas for higher education, including governance of higher education, privatisation, quality assurance and a vision for future higher education by 2020. HERA also emphasised on expanding the private sector, with enrolments at non-public higher education institutions to account for 40%, and market-oriented subjects, with around 70–80% of students requiring to be enrolled in profession-oriented subjects by 2020 (Harman, Hayden & Nghi, 2010).

Conclusion

This chapter looked at how the processes of the privatisation of higher education have been shaped and reshaped in the local contexts of five Asian countries over the last few decades. We have seen that a range of national sociopolitical and socioeconomic, historical and cultural ideologies, traditions and beliefs have shaped the processes in ways that were both similar and idiosyncratic. We have also seen that the notion of 'privatisation' itself and its perceived benefits for the state, for businesses and for the individual (both students and university staff) have been understood and utilised differently by different governments, even within the same country. Although sometimes these have broadly aligned with ideas from the West, highly distinctive features of the privatisation of higher education have also emerged in each country context.

Noteworthy is that the higher education systems of most of these countries originated from their colonial legacies, and therefore there was an inherent agenda of reform to transition beyond their colonial pasts once they became independent (see also Chowdhury & Kabir, 2014; Kabir & Chowdhury, 2017). Therefore, governments of these countries often adopted nationalistic ideologies and policies in their higher education systems to foster and nurture nationalistic views for the next generations. However, with changes in governments in these countries, policies have shifted and gradually the move has tended to gravitate towards the adoption of neoliberal policy doctrines to meet the demands of both local and international markets. In some countries, for example, China and Vietnam where communist parties have been in power, neoliberal elements have been imbibed within socialist policies in the name of shared responsibilities of communities and other private sector actors. These processes have helped governments of these countries to develop a very distinctive type of education, one which Appadurai (2004) calls the 'vernacular' form of private higher education.

A consideration of both common and unique features of privatisation of higher education in these five Asian countries highlights how neoliberalism has played out in this region. The discussion also helped trace some of the discursive mechanisms that have been historically shaped in the region and now contest with Western ideologies in shaping up distinct neoliberal practices in each of these countries. In the next five chapters we explore to what extent the Bangladeshi higher education sector has adopted or deviated from such trends.

4 Financial modes of higher education in Bangladesh

Politics, power and control

Introduction

Typically, under neoliberalism the state withdraws from the responsibility of funding some services, and leaves these to the market (Boron, 2006). Consequently, to raise funds to supplement the reduction in state funding, universities globally have adopted a range of strategies – for example, high tuition and amenities fees, student loans and grants, contribution to endowment funds, increased university-industry partnerships, market-related non-degree short courses and consultancy services (Mollis, 2006). However, in the case of Bangladesh, financial strategies adopted in both public and private universities seem to have been, primarily, a part of a political process rather than the considering questions of how and why these different strategies should be adopted in the university settings. This chapter explores not only how a diverse form of financial strategies adopted in the universities helped mitigate the financial burden of higher education in Bangladesh for the government, but also how these diverse strategies were adopted based on market fundamentalism and how these processes originated from and constituted political processes. As we will see, these political processes of adopting different strategies question the understanding and provision of social justice and equity in terms of financial viability of individual departments and institutions within university settings.

This chapter is developed in two parts: financing of private universities and financing of public universities. In each part, we look at what policies in the respective sector look like and the ways in which the policies are enacted at the ground level. By looking at both policies and their practices we attempt to explore the politics inherent in these policies as they have manifested in both sectors over the decades in post-independence Bangladesh. We argue that, over this period of time, the government has developed and rationalised a 'cost-sharing' approach in a way that not only ensures that the government has little financial responsibility for private universities, but also justifies sharing public higher education costs with its end-users – students in public universities.

Part I: Financing of private universities: what do policies say?

In the early stages of private university development in 1990s, the government did not explicitly define how the private universities would be financed; nor did it explain what financial roles the government and private universities' owners would have in operating them. Rather, the key concern for the government then was how to coordinate the bank accounts of the private universities – in other words, assign roles and responsibilities of bank-related activities. However, the government did allow private universities to receive money from domestic as well as foreign sources with prior knowledge of the Chancellor, a role designated to the President of the State. Such an arrangement was mandated by the first Private University Act 1992 which states that "No private university or any person or organisation on behalf of it shall raise any fund from within or outside the country, without knowledge or prior approval of the Chancellor" (Government of Bangladesh, 1992, p. 7586). The people who were involved in developing the idea of the private university in Bangladesh also insisted that from the very beginning the private universities did not receive any government funds or subsidies to set them up or to run them. This means that at the early stages, tuition fees were the single source of income and the key strategy to finance the system in Bangladesh (Alam, Haque & Siddique, 2007).

The participants of this study argued that the driving priority of the early Act 1992 was to expand the universities in the private sector and thus the government had turned a blind eye to where the universities' incomes were sourced from and how the owners generated finance to run these private institutes. However, many of the founders used a financing strategy loophole in the early Act 1992 to introduce a variety of structures of tuition and fees. For example, the policy administrators of the UGC, the Ministry of Education and academics who had moved from public universities to administrative roles in the UGC anticipated that many of the founders of private universities used these loopholes to run private universities much like business firms. These policy administrators argued that they were often targeted with allegations about the high tuition fees structures of some private universities. Nayan, a policy administrator of the UGC explained that "They [some founders] used the universities for every purpose ... after getting government approval the authorities abused the universities ... they even opened courses without having teachers in these areas". These interviewees from the UGC and the Ministry of Education also argued that the earlier Act of 1992 allowed anyone to set up a university and to be the vice-chancellor of that university. The journalists also appeared to be in agreement with these academics and policy administrators. One of the them, Nasir, who had produced reports on private universities in the 90s, stated that "Many founders used loopholes of the Act 1992 to run universities through family members".

In response, in the post-2000 period, the government set regulations imposing restrictions to make tuition and other fees more affordable. As pointed out in Ordinance 2008, "Each private university will formulate a student fee structure for their students based on the societal context of Bangladesh and will inform the government and the University Grants Commission" (Government of Bangladesh, 2008, p. 17585). Once the Cabinet division approved the draft of the latest Act 2010 in early 2010, it was found that the government had imposed further restrictions, requiring the UGC to approve tuition and other fees for private universities before they could be imposed. As stated in the cabinet approved Private University Act 2010, “In order to bear necessary expenses each private university will formulate a tuition and fee structure, which needs to be approved by the University Grants Commission, for their students based on the societal context of Bangladesh” (Government of Bangladesh, 2010a, p. 12).

However, the government brought further changes into it and relaxed this provision when the latest Act 2010 was enacted in the National Parliament. This Act stated that, “In order to bear the expenses each private university will formulate a fee structure for their students based on the societal context of Bangladesh and will inform the University Grants Commission” (Government of Bangladesh, 2010b, p. 7442). Shifting the provision of ‘approval’ from UGC to ‘informing’ UGC about induction of tuition and other fees for students in latest Act 2010 indicates that both parties negotiated the power of who should control the financial matters in what way – this is discussed later in this section. Along with this strategy, a provision also included Ordinance 2008 which allowed private universities to invest money from the university’s general funds – as per Section 43, subsection 3, “Money from general fund can be invested” (Government of Bangladesh, 2008, p. 17586).

Nevertheless, along with raising tuition and other fees, and money from investment, both the Ordinance 2008 and Act 2010 adopted a range of strategies in line with the global trend for raising funds. In particular, it identified the following strategies to be adopted by the private universities to manage their own finances:

1 Unconditional grants from public welfare-oriented person, assemblage of persons, charitable trusts or institution.
2 Loans from public welfare-oriented persons, assemblage of persons, charitable trusts, institutions or the government.
3 Donations from public welfare-oriented persons, assemblage of persons, charitable trusts or institutions.
4 Student fees.
5 University income from various sectors, and
6 Other sources approved by the government or the University Grants Commission.

(Government of Bangladesh, 2010b, p. 7442)

The above analysis shows that the latest Act 2010 shifted the financing of private universities from coordinating and maintaining bank accounts to financial management and governance. In terms of income generation, although a diverse mode of income generating system was adopted, in practice, the user-pays approach was still preferred as the key strategy for income generation for private universities. In the following two sections we look at how policies have been implemented on the ground and the micro-politics of financial management and governance of private universities in Bangladesh.

Policy in practice in private universities: it's all about 'user-pays'

Although Act 2010 adopted various strategies to generate funds, many founders and administrators of private universities found that some of these strategies were not contextually considered for Bangladesh. Many of them argued, for example, that the attempt of raising funds through private donations and grants are likely to be a difficult task, especially as there are currently more than a hundred private universities. As one of the VCs of a private university commented, "The concept of philanthropism does not work in Bangladeshi culture. The Bangladeshi people might contribute to religious institutes e.g. madrasahs, mosques, temples, but they don't have that kind of sense to contribute to university development". This participant further added, "While the government does not feel to do something about private university's funding, how can you believe general people would come forward to do something about it?"

Because of this, since its inception, private universities received little or no financial grant from either the government or others, except directly from its founders and foreign aids, and thus, all private universities adopted the *user-pays* approach for generation of funds. By incorporating aggressive strategies as sources of fund raising in the 2010 Act, private universities have been increasingly relying on tuition fees as the key source of financing. In addition, the idea of financing through external sources has also encouraged – and in some cases, compelled – many private universities to take loans from commercial banks.

Tuition fees: the key strategy of financing private universities

The way in which the government outlined how private universities will be financed encouraged these universities to use tuition fees as the key source to generate money for its operation. The Chairman of the Board of Trustees of a private university explained that they had to increase tuition fees every year in order to keep up with rising expenses. The University Grants Commission acknowledged in its report that the private universities were using high tuition fees as a strategy to generate funding. For example, in 2017, a total of 90 private universities together generated Tk. 320,160,000,000.02, which was BD Tk. 293,062,000,000.55 in the previous year. The average income of each private university also increased from BD Tk. 3,407,000,000.70 in 2016 to BD Tk. 3,557,000,000.33 in 2017 (University Grants Commission, 2018b). Although the general trend of average income of each university was upward from 2016 to 2017, the university's expenditure on each student decreased during this period, from BD Tk. 109,230,000,000.07 in 2016 to BD Tk. 81,182,000,000.54 in 2017 (University Grants Commission, 2018b). The following table shows how much on average a student pays for a 4-year degree in a private university.

Table 4.1 shows that on average a student spends BD Tk. 155,342 a year in the form of tuition and admission fees, and lab and other activities fees, which is almost twice as much compared to what the university spends on each student a year in the form of teacher and staff salaries, research, teaching and learning materials, laboratories, library costs and other expenses. This figure indicates the

Table 4.1 Tuition and other fees structure of a 4-year degree of a private university

Name of the programmes	*Costs for a 4-year degree (BD Tk.)*	*Cost involves in each year (BD Tk.)*
BBA	614,820	153,705
BSS in Economics	505,620	126,405
BA in English	497,220	124,305
BSS in Sociology	488,820	108,405
BSS in Information Studies and Library Management	433,620	108,405
LLB (Hons)	465,420	116,355
BS in Applied Statistics	511,220	127,805
B. Sc. in ETE	728,720	182,180
B. Sc. in ICE	728,720	182,180
B. Sc. in CSE	728,720	182,180
B. Sc. in EEE	728,720	182,180
B. Pharm.	816,920	204,230
B. Sc. in GEB	694,420	173,605
B. Sc. in Civil Engineering	811,370	202,842
Average costs per student a year		2,174,782/ 14=155,342

(Source: Data used in this table are collected from a private university)

extra money the university charges on students to generate funding for infrastructure development and other activities. For example, as the Chairman of a Board of Trustees explained, “The universities also charge students for the purpose of infrastructural development as Act 2010 instructed each university should have their own campus within a particular timeframe”.

External funding and loans

Although all private universities heavily rely on tuition and other fees, some indicated that they also generate substantial funding from external sources, including from foreign grants. In 2017, 27 out of 92 private universities generated around BD Tk. 15,517,000,000 from foreign grants and other funds (University Grants Commission, 2018b). In many cases, private universities also take loans from external sources, including commercial banks. In 2017, a private university loaned BD Tk. 23.75 million from external sources (University Grants Commission, 2018b). In order to get loans from commercial banks, universities often engage in the questionable practice of mortgaging the university land and reserving funds to commercial banks. As one of the administrators of the University Grants Commission explained, “Those universities going through financial hardships are sometimes taking loans from the commercial banks against the money they deposited in the commercial banks in a form of universities’ reserve funds. This is illegal”. In some cases, founders of the private universities also provide finance to the private university. For example, one of the VCs of one private university commented,

> The building of this university is owned by our founders and rent of this building should be at least BD Tk. 13 million a year, however our founders have not been charging any money for using this building since its inception.

Student loans: a new product offering by commercial banks

It is not surprising that the way in which government policies have developed for financing private universities in Bangladesh has encouraged many commercial banks to offer student loans as a new and lucrative product to enable them to pursue higher education. As of 2019, 59 commercial banks and 34 non-bank financial institutions are operating, and among them some big commercial banks including Prime Bank, Mercantile Bank, NCC Bank, BRAC Bank, IFIC Bank, One Bank, Eastern Bank, and Dhaka Bank currently offer students loans to those pursuing higher education either at home or abroad (Bangladesh Bank, 2019). In terms of higher education at home, most commercial banks indicate that their student loan products are mainly for students who are pursuing their degrees in private universities (One Bank, 2019). Banks set up their own rules and regulations on how to be eligible for higher education student loans. Although the interest rates and other conditions including age limit, loan amount and instalment varies between banks and other lenders, the key eligibility of having the students' loans is the parents' ability to repay the loans, rather than students' merit or future prospects.

There are certain reasons for commercial banks to target students who are pursing higher education in private universities at home and abroad. Banks generally treat education loan as a personal loan product and therefore it requires collateral or a fixed monthly income (*The Daily Star*, 2009). Therefore, the first reason for them is the students' economic background. Because private higher education is generally expensive, in general, students pursuing degrees in private universities are from middle and upper-middle classes. Second, in most cases big industrialists are involved in establishing private universities and therefore many universities have their own 'sister' banks. For example, BRAC University was established by BRAC – the leading NGO in Bangladesh – and under BRAC there is a large number of commercial enterprises operating across Bangladesh, including BRAC Bank. In some cases, some NGOs also offer education loans for both lower level education and higher education. For instance, the Grameen Bank, which is often known as the 'bank for the poor', has been offering education loans for a long time. In January 2018, the amount of outstanding education loans from Grameen Bank was BD Tk. 2,112.65 million (Grameen Bank, 2019).

Changing financial policies in different Acts: politics of power and control of private universities

Two important questions could be raised from the back-and-forth movement of policies related to private university's financing strategies and how financing matters have been handled over the last few decades. First, despite several efforts and in the face of sustained lobbying by the Association of Private University of Bangladesh (APUB), why has the government failed to adopt tighter measures in Act 2010 to ensure greater transparency on how funding is generated and spent in private universities? Second, is the failure of government initiatives a question of who will control the governance system of private universities? In the following discussion these two questions are considered by looking at the political processes of developing different ideas related to financial regulatory mechanisms of private universities.

Data has shown that there was a clear tension between the different key parties involved in the private universities regarding who controls the financial matters of these universities. Government apparatuses including UGC and the Ministry of Education took stand for greater freedom for VCs and other officials to control over financial matters to run the universities. These government apparatuses' positions were reflected in the Cabinet approved Act 2010 which clearly stated that the VC of the private university would be the chair of finance committees and these committees will look after the financial matters of the private university. However, founders soon lobbied with the political government to change this provision and successfully take greater control over all financial matters of private universities. As one of the leaders of APUB explained, "They [founders] created all facilities … They were committed to helping this sector flourish. A paid employer [the VC] wouldn't have the same commitment.... The board of trustees needs to play an important role in financial management". The founders therefore brought certain changes into the Cabinet approved Act 2010 by influencing the Parliamentary Standing Committee on Education. The APUB leader further explained, "So, instead of the VC, we made a board of trustees member the chairman of the finance committee.... We were less successful in gaining consensus at the Ministerial meetings, although we became successful in the parliamentary level meetings".

Indeed, the latest Act 2010 ensured greater authority and control of the board of trustees over the universities' funds. As Act 2010 states, "The general fund will be managed with a joint signature of a board of trustees' nominee officer and the treasurer" (Government of Bangladesh, 2010b, p. 7443). However, the government focused on managing the universities' funds in what Herbst (2007) explains as an effort to improve the governance system, which is similar to the accounts in the literature in other universities globally (Amaral et al., 2003). As stated in the latest Act 2010, "by informing the government and the University Grants Commission, money from the general fund could be invested in those sectors decided by the board of trustees" (Government of Bangladesh, 2010b, p. 7443). Alongside this measure, the government also imposed some restrictions to the use of the general funds of the private universities. For example, the latest Act 2010 stipulates that "the money from the general fund must not be used for any other purposes other than the necessary expenses of the university" (Government of Bangladesh, 2010b, p. 7443).

To ensure transparency, the government became more visible in auditing the income of universities, demanding that, "Every university must submit the annual expenses of the previous year by the 30th of September of each financial year to the Commission and the government" (Government of Bangladesh, 2010b, p. 7443). The government also imposed restrictions that prevented universities from receiving funds from international sources and vice-versa without prior approval from the Chancellor of the universities. By imposing such restrictions on the use and management of funding systems in the post-1998 Acts, the government tried to ensure that the private universities took on some public responsibilities, aligning with what scholars calls new public management (NPM), which will be discussed in more detail in the next chapter.

In fact, as financial issues have always been considered as one of the most sensitive and contentious issues for private universities worldwide, there is a tendency in the private university sector, in general, to maintain secrecy about the money they generate from different sources and the money they spend in running the university. As one of the Vice-Chancellors of a private university commented, "We don't want to disclose how much money we generate or how we generate money". The University Grants Commission (UGC) in its latest report published in 2018 also indicated that private universities are now generally reluctant in following the instructions for submitting financial reports to the UGC that was first adopted in Act 2010. In fact, in 2017 the UGC reported that only 23 out of 83 eligible private universities had submitted their audit reports. In 2016, this number was 25 and among them none followed the Private University Financial Report format as specified in the Private University Act 2010 (University Grants Commission of Bangladesh, 2018b).

To mitigate the financial burden of universities, neoliberal interests also often encourage the diversification of financial sources (Mollis, 2006). Although the government revised the financial strategies of private universities several times through the promulgation of different Acts since 1992, it did not specify in what way the government could or would finance private universities. In fact, in the early draft of Private Act 2010, the government included a provision allowing private universities to receive grants from the government; a provision, however, that was excluded once the latest Act was finalised. Such exclusion of government roles in the financing of private universities indicates that the government pushes private universities to adopt more aggressive financing strategies to run universities in the private sector. In addition, according to the Act of 2010, neither the founders or the board of trustees and the government have any role or obligation in financing private universities, although in effect they have assumed greater power and authority in running their institutes. Indeed, a specific provision was included in the Act of 2010 that allowed the general fund of the private university to be managed subject to joint approval from the treasurer and a board and trustees' nominee. This Act also included a provision that the general fund can be invested by the board of trustees, as stated in Section 44, sub-sections 2 and 3:

> The general fund will be managed with a joint signature of a Board of trustees' nominee officer and the Treasurer … informing the government and University Grants Commission capital from the general fund can be invested in those sectors decided by the board of trustees.
>
> (Government of Bangladesh, 2010b, p. 7443)

Although two powerful parties – the government and the founder or board of trustees of private universities – negotiated on how private universities should earn and how the money should be spent, they did not consider whether they should have any accountability towards students, academic and professional staff in terms of earning and spending money. It would therefore seem that both government, and founders and the board of trustees have worked to serve the interest of students and its teaching and other staff; neither the government nor the board of trustees acknowledge that private university authority should discuss every financial matter with its key stakeholders – students, as well as teaching and professional staff.

Although tuition and other fees are the main source of any private university, no private university considers students' voices in terms of increasing tuition fees and how money is or should be earned from tuition and other fees. Rather, it has been observed that students have often demonstrated their protest against private universities' decisions to introduce high tuition fees without consultation (Kabir and Greenwood, 2017). Money is also earned by private universities from the hard work of its teaching and professional staff. It is undeniable that these academic and professional staff commit to create good reputation and to build up reserve money for private universities, although they are not considered in the decision-making of how university finances should be structured. In its latest Strategic Plan (2017–2030), the UGC reiterated the financial regulation of private universities, but all of these have been considered from the governance perspective rather than a 'fair' practice involving the inclusion of everyone in issues related to generating and spending money in the private university setting.

Part II: Financing of public universities: what do policies say?

As we have seen, under neoliberalism, the 'cost-sharing' approach emerged as a much-preferred form of financing in public higher education sector globally since the 1980s (Johnstone & Marcucci, 2010, p. 1). In post-independence Bangladesh, higher education was exclusively the state's responsibility until 1990. However, with the government's promulgation of the first Private University Act in 1992, the private universities sector emerged, where students paid the entire costs of their education with no support from the government. Through policy traces and trails from the private sector, the government developed the first Strategic Plan for Higher Education (SPHE) in 2006 which stated that "the beneficiaries must share a reasonable part of the financial burden of the recurrent expenditure for providing public sector higher education" (University Grants Commission, 2006, p. 60). The SPHE also pointed out that most of the developed and developing countries all over the world have reduced public expenditure in the higher education sector by introducing different mechanisms in the public higher education sector.

To reduce the government's responsibility in this sector, the Strategic Plan came in with three different approaches as policy solutions to be adopted in the public universities. The first approach was more about the financial management system in public universities. By adopting this idea, the government wanted to ensure two things: that higher education in public universities was linked to the demands of the global market, and that "simultaneously, universities should gradually shift towards the system of zero base budgeting" (University Grants Commission, 2006, p. 28). The Plan argued that the budget allocation for the public universities "should be linked with the numbers of enrolments in each discipline, the importance of course offerings in the context of the job market, logistic requirements, research requirements and output, compliance of academic norms and standards by the departments" (University Grants Commission, 2006, p. 28). In doing so, the Strategic Plan adopted the idea of "formula-based funding" by the government to link to "categories of students or measurement of performance and competitive funding that reward the best institutional bids for new programmes or projects" (University Grants Commission, 2006, p. 27).

The second approach was about the 'cost-sharing' model "in conformity with its academic programmes, and ensuring a balance between economic rationality and social considerations" (University Grants Commission, 2006, p. 28). Johnstone and Marcucci (2010, p. 2) argue that 'cost-sharing' is mostly associated with tuition and other fees and 'user charges'. The Strategic Plan adopted various strategies to be adopted in public universities. The matter was explained as follows:

> Some modalities of cost recovery may include: increase in tuition fees, increase in fees for boarding and meals for the residential students, increased access to student's loans, and participation of private sector business entities and social organizations in supporting higher education through endowments, consultancy projects, establishment of academic chairs and other physical facilities.
>
> (University Grants Commission, 2006, pp. 28 & 29)

The third approach was the introduction of external involvement in the financing system of higher education in Bangladesh. Boron (2006) argues that the strategy is engendered to create dependence on foreign sources for the financing of higher education. To this apparent end, the Strategic Plan adopted the idea of 'external' involvement in the higher education sector. In terms of the financing of public universities, the role of state shifted towards the market worldwide (Marginson & Considine, 2000). Similarly, the Strategic Plan also adopted the idea of 'industries-universities' relations as a way of financing the public universities. The Strategic Plan emphasised the need to build up a partnership between the public universities and business communities to shift some financial burden to external bodies.

The Strategic Plan also brought the idea of the projection of self-funding strategies to be implemented by public universities over a period of time. It argued that 50% of internal income should be generated through tuition and other activities. The Strategic Plan pointed out, “Whatever growth rate occurs, public universities will need to generate a huge amount of money through internal sources to keep up with the total expenditure” (University Grants Commission, 2006, p. 62). The projection of self-funding strategies included 10% from leasing out land and buildings; 5% from the cafeteria, cyber cafe, book shops, souvenir and clothing shops, etc.; 15% from offering courses in evening shifts for professionals; 5% from consultancy services; 10% from alumni contributions; 15% from university endowment; 15% from partnership with industries and the private sector; and 25% from graduate taxes (University Grants Commission, 2006). It is also argued in the Strategic Plan that certain reformations should be carried out in the financial and management processes of the universities “if universities are to be operated in a commercial and profitable manner” (University Grants Commission, 2006, p. 63). By providing a project promoting self-funding, the Strategic Plan thereby redefined the concept of the state’s role in the higher education sector in Bangladesh.

Although the first Strategic Plan (2006–2026) emphasised that the public university should adopt a full cost recovery system, in the second Strategic Plan (2017–2030, awaiting official endorsement) provided a cautious observation of implementing such a full cost recovery system in public universities. As stated in the Strategic Plan 2017–2030, “It may not be possible to adopt a full cost recovery system for the public universities; however, they should attempt to recover costs as far as possible” (University Grants Commission, 2017, p. 76). However, the latest Strategic Plan 2017–2030 emphasised the financial regulation of public universities as part of controlling the public university system that will be discussed later in this chapter.

Policy in practice at public universities: shifting from the state to ‘user pays’

Public universities in Bangladesh still receive the lion’s share of government grants to run their academic activities. Most of these grants are spent on salaries and pensions for teachers and staff (73%) and building and other structural repairing (14%), as well as on education related activities (12%) (University Grants Commission, 2018b). In FY 2017–2018, the government allocated BD Tk. 33,590.02 million to 37 public universities, which is 8.03% of total education budget and 1% of GDP (University Grants Commission, 2018a). Only 120 million was allocated as research grant in FY 20 (University Grants Commission, 2018b).

Along with government grants, all public universities are also involved in generating money on their own. For example, in FY 2017–2018, public universities together earned around BD Tk. 6,910.51 million from own resources including students’ fees, lab fees, dormitory fees, and library fees (University Grants Commission, 2018b). As government allocation for public universities is inadequate, many public universities are allowing their own departments/institutions to use their resources for generating money for their expenses. Among these fee-earning evening courses, income from different projects and private-public partnerships are identified as the key sources for funding generations of public universities.

Fee-earning evening courses: a new mode of generating money

Although the Strategic Plan adopted a range of internal and external strategies to generate money for public universities, the key trend of public universities was to adopt the idea of opening fee-earning and commercially promoted evening courses to generate money (Kabir, 2013b). A large number of public universities, for example the University of Dhaka, University of Rajshahi, University of Chittagong, Bangladesh Agricultural University, Islamic University, Jahangirnagar University, Professional University of Bangladesh, Jatiyo Kabi Kaji Nazrul Islam University, Khulna University, Khulna University of Engineering and Technology, have already introduced fee-earning evening courses in order to reduce financial burden from the government (Kabir, 2020a). In most cases, and unsurprisingly, market-oriented disciplines have received priority in offering evening courses and generating additional income (Table 4.2). These fee-earning evening courses are designed to offer not just certificate courses and diplomas for various professionals, but Masters degrees too, allowing the attendance of students who are otherwise full-time employed.

Table 4.2 shows that 41 out of 84 departments and institutes under various faculties and institutes in a public university are engaged in offering a range of fee-earning evening courses for various professional groups. It can be argued if these fee-earning courses provide people with anything more just an alternative pathway and mere 'access' to higher education, aiming at helping business and non-business executives develop their professional careers. On top of tuition fees, students enrolling for these courses pay full administrative costs (Kabir 2010; 2011). As an example, Table 4.3 indicates the funding a department/institute generates from fee-earning evening courses at one public university in 2018.

This table shows that around Tk. 17,047,424 [US$213,000] was earned by one department/institute in a public university in 2018 from fee-earning evening courses alone. This fee-earning evening course has been offered along with the regular, day-time courses. The money generated from these fee-earning evening courses are spent on teachers and staff involved in these programmes, and examinations related costs. In 2018, this particular department saved around Tk. 2,836,573 [US$35,000] from these fee-earning evening courses with around BD Tk. 9,418,604 in total in the last three years. This income has not only been used for paying costs related to this course, but also for other development costs including improving classroom teaching-learning systems that are used for both regular and evening courses. In the following section we explore how public universities are involved in generating money from yet other sources.

Money generation through project management and consultancy services

Along with these fee-earning evening courses, many departments/institutions of public universities are engaged in a range of other money generating processes. Table 4.4 shows that the same department/institute of a public university used a range of ways to generate money in 2018. The key income modes included

Table 4.2 Evening courses offering by various departments and institutes of a public university

Faculty/ Institute	*Name of Department/ institute*	*Faculty/ institute*	*Names of Department/institute*
Faculty of Business	Management	Institute	Institute of Education & Research
	Accounting & Information System		Institute of Business Administration
	Marketing		Institute of Modern Languages
	Finance		Institute of Health Economics
	Banking & Insurance		Institute of Information Technology
	Management Information System		Disaster Management & Vulnerability Studies Institute
	Tourism and Hospitality		Social Welfare & Research Institute
	Organisation Strategy & Leadership		Institute of Statistical Research & Training
	International Business		Institute of Energy
Faculty of Arts and Humanities	Islamic Studies	Faculty of Social Sciences	Political Science
	Information Science & Library Management		International Relations
Faculty of Science	Theoretical Physics		Sociology
	Biomedical Physics & Technology		Public Administration
	Theoretical & Computational Chemistry		Population Sciences
	Statistics		
Earth & Environmental Sciences	Geography & Environment		Development Studies
	Oceanography Science		Television, Film & Photography
	Meteorology		Criminology
Faculty of Biological Science	Psychology		Communication Disorders
	Clinical Psychology		Printing & Publication Studies
	Educational & Counselling Psychology		Japanese Studies

(Source: Data used in this table collected from a public university)

renting out from conference halls and canteen, income from different projects and research consultancies, student fines and charges and bank interests.

Table 4.4 also indicates how the money earned from different activities was spent. Most of it was spent on infrastructural construction and resources maintenance, as well as payment for visitors and guests. Most importantly, this

Table 4.3 Income from a fee-earning evening course in 2018

Earning sectors	*Income (BD Tk.)*	*Expenses sectors*	*Expenses (BD Tk.)*
Course fees, centre fees and other fees	16,973,624	Teachers' honorarium	7,746,000
Curriculum fees	73,800	Centre Fees	2,601,500
		Staff honorarium	2,310,560
		Workshop for curriculum development	1,290,000
		Online service costs	182,800
		Curriculum publication	47,000
		Registration costs	19,000
		Bank Charge	13,991
Total Income	17,047,424	Total Expenses	14,210,851
Saving	17,047,424–14,210,851 = 2,836,573		

(Source: Data used in this table collected from a department/institute in a public university)

Table 4.4 Income from different sources 2018

Earning sectors	*Income (BD Tk.)*	*Expenses sectors*	*Expenses (BD Tk.)*
Renting out conference halls	645,000	Construction of teachers' lounge	1,678,800
Income from different projects	2,177,233	AC setting and servicing charge	1,243,950
Students fines/charges	204,500	Building and furniture repairing	919,284
Curriculum fees	125,700	Washroom renovation	775,800
Career centre	63,000	Honorarium for guests	225,300
Study tours	90,000	Support for teachers	200,000
Publication	42,500	Publication costs	125,000
Meetings	25,000	Curriculum materials development	150,000
Selling out old furniture	30,000	Security measures improvement	102,140
Renting out canteen	22,000	Stationeries	491,323
Bank interest	50,251	Vehicle maintenance and other services charge	95,200
		Teacher professional development	46,500
		Bank Charge	8,840
Total Income	3,475,184	Total Expenses	6,207,137
Deficit	6,207,137–3,475,184 = 2,731,953		

(Source: Data used in this table collected from a department/institute in a public university) department/institute spent almost twice the amount of money earned from the use of such diversified modes of money generation. This extra money they spent was defrayed by the income of fee-earning evening courses.

Higher tuition fees in newly established public universities

Since 2006, the government has adopted the idea of general public universities following the private university model (Kabir, 2013b) (this issue is discussed in detail in Chapter 8). Along with this, the government emphasised the introduction of higher tuition fees for newly established public universities. Although these newly established public universities already receive significant amount of funding from the government, they are also encouraged to adopt different strategies based on 'cost-sharing' approaches to generate more sustainable funding. In particular, public universities established since 2006 have charged more tuition fees than the older ones, which has led to a case of discrepancy. For example, as the former Chairman of the University Grants Commission explained,

> the reality is different. A student of Noakhali Science and Technology University (a regional university), which was established in remote area in 2006, is paying more tuition fees than the University of Dhaka (a metropolitan university) that was established in the heart of the capital city of Bangladesh in 1921.

Both of these universities are public but have adopted very different financial structures based on how long they have been in operation for.

Public-Private Partnership (PPP): a new bondage between public universities and industries

Both the government and the UGC also encourage public universities to develop direct links with industrial and non-government sectors to earn money from external sources. In the fiscal year 2010–2011, the government introduced the Public-Private Partnership (PPP) and under this scheme industrial and non-government sectors became involved in the funding of public universities. Many public universities signed up contracts with industrial and non-government organisations to develop their laboratories, commence joint research initiatives and improve other academic facilities (Kabir, 2011). For example, in 2017, with the support of a Base Project jointly funded by *Palli Karma Sahayak Fund* (PKSF) and Integrated Development Foundation (IDF), a laboratory named Halda River Research Laboratory was set up in the Department of Zoology at the University of Chittagong (Integrated Development Foundation, 2019; *The Daily Star*, 2017). It is noteworthy that some newly established universities have taken significant initiatives in building up university-industry collaboration. For example, since its inception in 2008, Bangladesh Professional University (BUP) signed a range of memorandum of understandings with some leading industries including Grameen Phone and Beximco Textile and Apparels Limited (Bangladesh University of Professionals, 2018; Grameen Phone, 2018). The key objective of these initiatives is to bridge the gap between industry and university sector.

National University: money surplus

The National University, which was established in 1992, operates in the public sector. Instead of taking in students directly, it offers degrees through various public and private colleges which they support with academic facilities, such as developing curriculum and content, arranging examinations and providing degrees (Kabir & Greenwood, 2017). Currently, about two million students are studying in more than 2,200 colleges and institutions located in different districts in Bangladesh, all affiliated to the National University (University Grants Commission, 2018b). Since 2014, the government has not allocated any grants for the National University and therefore it has resorted to adopting the above-mentioned *user pays* approach to generate money. This approach includes admission fees, tuition fees, examination fees, as well as amenities fees. Although the government has discontinued grants for the National University through using the user-pays approach, the National University generated BD Tk. 200 million in 2017 (University Grants Commission, 2018b). However, in January 2020, the Government of Bangladesh passed a new law titled the 'Deposit of Surplus Funds of Autonomous, Semi-Autonomous, State-Owned, and Public Non-Financial Corporations' into the Government Treasury Act 2020. According to this law, the surplus money of these of bodies must be deposited to the state after extracting from it the operational and other costs – including emergency and provident funds and pension for its staff. Accordingly, the National University is due to deposit Tk. 100 million to the state treasury in FY 2020–2021 (Byron & Rahman, 2020). This is but one example of the government's intention to use higher education as part of earning significant revenue.

It has often been alleged that the National University does not maintain quality in the degrees they offer (University Grants Commission, 2018b). However, about 100,000 students are forced to get enrolled into the National University because of lower enrolment capacities of other public universities. In addition, almost all public universities have adopted a set of policy guidelines for student admission – including students' need to have a minimum Grade Point Average (GPA) in the Secondary School Certificate (SSC) and Higher Secondary Certificate (HSC) to qualify for enrolment. Many allege that the National University takes advantage of this situation and earns a lot of money from prospective students.

One of key strategies the National University has adopted to increase the number of potential applicants is to commence the student's admission process well before other public universities. As enrolment in public universities becomes highly competitive, no student wants to miss the opportunity to get into the higher education sector. Therefore, most students are forced to get admission into the National University whether they eventually pursue their higher education in the National University or not. Through this strategy the National University surpluses their money and greatly relieves the government from financial responsibility.

Politics of government subsidies and the cost-recovery system: control over public universities

Two things need to be taken under careful investigation – the financial role of the government in public universities and the cost-recovery system – to understand of how controlling mechanisms have been working in the public university sector in Bangladesh. As indicated above, on the one hand, the government contributes the lion's share of public university expenditures; on the other hand, it also constantly encourages public universities to adopt a full cost-recovery system in order to make them 'self-reliant' academic institutions. The scope of this analysis is not to determine whether like in the case of the private university, the government's intention is to discontinue their financial role in public universities, or to ignore the role of ensuring equitable higher education for its citizens. Rather, we critically look at historical artefacts and events and how these historical processes have ensured and legitimised public universities to be continued as 'politically' empowered institutions and therefore, the government wanted to take this advantage through budgeting public universities.

As argued in the introduction of this book, and elsewhere (see Chowdhury & Kabir, 2014), the development of modern higher education in Bangladesh has always been a part of political processes. In particular, the agenda for the British ruler to establish the University of Dhaka in 1921 was to facilitate reconciliation between Muslims and Hindus in Bengal through which they wanted to continue and prolong their domination in the Indian Subcontinent. However, the University of Dhaka soon became the centre of intellectual activity in the East Bengal as well as politically empowered by voicing how colonial powers – both the British and the Pakistani rulers – suppressed and discriminated the majority Bengali people in East Bengal and East Pakistan. Public universities in Bangladesh have therefore not only ensured higher education for its students but have also played the key role of educating people about their moral, political, civic and democratic rights.

In particular, the University of Dhaka became the centre of organising all democratic movements since its inception and contributed to all democratic movements during the Pakistan era including the Language Movement in 1952, the Liberation War in 1971, and also post-independence movements against military autocrats from 1975–1991 and in 2007 to re-establish democratic governments (Kabir & Greenwood, 2017). These historical roles played by students and staff of public universities made the universities both intellectually and politically empowered in the Bangladeshi civil society. The way in which the public university system was developed and the way in which it became politically powerful helped them to assume a strategic position with a bargaining capacity with government apparatuses. Therefore, even as government apparatuses relentlessly created pressure on public universities to be financially (if not institutionally) self-reliant, it also believed that this would not be possible until national consensus was reached on matters of national interest.

We discuss the politically empowered status of the public university more broadly in Chapter 8 by showcasing the development of Jagannath University in the backdrop of the formation of first Strategic Plan 2006–2026 as a public university modelled on the idea of the private university. The government was compelled to amend the Act of Jagannath University in 2012 in the face of massive student unrest at Jagannath University during 2011–2012 when both students and teachers became aware of how the government planned to adopt the idea of the private university modelling of a public university. The policy shift from the first Strategic Plan 2006–2026 to second Strategic Plan 2017–2030 reflected the amendment made by the government with Jagannath University. While the first Strategic Plan emphasised that the government's financial contribution should be 'zero' by 2025, in the second Strategic Plan the government registered its concern that it would not be possible for the government to ensure public universities to adopt a full cost-recovery system. As stated in the new Strategic Plan 2017–2030, "This [a full cost-recovery system] would require wide spectrum consensus building with all political parties, students groups, civil society and public representatives. Without an agreement with all the stakeholders, this initiative will be impossible to implement" (University Grants Commission, 2017, p. 76).

This concern also came up in relation to other financial regulations from government apparatuses for public universities. Despite the government's reduced financial contribution to public universities over the last few decades, the government has employed more regulating mechanisms on how the public universities could spend the money they have received from both the government and that earned on their own e.g. from endowment funds or other sources such as fee-earning evening courses. As the latest Strategic Plan 2017–2030 states, "Budget management to be effective should have transparency and accountability mechanisms built into the system including monitoring, oversight and external and internal audit tracks; automation, electronic and online transactions, and periodic implementation reviews" (University Grants Commission, 2017, p. 86).

The 'duality' in the government's role in the mode of financing of public universities can be examined by looking at a recent decision made by the UGC. In December 2019, the UGC issued a directive to all public universities to stop all of their fee-earning evening courses. It urged the authorities of these public universities to maintain financial transparency and to seek approval from the UGC in opening any department or position, and for any matters related to employment and promotion (*The Daily Star*, 2019). This move came just two days after the President of the country (also the Chancellor of all public universities) heavily criticised public universities' fee-earning evening courses at a convocation ceremony at the University of Dhaka (The Daily Star, 2019). The Prime Minister also expressed her concern over this issue in the national parliament and insisted that the matter should be resolved by the UGC, rather than through parliamentary intervention (Mortuza, 2020; The BD News 24, 2020). Soon after the UGC directive, all public universities halted their fee-earning evening courses. The government's such recent move is an indication of its intention of using its financial role as a strategic position to impose control over the universities' activities.

Despite these fee-earning evening courses contributing significant revenue for the public universities, it is undeniable that some of these courses have been used as part of a 'business' tool and have created unequal facilities and services within the public university system. As indicated above, public universities have been suffering from financial constraints as government contributions have been slashed over the years – for example it was 0.92% in 2006 and this was reduced to 0.73% of the national budget in 2014–2015 (University Grants Commission, 2017). These fee-earning evening courses therefore became a way for the public universities to mitigate their financial burden. However, questions regarding how these courses were offered, how they aligned with regular (day) courses, and, perhaps most importantly – how the money earned from these courses were spent and reallocated across the departments to promote social justice and equity in the public university setting – were not addressed.

First, these evening courses were invariably market-related, and therefore in many cases, if not all, there was a tendency of some departments and faculties to use these courses as a business tool. For example, when the Faculty of Business Studies at the University of Dhaka introduced fee-earning evening courses in 2002, it offered only four courses under four departments and the number increased to at least 20 courses under 10 departments in just 18 years. Currently the faculty enrols students in different courses through 45 batches each year and the student enrolments in these courses are more than twice the size of the regular (day) programmes earning Tk. 750 million (approximately US$1million) each year (*The Bangla News*, 2020).

When the authority of the University of Dhaka began to take action based on the UGC directive to close all the fee-earning evening courses, a clear division became apparent in the teaching community based on faculties and departments that offered fee-earning evening courses and those that did not (*The Bonik Barta*, 2020). Both parties started an aggressive political uproar to justify their positions on whether fee-earning evening courses should continue or not. On neither side were justifications based on issues of social justice and equitable education. Yet many departments or institutes have not offered any fee-earning courses because either they do not have market demand or they are not able to nourish on the market logic within the public university setting. Regardless of the reasons behind not offering market-related courses, this has created huge inequality within the public university setting in Bangladesh, among academics, students and parents of students.

Conclusion

This chapter firstly explored the financial modes of higher education and secondly discussed how these budgeting systems have been used as part of controlling the university sector in Bangladesh. In the first part of this discussion we showed that although private universities have adopted different cost-recovery systems, they have still used user-pays as the main earning source to generate money for private universities. More importantly, this chapter examined that despite making no contributions, the government has developed a range of mechanisms to oversee and ensure control of the financial activities of private universities. However, in doing so, both government and founders or board of trustees have neglected the voices of students and the teaching and professional communities in terms of how the money should be earned and spent.

In the second part of this chapter, the discussion examined how public universities learned to adopt different cost-recovery systems to mitigate their financial burdens. This discussion showed how the public university sector has become politically empowered and why the government has played a *dual* role in the budgeting of public universities. More significantly, this discussion also looked critically at how the fee-earning courses offered in the public universities are tied to market demands and how they have been used as business tools to create an inequitable condition within the public university system. The overall discussion addressed how various financial systems in Bangladeshi universities have been used as essential tools in the play of power politics and the overall control of universities.

5 Governance system of higher education in Bangladesh[1]

> Neoliberal governmentality results from the infiltration of market-driven truths and calculations into the domain of politics. In contemporary times, neoliberal rationality informs action by many regimes and furnishes the concepts that inform the government of free individuals who are then induced to self-manage according to market principles of discipline, efficiency, and competitiveness.
>
> (Ong, 2006, p. 5)

Introduction

This chapter discusses the governance system of higher education by considering the key feature of the New Public Management (NPM) approach in Bangladesh in the form of the retention of the centrality of government control and the application of this control in both public and private universities. We argue that although NPM as governance system emerged from the private management model and has been applied to public sector in order to ensure public accountability of state-run universities in many Western countries, arguably in Bangladesh, a distinct *localised* form of NPM has developed over the last two decades. State involvement in the governance system of private universities increased in the late 1990s and extended significantly in the noughties, so that to date private universities in Bangladesh are significantly different organisations from what they used to be in the past.

Part I: The governance system of private universities

To dictate, regulate and oversee the administration of universities in the private sector, the state has so far introduced four legislations – the Private University Act 1992, the Private University Act 1998 (Amended), the Private University Ordinance 2008 and the Private University Act 2010. These various legislations have facilitated changes in the nature of state control over private universities. In this part, we analyse these Acts alongside data from face to face individual interviews with policy actors to explore in what ways, how, and why a mixture of deregulated and state-controlled governance system shifts have taken place within the private higher education system in Bangladesh, especially in the last two decades, and how these in turn have shaped the administration of both private and public universities.

Between 1992 and 2008: entrepreneur control over private universities

Global trends in the governance systems of universities are broadly concerned with the internal mechanisms of decision-making processes, patterns of authority and hierarchy, and the relationship of university as institute to the university's academics, the government and other external bodies (Marginson & Considine, 2000). In terms of the patterns of authority and hierarchy, the founders, who have established the private universities, often enjoy outright power over the universities in its early phase of the establishment. These founders typically make significant decisions including selecting and appointing top officials including the VC, Pro-VC and Treasurer. These top officials would be appointed by the Chancellor at "the recommendation of the founders for a period of four years on such terms as will be fixed by the Chancellor" (Government of Bangladesh, 1992, p. 7584).

In addition, the early Act 1992 gave the founders the right to constitute all administrative and executive bodies including the syndicate, the board of governors, the regency council, or the trustee board as authoritative bodies to administer the university, and set up any form of academic management structure to look after the academic affairs of the university. Although Syndicate members are expected to have considerable experience "in the field of education, culture, industry, science, technology or administration" (Government of Bangladesh, 1992, p. 7585), the founders could form the Syndicate of private universities on their own independent choosing.

The Syndicate, which is a key administrative and executive body within the private university setting, on the Chancellor's approval, could "formulate statutes containing provisions relating to the syllabus, curriculum, study schedule, and administrative or other necessary functions of the university" (Government of Bangladesh, 1992, p. 7586). The Syndicate also appoints other senior officials including the registrar, the departmental heads and the controller of examinations. Importantly, along with administrative tasks the Syndicate also manages and maintains the finances of the university. As mentioned in the Act 1992, "This fund, with the approval of the syndicate, the board of governors … as it must be deposited with any nationalised bank … and money may be withdrawn from the fund in the manner prescribed by the rule" (Government of Bangladesh, 1992, p. 7586).

Although the early Act 1992 ensured outright power to the founders of private universities, the government followed the old colonial practice of installing the head of the state as the Chancellor of the university.[2] As stated in the Act 1992, "The President of the People's Republic of Bangladesh will remain the Chancellor of all private universities and he or any person authorised by him will preside over the convocation ceremony for awarding academic degrees and honorary degrees" (Government of Bangladesh, 1992, p. 7584). However, the Chancellor does not hold any executive power on a day-to-day basis in relation to staffing, budget or the curriculum. The Chancellor is there more as a check and balance, in an 'honorary' position in the role of providing government 'advice', when needed. For example, the Act 1992 stated that when a complaint in relation to fraud, plagiarism or cheating in awarding certificates or a case of failure to maintain the standard of education arises, "the Chancellor may inquire into the complaint by appointing a sitting or retired judge of the Supreme Court and if the charge is sustained in the said inquiry the government may revoke the charter of that university" (Government of Bangladesh, 1992, p. 7586). Therefore, private universities were set up with a titular and tokenistic chancellor, although in reality, for all day-to-day decisions it was the founders who made appointments, controlled the curriculum and dictated the general operational direction of the university.

Six years after the development of a market-driven private higher education, the government first began to exert direct control over higher education institutes in the private sector. In 1998 the Ministry of Education and the University Grants Commission (UGC) extended its powers in relation to several aspects of the operation of private universities. As noted in the Act 1998 (Amended), "The government or Grants Commission can arrange to carry out inspections of a private university from time to time by an individual so authorized" (Government of Bangladesh, 1998, p. 5609). Following an inspection, the government or the UGC could issue directives for the university to undertake what they considered to be necessary action within a specified time period.

This move also seems to have coincided with changes that were introduced to restrict the operation of foreign private universities in the country. Arguably, the Bangladeshi government might appear not to have foreseen the problems of a rampant market-driven higher education which would have its own agenda and might not develop in ways the government had hoped. The government had regarded opening up to the market as a way of responding to new student demand and harnessing the entrepreneurial skills of some people. However, by 1998 private universities began developing in a direction the government had not foreseen and did not particularly like, as discussed below.

Post-2008 period: shifting to a blending of deregulated yet state-controlled system

The degree to which the government became involved in the governance of private universities through the Act 1998 was perceived by the government as not sufficient in improving the accountability and transparency of the private universities' activities. Interviews with policy actors who were involved in the early phases of the establishment of these private universities argued that because of the loopholes of the early Acts of 1992 and 1998, owners of many private universities became directly engaged in the governance system and used the private universities as profit-driven family businesses. For example, two academics who had moved from academic positions in public universities to positions of VCs in private universities, perceived that the involvement of family members in the private universities had intensified the development of higher education as a business in the post-1998 period. They argued that such education business was limited to only a few families across the country until 1998. However, after 1998 many families became involved in this highly profitable venture. For instance, an academic, who had become the VC of a private university, described how some families invested in private universities for business purposes in the post-1998 period. He explained, "There was a group of universities where family members invested money and expected a return from them. The extent of this business was not significant till 1998". Other academics involved with the UGC suggested that the business motives of some of these founders stimulated others to get involved in similar activities. For instance, the Chairman of the University Grants Commission, an academic himself, explained that "When some universities were able to attract students, they started to do business. Some other universities noticed that and were encouraged into adopting it".

By 2010 such practices became rampant. Many private university representatives acknowledged the concerns of academics and policy administrators regarding the governance of the private system in Bangladesh. For example, a private sector representative – who later became a founder of a private university after his retirement as a civil bureaucrat and went on to become the President of the Association of Private Universities of Bangladesh – commented,

> I heard about a university where the Chairman of the Board of Trustees has been serving the role of the VC. His wife and son have been playing the roles of Pro-VC and Registrar respectively, although this is not happening everywhere.

However, this group of private sector representatives claimed that the early founders really wanted to expand higher education through this sector, although as more organisations joined the sector after 1998, unscrupulous people were beginning to use higher education as a 'business tool'. Again, this participant explained, "Those who were involved in expanding higher education through the private sector really wanted to expand higher education and some of them – I don't wish to let them down – but I must say, were clearly profit motivated".

Given this situation, the government developed the argument in the post-2008 period that the previous Act 1992 and Act 1998 were ineffective in ensuring 'proper management' in the private universities – "As the existing Acts seem to be inadequate, it is necessary to repeal the existing acts and formulate a new act to expand standard higher education for establishing the private university and for its proper management" (Government of Bangladesh, 2010b, p. 7423). Accordingly, in the post-2008 Ordinance and Act, the government restructured some of the governing bodies and redefined the roles and functions of these bodies and those of top officials from private universities. Together these changes altered the founders' influences and increased government influence in the running of the private universities. Although the Ordinance 2008 continued to endorse the term 'founder(s)', the Ordinance ensured that founders had little or no executive or administrative authority. In order to establish and run the university, the founder had to form a 'board of trustees', which turned out to be the highest authority for the private university. The role of the founder(s) as defined in the pre-1998 Acts shifted to the 'board of trustees'. As stated in the Ordinance 2008, "On the terms as will be fixed by Chancellor [the state's head], the Vice Chancellor will be recruited at a recommendation of the 'board of trustees' for a four-year period" (Government of Bangladesh, 2008, p. 17576). The other top officials including the Pro-VC and the treasurer would also be appointed by the Chancellor at the recommendation of the board of trustees. Moreover, all top officials could be stepped-down by the Chancellor based on well-defined and acceptable allegations made by the board of trustees.

According to this Ordinance, the board of trustees' members could be in different executive and management bodies including in the Syndicate, Academic Council and various finance and teacher recruitment committees. Through the representations in different bodies, the 'board of trustees' could be involved in decision-making processes. Apart from this, the board of trustees could carry out certain specific tasks. The tasks included approving the university organisational structure and organogram, approving the university employment policy and sending the university's regulatory guidelines to the UGC, reviewing, investigating and reserving yearly expenditures, approving the university's yearly budget and sending it to the Chancellor for approval, organising consultation meetings with the student's parents, teachers, alumni and other stakeholders at least once a year in order to solve university related issues, and formulating a plan following the consultation meeting and implementing it (Government of Bangladesh, 2008).

In addition, the Ordinance specified the role of the syndicate: "The syndicate as an executive authority will supervise and administer the academic and administrative functions and oversee the general management of the university" (Government of Bangladesh, 2008, p. 17582). Furthermore, the syndicate could formulate the university's rules and regulations, appoint teachers and non-academic staff, develop the terms and conditions of the teachers and officers, and set the student fee structure. Along with the board of trustees and the syndicate, the finance committee became one of the powerful authorities because it dealt with financial matters of the private university. The key responsibilities of the finance committee included "prepar(ing) the annual budget of the university and send (ing) it to the syndicate for granting approval, and play(ing) an advisory role in the financial matters of the university" (Government of Bangladesh, 2008, p. 17583).

Although most of the provisions of the Ordinance 2008 were carried on into the latest Act 2010, some significant issues related to the governance had to change. Such changes ensured more authority for the 'board of trustees' over the university. The major changes in the latest Act 2010 included increasing the numbers of board of trustees members in different bodies, such as the syndicate, academic council, teacher recruitment committee and redefining their functions in the private university. Instead of the Treasurer, a board of trustees member was also made the chairman of the finance committee. As is pointed out in Subsection 2 of Section 25, "The finance committee will be formed by the following members: a. three members selected by the board of trustees from which someone will be chairman" (Government of

Bangladesh, 2010b, p. 7435). Along with other activities mentioned in the Ordinance 2008, the board of trustees would be monitoring the VC's activities as well. Similarly, some changes were also brought to the formation of the disciplinary committee in which a member of the board of trustees was made the chairman instead of the VC, also dictated by Ordinance 2008.

What this analysis of policy change over time shows is that while government involvement in the private university governance system was minimal in the first Act in 1992, it became more actively involved in the direct governance of private universities through the Act of 1998. A further step-change took place through the Ordinance of 2008, which is evidence of the increasing concern to promote the interests of the public in the private sector. Through the latest Private University Act 2010 the state is revealed as heavily involved in both the academic and administrative activities of the private universities while the role of the founders in the day to day activities of the universities is curtailed. Between 2008 and 2010, the most significant change has been in determining the composition of the Syndicate to ensure representation of the views of the government in the private university setting. Both the Ordinance 2008 and the latest Act of 2010 mentioned that an educationalist or a person who has an interest in education and a professor from outside of the UGC will be nominated by the Ministry of Education and the UGC respectively to be a member of the syndicate to oversee the activities of private university (Government of Bangladesh, 2008, 2010b).

Although the Ordinance 2008 and the latest Act 2010 still propound the idea that the establishment of a private university can be initiated by a private individual and that the founder or 'board of trustees' can always have power over the university, a private university is not considered as one running the same type of activity as any other business or commercial outlet. Instead, the changes in these policy texts indicate that in Bangladesh private universities are regarded as serving what Marginson (2011) describes as both public and private interests or goods, which need to be managed by the state. To understand how these policy shifts towards a mixed economy of private and public higher education have identified a new role for the national state and its administrative organisations, we return to a discussion of 'new managerialism', which was discussed in Chapter 2.

Arguably, New Public Management (NPM) was developed in order to shift responsibility away from direct state control to "arm's-length" bodies and self-regulation (King, 2004, cited in de Boer, Enders & Schimank, 2007, p. 141). The theoretical underpinning for this process stems from Foucault's (1978) concept of 'bio-power' or regulation of the self. The notion of 'bio-power' refers to the way citizens are governed by the modern state through "an explosion of numerous and diverse techniques for achieving the subjugations of bodies and control populations" (Foucault, 1978, cited in Baker & Brown, 2007, p. 12). In line with 'new managerialism' or NPM approach, the government in Bangladesh has expected private universities to adopt purposes and standards that align with those of public higher education and to take management responsibility for reporting to the government on the practices and outcomes of their activities, as well as to their own 'boards of trustees' or even founders and shareholders.

Since the early 1990s when policies in Bangladesh first afforded the development of the modern private university, to the present situation, there has been a *double* strategy at work. On the one hand, government policies have enabled the higher education system to expand under the direction and interests of the private sector; but on the other hand, increasingly, the government has set in place arm's-length policies to circumscribe the form of this expansion. In the post-1998 periods, the government legislated that the UGC and the Ministry of Education must be included in the governance structure of all private universities. Through the changes introduced over the past almost two decades, the state has required that government representatives and academics from outside of the private universities must be involved in the day-to-day work in the private universities – to ensure these universities act in the interests of and with the advice of the civil society. Arguably, this mixed governance model means that although private universities in Bangladesh are still privately owned, they are regarded by the state as bodies that provide what Marginson (2011) calls 'public good' and therefore need to be under the control of the government. Models of NPM that ensure state control through arm's length government bodies and self-regulation have provided a regulatory framework to reduce the drive of private universities to pursue the private interests and private goods of some of the founders.

In the following theme, we further look into how the roles of top officials have changed within the private university setting to understand the distinctive Bangladeshi form of NPM manifested in the private universities.

Shifting role of the VC: from 'manager' to 'chief executive and academic officer'

Changes that have taken place in the roles of top officials in the private universities in Bangladesh are also a classic neoliberal move, based on the managerial approach in which the president or the Vice Chancellor of the university is now often called university 'chief executive officer' (CEO) (see McClenaghan, 1998). Both the previous and the latest private university Acts and the Ordinance have had a major influence in shaping the roles of the top officials in universities and the corporate culture they have gradually moved into. In the first Act of 1992, the VC of a private university was recognised as the Chief Executive Officer – as stated in the Private University Act 1992, "he [VC] will be the chief executive of the university" (Government of Bangladesh, 1992, p. 7584).

Arguably, the executive leader has become a "generic rather than localised manager", who mediates the external relations of the university and develops its overall strategy (Marginson & Considine, 2000, p. 9). However, the early Act 1992 did not define who the VC would be, nor was the VC considered to be a powerful enough position to develop university strategies. As discussed in the earlier section, the power, instead, resided with the founders who ran the university as per their wishes. The VC was not included in any executive bodies including the syndicate or trustee board as the chief executive officer. Although the academic operation of the private university was managed by designated academic officials with specific responsibilities, they were more managers than academic decision makers. For example, the early Act 1992 stated that with the approval of the Chancellor, the syndicate or trustee board would formulate statutes containing provisions "relating to the syllabus, curriculum, study schedule, and for the performance of administrative and other necessary functions of any private university.... All the educational certificate, degree and diploma of any private university shall be signed by the Vice-Chancellor" (Government of Bangladesh, 1992, p. 7586).

Although the universities were private, the government dictated the governance structure and the roles and the qualifications of different positions of these institutions in the post-1998 period. In Ordinance 2008 the government shaped the role of the VC as the 'executive and academic officer' of the private university – as stated in Subsection 1 of Section 15, "Following the prescription the appointed VC will be the Chief Executive and Academic Officer of that university" (Government of Bangladesh, 2008, p. 17576). The Ordinance 2008 also set up the academic qualifications of the VC – "the VC's must have a first class or equivalent honours and postgraduate or PhD degree and twenty years of teaching or research or administrative experience of which ten years [must be] of advanced research or teaching experience" (Government of Bangladesh, 2008, p. 17576). Whilst the Ordinance 2008 began to shape the role of the VC, the latest Act 2010 advanced the same idea, namely, that the VC should be the "executive and academic officer" of the private university (Government of Bangladesh, 2010b, p. 7438).

Through the Ordinance 2008, the government also brought in a number of significant changes to create a division of executive power between the founders and the VC as the chief executive and academic officer of the university. Although the early Act of 1992 allowed the founders to form different bodies to run the university, it did not specify whether the VC could be part of these bodies of authority. To empower the role of the VC in different decision-making bodies, Ordinance 2008 included the VC as the ex-officio chair of syndicate, academic council, teacher committee, teacher and staff recruitment committee and disciplinary committee. The Ordinance clearly mentioned that "the VC would be a member of the board of trustees by virtue of position" (Government of Bangladesh, 2008, p. 17576).

The Ordinance 2008 also shaped the positions of senior management and their roles in the private university and emphasised the significance of professional expertise of senior management staff. The Ordinance identified the role of senior management in implementing the academic strategy effectively. As for the VC, the Ordinance 2008 specified the academic credentials and the experience required of the senior management. As stated, "The Pro-VC must have at least a postgraduate degree and at least fifteen years of administrative or teaching experience" (Government of Bangladesh, 2008, p. 17577). However, the latest Act 2010 placed more emphasis on creating a centralised control mechanism to ensure the accountability of all senior management staff to the VC. The latest Act 2010 stated that the VC will appoint and control all deans and departmental heads. In order to ensure the VC's role in financial matters, the latest Act 2010 also included the VC as a member of the finance committee (Government of Bangladesh, 2010b).

De Boer, Enders and Schimank (2007) argue that under the NPM approach, corporate management structures govern through layers of regulation and audit in which university top and middle management are expected to be responsive to external government by implementing internal goals that fit with external drivers and taking responsibility for the activities and expenditure of the university. Similar to what they argue, analysis of the post-1998 Acts shows the inclusion of the VC in different executive bodies, for example in the Syndicate confirmed the new powers of the VC, but also made clear that their power was constrained by their accountability to others. It states, "s/he will implement the Syndicate decision … VC will be responsible for his [sic.] work to the 'board of trustees'" (Government of Bangladesh, 2008, p. 17576).

Similarly, the latest Act has brought changes into this provision in making the VC responsible for carrying out decisions made by both the board of trustees and the Syndicate. Both the Ordinance and latest Act again included another subsection which states, "She/he (VC) will be responsible to implement the decision of the Syndicate and the board of trustees" (Government of Bangladesh, 2010b, p. 7438). Consequently, the management structure of the private university was developed in a particular way in which the top officials were empowered to some extent, but they were only implementing the decisions of the board of trustees. However, compared to their role prior to 2008, the latest Act 2010 gives the VC a more explicit academic role in the university that will allow them to make day-to-day academic and operational decisions and determine the general strategic direction of the academic work.

Part II: Managing the governance system of public universities

As mentioned earlier, each public university was set up by an individual Act, unlike the one Act that applies to the entire range of private universities in Bangladesh. Consequently, all public universities have an independent one-to-one relationship between themselves and the state. From independence in 1971 until 1986, the country had four general and two specialised universities (Kabir, 2010). Of them, four public universities were operated by four University Ordinances promulgated in 1973, which are known as the '73 Ordinances. Between 1987 and 2004, 16 more public universities were added and among them only two were general universities while rest were specialised universities, including medical science, agricultural science and science and technology universities (University Grants Commission, 2018b). Except for three universities – Islamic University, Shahjalal Science and Technology University, and University of Khulna, 11 universities were transformed and upgraded from either colleges or institutes to standalone, full-fledged universities through promulgated individual Acts for each university (University Grants Commission, 2019). In fact, more public universities were added by the government in the post-2005 periods compared to the previous period.

In looking into the governance system of these public universities, a variety of governance systems can be seen to have emerged based on the NPM approach.

For convenience of discussion, we divide all public universities into three categories based on the different phases in which these universities were established by the governments of the time. These categorisations would be useful not only in understanding how the government developed different governance systems for different public universities, but also understand how the neoliberal penetration into the higher education sector impacted the governance systems of the post-2005 universities. The two major phases are: universities established before 2005 and the universities established after 2005; within the phase of before 2005 we categorise them into two: universities which operated with the '73 Ordinances and universities that operated with other than '73 Ordinances.

Governance system of universities operated through '73 Ordinances: neither fully autonomous nor fully government-controlled

Upon Bangladesh's Independence in 1971, the government attempted to ensure academic freedom of all universities. There were certain reasons for taking such initiative in ensuring the university's academic freedom. As discussed in the previous chapter, among them, the role of the universities in Bangladesh's movement towards sovereignty and eventual Independence was immense. Throughout the Pakistan period (1947–1971) universities in Bangladesh had played the key role in organising resistance movements to political oppression led by the then Pakistani government on its East Pakistan region. Earlier, in colonial times, the British rulers established the University of Dhaka in 1921 in East Bengal as means of dealing with socio-political unrest (Chowdhury & Kabir 2014; Kabir & Greenwood, 2017; Rahman 2009) and "it continued to be seen as a catalyst to achieve political goals during the Pakistani regime" (Kabir & Greenwood, 2017, p. 70). Under the Pakistani regime, both students and academic staff used the university as the centre of resistance movements that ultimately helped the country to be an independent nation in the world (Kabir & Greenwood, 2017; Quddus & Rashid, 2000).

The way in which both academics and students contributed towards the freedom of the country influenced the then leadership of the newly born country in ensuring and upholding the autonomy of the few universities at that time. The state under Prime Minister Sheikh Mujibur Rahman took initiative to formulate new laws for universities. As part of this initiative, there were four public universities – University of Dhaka, University of Rajshahi, University of Chittagong and Jahangir Nagar University – which operated through four different Acts – commonly known as the '73 Ordinances – "with a view to ensure academic, intellectual and political freedom of the public universities" (Kabir, 2010, p. 622). The key characteristic of these four universities was that the VC of these four universities had power in the decision-making process. For example, the VCs of these four universities were all ex-officio chair in all academic and administrative bodies and committees including the senate, syndicate and academic councils.

The key roles of the Senate, which is the highest authority of the university, are to ratify the status of proposals from the Syndicate, consider and pass resolution of annual reports and annual budgets, and nominate a three-member panel for the selection of VC, from which the Chancellor would appoint someone as the VC of the university (Government of Bangladesh, 1973a). On the other hand, the Syndicate is formed as a day to day executive authority in the university. The key roles of the Syndicate include holding, controlling and administering the property and funds of the university and regulating and determining all concerns relating to university. Finally, the Academic Council is formed as an academic body of the university to

> have the control and general supervision over, and be responsible for maintenance of standards of, instruction, education and examination within the University, and shall exercise such other powers and perform such other duties as may be conferred or imposed upon it by the Statutes.
>
> (Government of Bangladesh, 1973a, p. 19)

The Academic Council would have the right to advise the Syndicate about academic matters, although decision making responsibilities remain the prerogative of the latter.

It appears then, that these four universities enjoyed relatively more freedom in terms of appointing their top officials including the VC and Deans and could make their own administrative and academic decisions. However, through this system, the government developed a solid and consistent mechanism to intervene in the governance of these four universities. For example, as per the '73 Ordinance, the VCs of these four public universities are all recruited by the Chancellor – who of course happens to be the President of Bangladesh – from a three-member panel elected by the Senates of these four Universities (Government of Bangladesh, 1973a, 1973b, 1973c, 1973d). According to the '73 Ordinances of these four universities, more than 40% of Senate members are to be nominated by the Chancellor and the government, and therefore, it becomes obvious how the government can easily influence the entire recruitment process of the VCs of these four public universities.

Not surprisingly therefore, since the 1990s, the VCs of these four universities have been stood down and new appointments made right after the change of a partisan government following a General Election, applying the British Black Act of 1897 (Kabir, 2010). Similarly, both the Syndicate and the Academic Council are formed with the representatives from the government. In particular, along with the VC, Pro-VC(s) and six elected academics from teachers' community of the university, almost half of the syndicate members are nominated by either by the government or the Senate (Government of Bangladesh, 1973a). It can be said that the mechanism the government has developed over the periods can be used not only to influence the university administration, but also to oversee the day to day activities of the universities.

Governance system of public universities established before 2004 and operated with other than the '73 Ordinances

Apart from these four universities mentioned above, 18 public universities were added until 2004, and of them two were specialised universities – the Bangladesh

University of Engineering and Technology (BUET) and the Bangladesh Agricultural University (BAU) – established in 1961. After Independence in 1971, the government of Bangladesh promulgated the Ordinances for these two universities in 1973 (Government of Bangladesh, 1973e, 1973f). Similar to other four public universities operated with the '73 Ordinances, the President of Bangladesh was once again made the Chancellor for these two universities. However, the key difference between these two types of universities is not having the provision of the Senate for these two specialised universities. Therefore, unlike the four public universities that operated with the '73 Ordinances, the VCs of these two specialised universities were to be appointed by the Chancellor on such terms and conditions as the Chancellor may determine (Government of Bangladesh, 1973e, 1973f).

Although most of other public universities established between 1971 and 2004 would have the provision of the Senate, the role of the senates of these universities was quite different from that of the first four public universities which operated through the '73 Ordinances. Specifically, the Senate of these universities are supposed to approve the decisions made by the Syndicate of the respective university. Moreover, the Senates of these universities were composed of a government-majority membership, with more than 50% of the Senate members being nominated by the government. More importantly, for example, in the case of Shahjalal Science and Technology University established in 1987, and the Khulna University established in 1990, to ensure the business and community participations in the Senates of these universities, the government included the provision of nominating representatives from the business and industry communities (Government of Bangladesh, 1987, 1990).

As stated earlier, similar to the first four universities which operated with the '73 Ordinances, there were various administrative bodies including the Syndicate and the Academic Council in these specialised universities. However, unlike the other four public universities, the formation of the syndicates of these universities was quite different. For example, no syndicate member of these universities was elected by the university academic community of the respective university. Rather, all syndicate members were either nominated by the government and the VC or Senate and Academic Council of the respective university. For example, in the case of Khulna University, the Syndicate – the highest executive body and chaired by the VC – comprised of at least 16 members including the VC and Pro-VC(s). Of them, nine members were to be nominated by the government and the VC and the rest by the Syndicate and the Academic Council (Government of Bangladesh, 1990).

As the Syndicate is overwhelmed by the government, the decision-making processes of these public universities are directly influenced by what the government intends to do in these universities. Moreover, the laws of these universities created scope for the government to be involved in investigating any matter relating to the university. For example, both in the BUET and the BAU, there is provision for visitation into the university affairs. As it mentioned in provision 9(1) of the Bangladesh Agricultural University Act of 1961:

> The government shall have the right to cause an inspection to be made by such a person or persons as it may direct, of the university and its buildings, laboratories, libraries, museums, workshops and equipments, of any institutions or colleges maintained and recognised by, or admitted to the privileges of, the university, of the teaching and other work conducted by the university and of the conduct of examinations held by the university, and to cause an enquiry to be made in respect of any matter connected with the University.
>
> (Government of Bangladesh, 1973f, pp. 4 & 5)

The above analysis has shown that although each public university is operated on their own law, they are effectively still highly controlled by the government. The laws of each of these universities after all allow the government to be involved in the university activities by deploying government representatives in different administrative bodies including Senate, Syndicate and Academic Council. However, both the Strategic Plan 2006–2026 and the Strategic Plan 2017–2030 argue in favour of adopting a single Act like the Private University Act for all public universities. In the following section we analyse how the idea of a single Act for all public universities has been justified and some of the key aspects of the governance system of this single Act.

The Strategic Plan and the governance system of public universities established post-2005

The new economy demanded a new role of the universities (Slaughter & Rhoades, 2004) and thus, a particular form of governance emerged in higher education worldwide (Altbach, 2005) in the new century. As mentioned earlier, in 2006 the government adopted a 20-year Strategic Plan aimed at reforming the higher education sector based on a predominantly neoliberal doctrine. In order to introduce a new kind of governance system drawing on NPM, the Strategic Plan identified a problem in the governance system across the entire higher education sector, and then specifically raised this as an issue across public universities in Bangladesh. The Strategic Plan posited that the governance 'problem' of public universities in Bangladesh that needed to be overcome was the politicisation of public universities that had resulted in sliding quality in public higher education. It identified two major issues in the public universities that were deemed to be the subtle politicisation of public universities. First, the VC, Pro-VC and Treasurer of all public universities were recruited by the government based on their political affiliation with ruling political parties. Second, according to public universities' Acts, deans of different faculties as well as a significant number of Senate and Syndicate members were directly elected by the teachers. To elect representatives for the Senate and Syndicate, the teachers of the public universities became divided into two main groups based on their political ideology. It further argued, "Politicization has taken its tolls in terms of quality slide, substandard faculty, distribution of grants and other incentives along party lines and intensification of students' and teachers' politics" (University Grants Commission, 2006, pp. 23 & 24).

One of the principal trends of governance of the 'enterprise university' is to introduce "a new kind of executive power, characterized by a will to manage and, in some respects, a freedom to act greater than was once the case" (Marginson & Considine, 2000, p. 9). Similarly, in order to improve the governance system of the public universities, the Strategic Plan emphasised the importance to ensure the 'de-politicisation' of public universities by abolishing the existing system of appointing the VCs and Deans for faculties. It also underlined the need to redefine the accountability and institutional autonomy of the public universities by restructuring the governing bodies – the syndicate or regent board – "under the legislation to the UGC and the MOE [Ministry of Education]" (University Grants Commission, 2006, p. 23).

As explored earlier in the first part of this chapter, in the early 1990s the government began to use a single Act to regulate all private universities as a group. The idea of the single Act facilitated the introduction of a new kind of governance system where external bodies became a part of the governance system of the private universities and all private universities had to have a collective relationship with the state. In contrast, the governance system of the public universities was very different from that of the private universities. All public universities were established by their own Acts and these public universities therefore had a one to one relationship to the state. This also meant that top officials of these universities enjoyed relatively more academic freedom. By 2006, when the Strategic Plan was developed, a lack of cohesion and uniformity among the public universities Acts was identified. Arguably through policy tracing from the policy development for the private sector, the Strategic Plan developed the idea of a single Act – the "Umbrella Act", designed to regulate all public universities. As it is argued in the Strategic Plan, "As the existing acts for the public universities lack of uniformity and cohesion and are, in many cases, there is an immediate need for rationalizing the different University Laws by developing a single 'Umbrella' legislation for all public universities" (University Grants Commission, 2006, p. 21). Through this idea the Strategic Plan brought in a new governance system that introduced a new recruitment policy for top officials and reorganised the existing governing bodies for all public universities.

In terms of the recruitment of the VCs for all public universities, the Strategic Plan adopted two alternative ways that would remove political manoeuvring in the public university system. First, the Plan enacted new legislation that empowered the governing body of each public university to appoint their own VCs. Second, the Chancellor was required to "form a national search committee with adequate legal backing in order to recommend the appointment of VC" (University Grants Commission, 2006, p. 25). It also proposed the introduction of changes to institutional regulations and statutes to empower the deans and departmental chairpersons to take action against academic and administrative staff for violating rules and for irregularities of conduct. Moreover, the Plan also argued that the "appointment of faculty Deans should be based on academic excellence and leadership qualities instead of election" (University Grants Commission, 2006, p. 24).

In terms of restructuring the governing bodies of public universities, the Strategic Plan proposed that there should be representations from civil society and the

UGC in the Senate, Syndicate and finance committees of every university. Although the Strategic Plan identified that the wrong kind of external influence causes 'bad' governance of the public universities in Bangladesh, it adopted the idea of the value of external influence, which had been introduced into the private higher education sector, to ensure external forces would continue to be involved in all public university settings.

Deem (2001) argues that the new discourse of managerial systems of universities derives from the *for*-profit sector. The idea of involving external forces in universities derives from the neoliberal idea that there should be commercial benefits from academic and non-academic products (Slaughter & Rhoades, 2004). The Strategic Plan adopted the idea of reducing teacher representations in the senate and syndicate and empowered the VC to nominate Senate and Syndicate members from different categories on a rotation basis rather than through election. As stated in the Strategic Plan, "the teachers' representation in the university senates needs to be reduced for creating a premise for better governance" (University Grants Commission, 2006, p. 25). In the Strategic Plan, the role of students in universities was also redefined such that the students could be mainly involved in academic matters and socio-cultural issues rather than with the national political parties.

The Strategic Plan also reflected concerns about political manoeuvring by the political party in power. It argued that representatives from the ruling parties in different governing bodies "make the university administration vulnerable to government interference and limits its required autonomy for ensuring academic freedom" (University Grants Commission, 2006, p. 25). However, the Strategic Plan still argued for government involvement in the governance of the public universities. In order to strengthen the government and the UGC power over the university settings, the Strategic Plan suggested significant amendment into the UGC Act.

It was proposed in the Strategic Plan that the UGC needed more freedom for executing its decisions. The Plan argued that "this regulatory body [the UGC] has not been able to carry out its charter due to lack of adequate authority and resources in enforcing norms and standards for ensuring good governance in the universities" (University Grants Commission, 2006, p. 22). The Strategic Plan solved this problem by upgrading the status of the UGC's Chairman, asserting it should be equal to a Cabinet Minister, and upgrading the status of full-time members to that of a State Minister. The Plan argued that consolidating the legal support ensured the UGC would act and intervene in the university settings as a strong 'oversight' body. As stated in the Strategic Plan, "the UGC might be renamed 'Higher Education Commission' (HEC), with an appropriate set of terms of reference. This will give the commission a better image and help to signal the strengthening of its authority and roles" (University Grants Commission, 2006, p. 23).

In the same way, the Strategic Plan identified the strategic role for the Ministry of Education (MOE) in public universities. The MOE should work in three broad areas of the universities: policy development, private participation and endowment support; establishing a specialist planning function to watch the labour market; and monitoring demographic changes and observing international developments in higher education. In addition, "MOE can participate in university affairs through representation in different governing bodies such as the university senates and syndicates and the role it plays in the process of appointing Vice-Chancellors" (University Grants Commission, 2006, p. 21).

Based on these recommendations, the government attempted to bring significant changes into the public universities in the post-2005 period. For example, the government formed a 'search committee' in 2008 to appoint the VCs of all public universities. Eventually this, however, failed because of pressure from academics from public universities. As an academic from the University of Dhaka commented:

> When the government formed a search committee I was nominated by the government in the committee. But I resigned from the committee when I noticed that the head of the committee was the Secretary from the Ministry of Education. I wanted not to work under a Secretary because it was mentioned in the Strategic Plan that the head of the search committee should be either a Justice of the Supreme Court or the former VC. Through nomination of the Education Secretary the government ultimately wanted to influence to appoint someone as the VC of a public university who might be loyal to the government.

Although the idea of a search committee had not met expected success, the government shaped the governance system of public universities established in the post-2005 period based on the Strategic Plan. For example, during the time of the formation of the Strategic Plan in 2005, the government set up three public universities – Jagannath University in 2005 (see Chapter 8), University of Comilla and the Jatiya Kabi Kaji Nazrul Islam University in 2006. The governance system of these three universities was shaped in a way that not only ensured the government was involved, but also created the University Grants Commission (UGC) as an at arm's-length body in the university setting. Similarly like with other universities, the President of Bangladesh would be the Chancellor of these universities with the key roles of the Chancellor to appoint the VCs of these universities and determine the terms and conditions of the VC's appointment. Regardless of what was stated in the Acts of these universities, the VCs of these universities would continue their roles to the satisfaction of the Chancellor and be responsible and accountable to the Chancellor. The Chancellor could investigate any matter related to these universities and could send the findings of investigation to the Syndicate to take necessary action on them.

The UGC, which was originally established by the government in 1973 to only look after financial matters of public universities, was empowered through these Acts into overseeing *both* academic and administrative activities of these universities. For example, it is mentioned in the Acts of these universities that the UGC could form a committee comprising of a person or persons in order to inspect the university and its buildings, laboratories, workshops and equipment and associated institutions run by these universities. The universities also must maintain the documents and registers directed by the UGC and must supply the statistics, information and report as per the demand of the UGC (Government of Bangladesh, 2005, 2006a, 2006b). Moreover, it is also mentioned in the Act of the Jagannath University that along with government representatives, the UGC would also nominate someone as its Syndicate member.

Conclusion

The idea of NPM emerged from a desire to reduce the role of the state yet still ensure regulation of the education sector. By taking a model of regulation and control that had been used in the management of private sector organisations and applying this to the education sector, NPM models ensured accountability in the public sector without the direct involvement of the state.

In the context of Bangladesh, the government developed the idea of NPM to the governance of universities yet retained a strong central control mechanism over both public and private universities. Although the earlier Private University Act 1992 shaped a 'founder-controlled' or 'entrepreneurial-controlled' governance system, the post-1998 Acts focused on incorporating new managerial values in the private universities through the involvement of the state in the governing bodies of the private universities. In the post-1998 period, the state introduced government representatives and academics from outside the private universities who could reflect the interests of parts of the civil society to provide advice on the day-to-day work of these universities. The VC of the private university was given a more explicitly academic role in the university that allowed them to make day-to-day academic operational decisions and control the strategic direction of the academic work. This shows the modification of some aspects of neoliberalism – the move to the market and founder control – by the cross-field effects of quality assurance and expansion of the role of VC.

The idea about the governance system the government introduced in the post-1998 Acts could be defined as a 'mixed private-public' controlled governance system. The shifting to change from the 'entrepreneurial controlled' to a 'mixed private-public' controlled governance system indicates that the private universities could still be owned privately; however, the Ministry of Education and the UGC as state agencies in the higher education sector could still play the roles of what King (2004) calls 'arm's-length' bodies to ensure the accountability of private universities (cited in de Boer et al., 2007). In line with the 'new managerialism' or NPM approach, the government in Bangladesh has expected the private universities to adopt purposes and standards that align with those of public higher education, and to take management responsibility for reporting to government on the practices and outcomes of their activities, as well as to their own 'boards of trustees' or even founders and shareholders.

In looking into the similarities and dissimilarities of the governance systems of the public and private universities, the findings show that between 1992 and 2010 the government developed a similar kind of governance system for both public and private higher education systems based on NPM. In both the systems, although the ultimate power resided with the government – for example, the President of state continued to be the Chancellor of all universities – the government increasingly relied on a more indirect role to control the universities. The government deployed the Ministry of Education and the UGC as arm's-length bodies to oversee the day to day activities of the public and private universities. In both models, this ensured new roles for the civil society body and at the same time limited the roles of academics in the governing bodies.

Note

1 Parts of this chapter are based on a study by Kabir and Webb, 2018. Reproduced with permission.

2 The University of Dhaka was the first university in East Bengal (now Bangladesh) established by British rulers in 1921 through the Dacca University Act of 1920 [Act number XVIII], where the Governor of Bengal would be the Head as well as the Chancellor of the University of Dhaka. Among others, the key powers of the Chancellor were to preside at the meeting of the Court and at the Convocation of the University, appoint the members in different selection committees including Professorships and Readerships, and appoint the Vice Chancellor of the University after consideration of the recommendation of the Executive Council of the University (see the Dacca University Act, 1920 (XVIII of 1920) (Indian Legislative Council, 1920)).

6 Quality control mechanisms

Rhetoric vs. reality

Introduction

This chapter discusses the forms of quality controlling mechanisms in private sector higher education in Bangladesh, and how far they 'deviate' from the dominant discourses including market norms and expectations. It addresses the causes and effects of the forces of marketisation discourses and the political motives and interests in relation to the quality of higher education. We argue that although the idea of external audits was introduced in line with global trends, the government's involvement was also ensured in the quality assurance process through its arms's-length bodies – in particular, the University Grants Commission (UGC).

The first part of this chapter looks at the politics of quality in private higher education. We begin this part with providing an understanding of how the issue of 'quality' was used in the higher education sector to justify the introduction of higher education in the private sector; following this, we look at the politics of quality maintenance in Bangladeshi private universities. In the second part, we critically explore the process and operation of quality assurance mechanisms in public universities by first examining what processes have been used in these public universities, and then looking into the politics of external quality assurance bodies' involvement in these universities.

Quality assurance mechanisms in private universities

Before moving into exploring how quality assurance mechanisms have developed in the private university sector over the last three decades, we explore how the idea of 'quality' was used as an instrument to justify the introduction of private sector higher education in Bangladesh in the first place. Such discussion would help to understand and situate how the issue of quality became the central concern in the politics of higher education in Bangladesh in subsequent decades.

The politics of 'quality' and the introduction of higher education in the private sector

In the context of Bangladesh, 'quality of higher education' is an overused expression, ubiquitous in both mass media and government discourses. When the private university movement began through the involvement of a group of key drivers including academics from public universities, politicians and private sector representatives in the late 1980s (see Chapter 7), they had perceived that the quality of public higher education was in general decline; the idea of the private university was therefore framed as a policy solution to this problem. They questioned the effectiveness of the teaching-learning methods the public universities used in the 1980s; they argued that the public universities had not brought modern teaching-learning instruction into the classroom and that teachers used traditional and outdated curriculum, and teaching-learning methods that required students to uncritically memorise rather than to learn real life knowledge. For instance, Dr Asim, an academic who was involved in the development of a private university and was later the VC of one, argued that "higher education at that time was too memorisation-based ... our higher education was not linked with practical life. It failed miserably to interplay between practical life and philosophical thought".

The key movers' group in the late 1980s perceived that the higher education sector in Bangladesh could not prepare its citizens to meet market demands as long as it remained dominated by public institutions. Dr Asim's large-scale survey involving 360 organisations in Dhaka and Chittagong in the late 1980s about what types of graduate entrepreneurs generally expected for their organisations revealed that the business-related degrees were the ones most in demand in the labour markets. It was generally perceived that the public universities of that time had largely failed in preparing employable graduates with attributes entrepreneurs and business owners were most desiring in their businesses.

In addition, these key movers also believed that both students and many teachers from the public universities were actively involved in national politics. In particular, academics who had moved to private universities from public universities also assumed that such political activities by both students and teachers ruined institutional cultures and academic activities in the public universities. However not everyone had the same view. One academic argued that teachers who kept their distance from politics often failed to bring about academic changes in higher education. A senior academic, Professor Nasim, who had moved from a public university to a private university, explained that he could not introduce a Bachelor of Business Administration (BBA) programme in the public university because of resistance from teachers. Another academic argued that the teachers of public universities had spent more time in politics than in the development of their own professional development, research or teaching. Dr Asim, who also moved to a private university, explained that "our universities, particularly the University of Dhaka, has no doubt contributed to the formation of our national identity, but it was barely running as a university. The teachers were not involved in teaching; they did not like to go to the classroom".

Through the construction of the rhetoric that the public universities are not able to provide 'quality' education, these key movers sought to explore ways of linking the Bangladeshi higher education system to contemporary global demands. They constructed the idea of 'quality' as part of economic process, rather than what Biesta calls 'good' education used for promoting student values, personhood (morality) and society (politics) (Webster & Whelen, 2019; Webster & Ryan, 2019). They understood that addressing the need to expand higher education through private universities could also help national economic growth. Mohosin, who was involved in the establishment of a private university in 1996 after his retirement from civil bureaucracy, explained that "the global world was far ahead, our country needed to move faster ... needed huge human resources to expand the economy. The public universities were unable to generate a huge number of human resources because of their limited resources". The widely recognised failure of public universities in meeting global demands helped these key movers to construct the discourse of the 'private university' as a solution to meeting the economic needs of the country. Another academic, Professor Kowsar, who had moved from a public university to the position of the VC of a private university, stated that "when we realised public universities were unable to meet the increasing demand for market related degrees ... this demand needed to be fulfilled by the private sector".

Now we turn to explore how the issue of quality was addressed by stakeholders in the private university setting over the years after their first establishment in 1992 with reference to the Private Universities Acts of 1992, 1998 and 2010 and the Private University Ordinance of the non-political caretaker government in 2008. As we will see, in this chronology, 2008 marks a significant milestone.

1992 and 2008: situating the notion of 'quality' in private higher education discourses

Although the key players of the private university movement had framed the quality of public higher education as a policy problem to influence the government in favour of supporting the introduction of the private university as policy solution in 1992, the quality issue was not acknowledged or addressed explicitly until the first Act of 1992. Indeed, the Act of 1992 did not offer any guidelines as to how to maintain the 'quality' of private higher education; instead the state positioned the UGC as an arm's-length body to monitor the 'standard' of private higher education. As the state statutory body, the UGC had to approve "the plan in regard to educational programmes, curriculum, syllabus and the *standard* of the education of any private university" [italics added] (Government of Bangladesh, 1992, p. 7585).

However, by 1998 the general declining quality of private higher education became a major concern. The government perceived that the private universities often became involved in unlawful activities because of the lack of adequate monitoring mechanisms. Both the Ministry of Education and the UGC noted the 'mushroom growth' of private universities causing its own problems in quality maintenance. They further pointed out that the 1992 Act did not ensure a legal basis for the Ministry of Education and the UGC to monitor the private universities' activities. A policy administrator from the UGC explained the problems the UGC faced in monitoring private universities' activities: "if we asked them to audit the financial expenditure and send back the report to us, they did not do that. If problems like dismissing staff without proper reasons were there, the UGC had nothing to do with that either".

Although the government insisted on their concerns regarding the deterioration of quality in private higher education, private sector representatives argued that from the very beginning a number of leading private universities had consistently focused on creating a good reputation to attract high quality students. They further argued that some leading private universities had adopted a Western – in particular an American – model, developed collaborative programmes with foreign universities, and hired reputed academics from home and abroad. One of the private sector representatives, Mohosin, who established a university in 1996 after his retirement from civil bureaucracy, explained that "almost all universities adopted the Western model.... From the beginning, we strictly managed semesters, adopted an English-medium curriculum, and ensured a non-political environment in the campus". However, academics who had moved from public universities to administrative roles in the UGC believed that business-led and commercially inspired activities contributed to a general reduction in the quality of the private universities in the post-1998 period – as Professor Khairul argued, "as most of the private universities were motivated in doing business, they could not emphasise the quality issue at the same time".

In the interviews, several groups of policy actors identified various interrelated factors they thought were behind the deterioration of quality in private university education. For example, politicians who had served as the Ministers of Education at different times argued that over the years, most private universities had failed to ensure a proper academic environment. These politicians explained that although private universities were expected to have their own academic and physical infrastructure within five years of their establishment – according to the earlier Act 1992 – most private universities had failed to comply with this condition. Ohedul, a former Minister of Education in the post-1998 period, explained that "at that time about 4 to 5 private universities met this condition. Although some universities were established more than 10–15 years ago, they didn't meet the conditions of the Private University Act 1992".

These politicians also noted that instead of having their own academic buildings, a significant number of private universities conducted their academic activities in rented properties shared with other businesses and commercial outlets in the same building. They also explained that from the beginning private universities relied on part-time teachers to reduce the expenses of the enterprise. Ahmed, who had also served as the Minister of Education, said, "one of the main reasons behind this situation was the scarcity of permanent teachers ... all private universities hired public universities' teachers".

Policy administrators, as well as academics who had moved from public universities to the UGC were in agreement with these politicians; however they argued that the UGC and the Ministry of Education often received allegations against some private universities about not holding classes regularly and students being awarded degrees without appearing in the examinations. For example, Professor Khairul, a former UGC member, explained that "some universities did not ensure minimum facilities for students.... We even received complaints about some universities where students were not required to attend classes and exams".

They also reported that many universities opened 'branch campuses' unlawfully across the country. As a policy administrator of the Ministry of the Education, Podder explained that "once I travelled to a remote area in the country, I found a private university offering courses through branch campuses. Students were just needed to come to sign the papers only".

Although journalists were generally in agreement with the policy administrators, politicians and UGC academics, they believed that the lack of qualified administrators, as well as the operation of fringe campuses operated by foreign universities across the country also contributed to the deterioration of quality in the private universities. One journalist, Plabon, explained that "anyone could become the VC of a private university without having higher degrees and teaching experiences". Another journalist, Rason, who had produced reports on fringe campuses operated by foreign universities, said, "I found that in the name of foreign universities, hundreds of outer campuses were operating across the country illegally without having qualified teachers and proper academic infrastructure".

In contrast, representatives who had been involved in the private universities from the 1990s perceived the problem in quality differently. They argued that many private universities could not afford full-time and qualified teachers because of financial constraints, although they also agreed that the lack of qualified teachers in the private universities affected the quality of education. Mohosin, who became involved in a private university in 1996, explained, "another problem was the lack of quality faculties". As stated earlier, they also had concerns about branch campuses with no qualified teaching staff and academic facilities which they knew contributed to slide in – Zafor, the former President of the Association of Private Universities, commented that "quality also deteriorated through opening branch campuses here and there".

Failing to ensure quality teaching-learning facilities by private universities in the post-1998 period assisted policy administrators of the UGC and Ministry of Education as well as academics who had moved from public universities to positions in the UGC, to construct the policy rhetoric of 'private universities cannot be trusted to ensure quality' and emphasise the urgency of the need to improve the quality of private higher education. Professor Khairul, who was an academic at a public university and later moved to an administrative role in the UGC explained that "the UGC and the Ministry of Education were thinking for a long time how to stop this worsening situation that existed in the private universities". To improve quality policy administrators emphasised the need to bring in different ideas, for example, an external quality assurance body, into the private universities.

Post-2008: shifting from control by state to external quality assurance bodies

In the post-1998 period, the rapid expansion of private universities caused its own problem of lack of quality. No doubt in the post-1998 Acts concern about and emphasis on quality emerged and therefore instead of having a completely free market approach, successive governments came in with various ideas for controlling quality. Although there is no straightforward consensus on the nature of good quality tertiary education or what it really entails, it could be presumed that the issue of quality was related to market demands of the day, since quality always plays a critical role in the function of the market (Morley, 2003). This is clearly reflected in Ordinance 2008, "The previous Acts were reasoned to be inadequate in improving higher education's standard and meeting the fast growth and gradually increasing multiplex demands of higher education" (Government of Bangladesh, 2008, p. 17569).

Under the neoliberal state, both internal and external quality assurance systems are developed to ensure the efficiency and effectiveness of universities (Sing, 2000, cited in Mollis, 2006). In the post-1998 Acts, private universities were required to submit their academic activities to the reviews of internal and external bodies to ensure assurance of quality. Ordinance 2008 specified the Academic Council as the internal body each university should have to design and implement the day to day academic activities in maintaining and improving academic quality. As stated in Subsection 1 of Section 31, the "academic council ... will be responsible for improving and the continuity of the private university's learning, teaching and examination system, and will have the power to supervise and control these kinds of issues" (Government of Bangladesh, 2008, p. 17582). Ordinance 2008 also ensured the role of the board of trustees in improving quality. It stated that the board of trustees should formulate a 3-year or a 5-year 'strategic plan' to improve quality and the overall development of the university. However, alongside the academic council's and trustees' roles, the latest Act of 2010 adopted the new concept of the 'Internal Quality Unit', which would be established in every private university in order to strengthen the internal quality assurance mechanism. As specified, "In order to ensure the quality of education each private university will have an internal quality unit and will have a written account in the concerned University Yearly Report about the activities which are taken up" (Government of Bangladesh, 2010b, p. 7441).

As argued above, under neoliberalism some of the controls over such quality assurance activities in the universities were being delegated to external agencies. In the post-1998 Acts, the state stepped in with different kinds of quality control mechanisms and did not leave the universities to ensure and monitor quality themselves. The Ordinance 2008 adopted the idea of an 'accreditation council', which Morley (2003) refers to as external body to audit the quality of private higher education. As stated, "In order to evaluate overall academic activities at the universities' level, to improve quality towards world standards, and to continue that world standard in quality, the government will form an accreditation council" (Government of Bangladesh, 2008, p. 17585). The Ordinance 2008 pointed out that the accreditation council will develop a rigorous monitoring and assessment system to audit quality. The Ordinance required all private universities to have "membership" and an approval on all academic programmes from this body for all courses offered at the undergraduate and postgraduate levels with permission of the UGC (Government of Bangladesh, 2008, p. 17585). In the latest Private University Act 2010, the government adopted the idea of the accreditation council as an independent and autonomous body to enhance quality in private universities.

The quality assurance mechanisms of public universities

As indicated in Chapter 5, the public universities have their own Act and a one to one relation with the government and the UGC, which, at least on paper, ensures freedom on what courses to offer and how. Specifically, universities which operated under '73 Ordinances would have power to "provide for instruction in such branches of learning as the university may think fit, and to make provisions for research and for advancement and dissemination of knowledge" (Government of Bangladesh, 1973b, p. 3). The courses and curriculum of these four universities are prescribed by the University Ordinances and the Regulations (Government of Bangladesh, 1973a). Other universities that did not operate under the '73 Ordinances also enjoyed freedom to develop their own curriculum and courses and could decide what degrees they wished to offer, however they needed to have permission from the UGC in terms of opening new courses. The government thus created the UGC as arm's-length body to these universities to mainly regulate the universities' financial activities, rather than to assume control over the formation processes of courses and curriculum. The key mechanism behind this was that if any university in this category introduced any courses without permission from the UGC, it would not be financed by the government (Government of Bangladesh, 1973g).

Whatever the processes used by different public universities in terms of producing courses and curriculum, all public universities, in fact, used their own internal quality assurance mechanisms to improve their quality. Generally, two-tiers of internal quality assurance systems have been used in all public universities. First, at the micro-level, all departments and institutes would have their academic body, usually known as the 'academic committee' that is formed with all teachers of the department, faculty, school or institute, and this committee dealt with all academic matters including the production of courses and curriculum, examinations and the development of teaching learning methods within the framework developed by the highest authority of the university.

The Second Statute which adopted to establish the Institute of Education and Research, the University of Dhaka stated, "The academic committee shall deal with admission of the students; syllabuses; examinations; teaching in the institutes; co-curricular activities of the students in the institute" (University of Dhaka, 1996, p. 140). Sometimes the decisions the academic committee of a department/school take are sent to the higher authority through the faculties if further advice is needed. In addition, in many cases, 'institutes' within a university enjoyed greater freedom than the department/school as they are set up through a separate Statute. For example, the Institute of Education and Research at the University of Dhaka operates through a Statute, where a Committee of Advanced Studies in Education is formed with all professors and other representatives from various education bodies. The Committee of Board of Advanced Studies in Education prepares courses and syllabi for postgraduate examination in education (University of Dhaka, 1996).

Second – and at the macro-level – all public universities would have a body, which is most commonly known as the 'Academic Council', which would play the key role in not only auditing what the Academic Committee produces, but also develops the policy guidelines for academic issues for the university. For example, the following excerpt describes the power of the academic committee on academic matters:

> The Academic Council shall be the academic body of the University, and shall, subject to the provisions of this Order, the Statutes and the University Ordinances, have the control and general supervision over, and be responsible for maintenance of standards of, instruction, education and examination within the University, and shall exercise such other powers and perform such other duties as may be conferred or imposed upon it by the Statutes. It shall have the right to advise the Syndicate on all academic matters.
>
> (Government of Bangladesh, 1973a, p. 19; Government of Bangladesh, 1973b, p. 16; Government of Bangladesh, 1973c, p. 16; Government of Bangladesh, 1973d, p.16)

Along with the Academic Committee, there is also a body, commonly known as Boards of Advanced Studies, at the macro-level, "for organising post-graduates studies in the University which shall be constituted in such manner as may be prescribed by the Statutes" (Government of Bangladesh, 1973a, p. 26).

Strategic Plan: the blueprint of adopting external bodies' involvement in the 'quality' of public higher education

As discussed previously, the NPM approach has been identified as changing the prevailing meaning of efficiency, accountability, transparency and quality of higher education (Lorenz, 2012). Morley (2003) argues that under a neoliberal state, quality is linked with knowledge economy because corporate interests play a significant role in identifying the purposes of higher education. Similarly, analysis of the Strategic Plan can reveal the idea of the importance of a focus on the quality of higher education to support the development of a knowledge-based society, although in the Strategic Plan the focus is given only to the public sector. The Plan states that "The public universities in Bangladesh, over the last two decades, have seen a slide in the quality of both teaching and learning" (University Grants Commission, 2006, p. 33).

While operating under the logic of neoliberalism, quality assurance systems usually involve increasing professional development (Morley, 2003), and producing market-related knowledge (Sing, 2001, cited in Mollis, 2006). In this vein, the Strategic Plan addressed two key issues in the quality enhancement process in higher education sector in Bangladesh: "promoting a culture of teaching quality", and "making courses more relevant and of high quality" (University Grants Commission, 2006, p. 32). The Strategic Plan identified academics as professional bodies and argued that academics needed to enhance and update their skills and should be committed to improving students' learning needs. The Strategic Plan stated that modern teaching-learning methods could help to establish a knowledge-based society.

Alongside modern teaching-learning approaches, a market-responsive curriculum has also been adopted in universities worldwide (Mollis, 2006). In line with this, the Strategic Plan focused on a distinctly market-responsive curriculum to be adopted in the universities in Bangladesh. The Strategic Plan developed two arguments to make academic courses more relevant and of high quality. First, "if a university has to function as a centre of excellence", the universities need to promote new knowledge that will continuously update the process of learning and fill the gaps in any existing programme (University Grants Commission, 2006, p. 32). Second, "in a globally competitive environment a university needs to teach courses and programmes that are relevant to the needs of the community and the country as well as global society" (University Grants Commission, 2006, p. 32). The course curriculum could be developed through constant updating of existing syllabi, discussion with the stakeholders and building up partnerships with reputed foreign universities. In the curriculum, English language acquisition was seen as needing to be emphasised. Although it was not clear who the decisive 'stakeholders' were, it could be presumed that the market was one of determining factors in setting up course curricula across the board. As stated, "a partnership with the "real world" of industry, business and the public services is essential if our higher education institutions are to be nationally and globally competitive" (University Grants Commission, 2006, p. 29).

The Strategic Plan reflected concerns over the current practices of teachers' promotion and its relationship with poor quality education in the public universities. Many universities around the world had already adopted 'output measures' – for example, publications, citations, citation impact measures and research user impact measures for academics as part of quality measurement in higher education (Marginson, 2008). To improve the quality of the public universities, the Strategic Plan argued that there should be a link between the quality of teachers' outputs and teachers' promotions. It emphasised the need to ensure academic excellence, teaching performance, research ability and number of publications in ranked journals as 'output measures' for teachers' promotions. As stated in the Strategic Plan, "the range of publication and research, the quality of research and not mere quantity, and the promise of further scholarship should be the main criteria influencing promotion" (University Grants Commission, 2006, p. 33).

The Strategic Plan adopted the idea of what Marginson (2008) calls performance-based incentives for teachers of public universities. It stated: "Teachers who perform well should also be given incentives by way of salary increase, research grants etc." (University Grants Commission, 2006, p. 32). The Strategic Plan underscored the importance of research by setting up the National Research Council which "will conduct and coordinate research areas where Bangladesh has the most potential" (University Grants Commission, 2006, p. 40). In addition, the Strategic Plan emphasised the need to build up links between universities and research institutes at home and abroad. Similar to India and Pakistan, it emphasised the importance of setting up a Postgraduate University. It is argued in the Strategic Plan that "The proposed university will be an apex research institute for advanced level studies … provide training and high quality academic programmes" acknowledging that "exclusive post graduate universities already exist in India, Pakistan and other countries" (University Grants Commission, 2006, p. 42).

Under the neoliberal state, academics become less trusted (Connell, 2009) and professional autonomy and responsibility are reduced, as professional controls are shifted to external and internal 'audits' or review systems (Lorenz, 2012; Marginson, 2008). Indeed, the Strategic Plan emphasised the importance of setting up internal and external auditing systems to control quality in public higher education. It stated, "unfortunately the public universities in Bangladesh have no external system ... there is no internal auditing processes or review" in this sector to control its quality (University Grants Commission, 2006, p. 34).

The Strategic Plan therefore adopted the idea of an 'accreditation council' as an external body to oversee the improvement of quality in higher education. It argued that the accreditation council would set a level of performance, integrity and quality and would help students take advantage of structured programmes. This external review aimed to promote and enhance quality, to inform students and other stakeholders about programmes offered by universities that meet national expectations, to identify the deficiencies of quality in higher education and to ensure accountability for the use of public funds. The accreditation council would be "undertaking formal accreditation reviews, promoting internal quality enhancement and quality improvement in universities and carrying out external audits of the self-assessment and self-review of quality" (University Grants Commission, 2006, p. 35). The Strategic Plan also argued that the Accreditation process would take into account four aspects of how universities operate: process and goals, organisational structure, resources and support, effective planning mechanisms, high quality programmes, fairness and accessibility in terms of admission and institutional management and outcomes and effectiveness. Significant issues were the Council's involvement in the university's governance, management, transparency, accountability, democratic practices and accessibility of admission system.

Accreditation Council: a mechanism for controlling higher education institutions

The insistence on the Strategic Plan, along with the government's pushing forward with the issue of quality of higher education, justified having an Accreditation Council for the higher education sector. However, the question was to whether the Accreditation Council would be an autonomous body or a controlling agency. During the time of Private University Act 2010, there was debate on this issue between Ministry of Education and the UGC. In terms of roles of the Accreditation Council, policy administrators of the Ministry of Education identified the Accreditation Council as a monitoring and supervising agency to improve quality. However, policy actors of the UGC argued that the Accreditation Council, as an external body, should play no more than a voluntary role in overseeing and improving quality. A policy administrator of the UGC, Nasim stated, "We [the UGC] wanted the Accreditation Council as a voluntary organisation to help improve quality. But the ministry officials saw this council as a controlling agency for quality".

Although the Private University Act 2010 adopted the idea of the Accreditation Council for private universities, the founders of the private universities identified the incorporation of this external body as a policy solution intended to work as a mechanism of control. The founders also argued that the controlling attitudes of the policy administrators would further reinforce the bureaucratisation of private universities. A private sector representative, Anzus, who had founded a private university and become a leader of the Association of Private Universities of Bangladesh (APUB), spoke at length about his recent experiences of how the bureaucratisation process had been working in the private universities at that time.

The founders of the APUB argued that the government developed a top-down bureaucratic system over the years which contributed to developing a typically bureaucratic setup. Reflecting on his personal experiences on this, Anzus explained, "He was a joint secretary to the Ministry of Education and a few years after he could be the Secretary to the Government. Therefore, this kind of person wants to have the upper hand. They don't like to hear from others". The founders emphasised that the Acts needed to be more rational and balanced for all stakeholders. Therefore, they raised question as to why the Accreditation Council was incorporated *only* for private universities. According to Mohosin who founded a private university of which he later became the VC, and who also later served as the Chairman of the board of trustees, "We just wanted to ensure the rules would be updated and rational. Our motivation was to generate human resources for the society". These founders of the private universities considered the introduction of quality assurance as global idea that served the interests of 'multinational organisations'. For instance, Professor Nasim, an academic who founded a Private University in which he played the role of the VC and later became the Secretary of the APUB, explained: "I started to worry, this homegrown reform agenda was going to be ruined by the multinational concepts because these concepts were different from ours".

Eventually the government promulgated the Accreditation Council Act 2017, which has been effective since 6 March, 2017, for the entire higher education sector. In the Accreditation Act 2017, the government defines the term 'accreditation' as the recognition of the curriculum and the academic activities according to the curriculum developed by different public and private higher education institutes across the nation. In providing the 'confidence' or 'accreditation' certificate for a particular academic programme, the Accreditation Council will assess the curriculum and its academic activities through a standard quality framework developed by the Accreditation Council. Moreover, in terms of defining quality assurance, the Accreditation Council Act referred to assess higher education institutions and their academic programmes, development and assurance based on the standard quality framework (Government of Bangladesh, 2017).

Within neoliberal discourses of quality assurance, the relations between universities and state have changed so that the role of the state has shifted from promoter of intellectual activity to controller of it (Morley, 2003). Although the Act does not make it clear whether the Accreditation Council would be operating as an autonomous body or not, the way in which the government determines the formation criteria of the Accreditation Council essentially shapes the Accreditation Council as another arm's-length body of the government. For example, the Council is led by a chairman and four fulltime members – all of them either from public university or government bureaucrats. In the Acts, the government defines the criteria and experiences of persons who could be considered as a member of the Accreditation Council. As stated in the Accreditation Act 2017, "The government will appoint four persons as fulltime members of the Council either with the experiences of professorship from the public university or with administrative experiences within government" (Government of Bangladesh, 2017). In addition, there are eight part-time members from different bodies including government bodies, representatives from private university associations, experts from international quality assurance bodies, representatives from civil society bodies, representatives from medical and dental councils, and educational administrative experts and ICT experts – although all of them will be nominated by the government. The Accreditation Act also mentions that the Chairman of the Accreditation Council would have at least 25 years of teaching experiences at public universities with at least ten years of professorship as well as with extensive knowledge about higher education sector and accreditation and quality assurance processes. All members and the Chairman of the Accreditation Council will work for as long as the government is satisfied with their performance.

The way in which the government defined the responsibilities and functions of the Accreditation Council not only promotes the accountability of higher education institutions, but also extends control over the whole range of academic activities in higher education institutions. For example, the Accreditation Council Act 2017 defines the responsibilities and functions of the Council and how it operates stating that the key responsibilities and functions include providing the confidence or accreditation certificate, as well as suspensions and cancelations of confidence and accreditation certificates. The Council can not only provide or suspend accreditation certificates, it can also form discipline-specific accreditation sub-committees and determine the terms and conditions of the confidence and accreditation certificates. In order to receive expert advice, the Accreditation Council can also form expert committee(s) and develop quality frameworks with permission from the government.

Without securing a confidence or accreditation certificate, no higher education institution could operate their academic programmes. If any higher education institution failed to follow the terms and conditions of the confidence or accreditation certificate, the Council could cancel or suspend their confidence or accreditation certificate and they would have to stop or discontinue their academic programmes. Representatives of Accreditation Council could visit any academic programme offered by any university and during their visit the institution had to make sure they did not provide any misleading information or hide any information asked from them.

Conclusion

This chapter has critically considered the politics of adopting quality assurance mechanisms in the higher education sector in Bangladesh. Under the neoliberalist movement, different mechanisms – such as *internal quality assurance* and *external quality assurance* – were developed both within and outside universities to ensure assurance of quality of higher education across the world. In the early years of the establishment of the private university in Bangladesh, the key movers identified the declining quality of education in public universities as a policy problem and the establishment of higher education in the private sector as a policy solution to that problem. However, in the early years, the expansion of private universities was the key focus, and thus compromised quality. Until 2008, the UGC as the state-funded statutory body in the higher education sector became heavily involved with the private universities and was given a new role in approving educational programmes, curriculum and course content, as well as quality standards of private higher education.

The role the UGC played in the private universities ensured that the quality issue in this sector became part of 'state evaluation' (Neave, 1998, p. 265). By 2008, the government made the private universities subject to institutional performance evaluation through both internal and external quality assurance bodies. The Academic Council, as an internal academic decision-making body of the private universities, played a crucial role in improving the programmes and learning outcomes under the direction of the UGC. However, the university would need to have an 'internal quality unit' to provide progress reports about the quality to the Accreditation Council. The government identified that the Accreditation Council, as an external auditing governance body, would use specific benchmarks to assess the institutional performance of quality and to ensure 'external accountability' of the private universities (Vukasovic, 2014, p. 46). Consequently, the UGC and the Accreditation Council would play important roles in the private universities in auditing quality, so that they not only transform the private universities into institutes that contribute to the knowledge economy, but also affect their governance systems.

By 2006, the government had developed the argument through the Strategic Plan that public universities were also required to demonstrate institutional performance of quality. Traditionally, the quality issue of the public universities was solely the responsibility of the faculties and the universities themselves. The formation of the Accreditation Council in the Strategic Plan echoes the characteristics that are already identified in scholarly literature (see for reference, Sanyal & Martin, 2007) where the quality assurance process is shifted from the institution to an external body. In addition, the Strategic Plan adopted the idea of internal and external evaluation processes in which student and staff outcomes and publications would be evaluated by various participants and standards: for example, students' assessments and number of publications in ranked journals. Based on the policy recommendation in the Strategic Plan, many higher education institutes came under intense government and public pressure to respond to the demands of the market. However, the way in which the government established the Accreditation Council in 2017 as arm's-length body would continue to control the entire higher education sector in Bangladesh.

7 Higher education in the private sector

'For-profit' vs. 'not for-profit'

Introduction

This chapter discusses the complexities that have characterised discourses situating higher education in Bangladesh as neither 'for-profit' nor 'not for-profit', or both. By employing various central controlling mechanisms based on NPM approaches into the private universities (see Chapter 5), and by refraining from clearly defining whether private universities should be run as 'for-profit' or 'not for-profit' institutions, the government has developed a distinctly Bangladeshi form of private university model. In other words, this chapter explores the concept of the private university in Bangladesh through reference to the understanding that an academic institution could be set up by a person or a group of people in a way that is neither 'for-profit' nor 'not for-profit', or both, although the government might *still* control its existence through regulations and the state-sanctioned power of the quality assurance bodies, such as the UGC.

In the first place, we attempt to understand how the idea of the private university has shifted over the world, and second, we look at how the idea of private university has moved into a third space of non-committal rationale in the context of Bangladesh. In looking into this debate, we particularly focus on how the 'for-profit' and 'not for-profit' dichotomy has created a grey area that has been utilised by both the government and owners and founders who control over the private university sector for their own socio-political and personal gains.

Global shifts in the concept of the private university

The privatisation of higher education is not a new phenomenon in world economy as the private provision of higher education in many countries can be traced back a few centuries (Tilak, 1991). However, as we have seen in Chapter 2, in the late 20th century, following the wide proliferation of neoliberalist ideas in the higher education sector, the development of a distinct private sector in higher education emerged as a policy strategy worldwide (Tilak, 1991). Levine (2001, p. 1) argues that six forces helped promote the spread of privatisation in higher education worldwide – these forces are "the rise of information-based economy, changes in demographics, an increase in public scrutiny, the advent of new technologies, the convergence of knowledge-based organizations, and a decline in public trust in government". Consequently, private higher education has become one of the most dynamic and fastest growing sectors at the turn of the 21st century around the globe (Altbach et al., 2010), with private university enrolment seen to be much faster than in the public sector in many countries, sharing around 30% of total student enrolment in the private universities in recent times worldwide (Gürüz, 2008).

Altbach et al. (2010, p. 75) was probably the first to argue that "privatization means many things in higher education". The term "privatisation" generally refers to a change of ownership from public to private, resulting in a distinct form of finance, governance and functions (Marginson, 1997). This is not to say private universities reflect a consistent model (Altbach et al., 2010) globally, or even in a given country – as we have seen in the preceding chapters. Whereas higher education at public universities tends to be largely supported by taxpayers' money offering more complex and more broadly based education, private universities are funded by private entrepreneurs offering mostly business and technology-oriented education (Marginson, 1997). Sometimes private higher education institutes are partially supported with public money based on being 'for-profit' or 'not for-profit' in terms of preference; they may also be accountable to the government or other authority outside the country (Altbach et al., 2010). On the other hand, public universities can also be shaped after private models, as we see in the case of Jagannath University (see Chapter 8).

Both Tilak (2006) and Altbach et al. (2010) discuss four types of private higher education, but in slightly different ways. For Tilak (2006), the first type of private higher education, which is identified as *identity institutions* by Altbach et al. (2010), is founded mainly by religious bodies in order to support the government in serving the public good. The second type of private higher education emerged with the support of the state but was privately managed. Following the proliferation of neoliberalism, the third type of private higher education does not rely on the state or philanthropy, but on 'hidden' subsidies from the state in various forms. Often this type of institution operates in a for-profit manner (Tilak, 2006). Altbach et al. (2010) argue that most such for-profit institutions could be included in the non-elite sector of higher education institutions because their goal is primarily to earn money through providing higher education, rather than to achieve academic reputation.

This type of institution is often characterised by a business model in which power and authority are concentrated in a board of trustees and a chief executive, and academics have less autonomy. The *raison d'etre* of this institution is to deliver a product by receiving money, and thus students are positioned as *consumers* (Naidoo, Shankar & Veer, 2011; Tilak, 2006). Altbach et al. (2010) point out that the 'for-profit' higher educational institutions are the faster-growing sector worldwide, a growth that sometime takes place across national boundaries with private local partners. Some universities that may be public in their home countries operate as private universities abroad. The fourth type of private higher education is known as financial privatisation which involves cost sharing or cost shifting in public institutions (Tilak, 2006).

Apart from the above-mentioned categories, Altbach et al. (2010) discuss two types of private higher education: *elite* and *semi-elite* and *demand-absorbing institutions*. They identify such elite and semi-elite institutions based on academic ranking of world universities. They argue that a few universities – for example Harvard University, and others mostly from the USA, Europe and Japan – are subsumed into the elite subcategory, but a large number of private universities could be included into this semi-elite subcategory. Universities included in this subcategory could be leading universities in their countries. They might not be in the very top in their country context, nonetheless they produce a large number of graduates for the market. Bangladesh, Pakistan, Poland, Thailand and Turkey are just a few national examples where this type of subcategory can be found (Altbach et al., 2010). The other category – demand-absorbing institutions – is mostly comprised of non-elite institutions that have emerged as students demand access to higher education. Altbach et al. (2010) argue that such types of institution are identified as technical and vocational institutions in many countries and operate in the third space between for-profit and non-profit.

As discussed in Chapter 3, despite the different approaches of private universities in Asian countries, their key characteristic is to develop a hybrid-form of private university through a blending of the neoliberal model and the pre-existing state-model of public universities (Mok, 2008). For example, as we have seen in Chapter 3, Malaysia has introduced tight regulatory measures in the private university system than would be typical of the private system in more developed economies (Mok, 2008). Consequently, as Naidoo (2011) reports, while universities in USA and UK are expanding as elite/semi-elite or demand-absorbing institutions by attracting a large number of revenue generating students, universities in developing countries, such as China and India have shaped this kind of revenue generating interaction in the private sector by imposing policy and regulation in order to control low quality universities. In many cases, such distinctive and hybrid forms of the neoliberal model have been transferred between regional countries – for example, instead of adopting a Western model, Indonesia has developed a higher education model derived from other East Asian countries such as China, Singapore, Malaysia and Hong Kong (Rosser, 2016). On the other hand, since the late 1990s Singapore has adopted its own distinctive form of the Global Schoolhouse Initiative where local universities build up alliance with elite universities. While initially this emphasised building up alliance between Singaporean universities and overseas elite universities including the MIT, this kind of alliance expanded across to other global elite universities e.g. INSEAD, a European Business School and the Indian Jain School of Management (Sidhu, Ho and Yeoh, 2011).

Such trends towards privatisation have also shifted the role of these universities towards society. Traditionally, the role of higher education was to generate 'public good', but such a concept is disappearing and being replaced by the needs of the 'private good' (Marginson, 2011). Slaughter and Rhoades (2004) point out that universities have been shifting from the public good knowledge to an 'academic capitalist knowledge' regime in which knowledge is constructed as a private good.

Because of privatisation, knowledge here is no longer seen as merely a 'scientific' or scholarly practice and teaching is no longer confined within the faculties. Rather, people who are involved in higher education use different strategies to generate "new circuits of knowledge" for the global economy (Slaughter & Rhoades, 2004, p. 1). Consequently, the traditional broad-based knowledge produced from the humanities, arts and social science disciplines has been ignored (Nussbaum, 2010) and corporate culture has gradually become the model for the perfect life and for individual success in contemporary times.

Giroux (2002, p. 425) argues that "civic discourse has given way to the language of commercialization, privatization, and deregulation and that, within the language and images of corporate culture, citizenship is portrayed as an utterly privatized affair that produces self-interested individuals". The growing influence of corporate culture on university life undermines the relationships between higher education and business. The corporation dictates the research they value and therefore sponsor, while business representatives often sit in the faculty meetings to determine how research funding is to be spent and allocated. Giroux (2002) contends that such shift towards privatisation colonises the university as public spheres and sites of critical learning. The number of part-time professional academics with a low salary has increased worldwide, and often faculty staff are encouraged to be involved in extra work to supply their own salary and subsidise the university's own budget (Altbach et al., 2010).

Conceptualising 'private' higher education in Bangladesh

Private higher education in Bangladesh is not a new phenomenon – private sector provision of higher education in the Indian Subcontinent in the then Bengal (now Bangladesh) can be traced back more to than two centuries. During the medieval period and even in the British colonial period (1757–1947) many philanthropists established higher education institutes in Bangladesh, for example the Jagannath College (see Chapter 8 for a detailed history), Mymansingha Ananda Mohan College, Sylhet Murari Chand College, with a view to serving the society rather than to using them as businesses for profit (Kabir, 2013b). Once Bangladesh became independent in 1971, most of these private colleges were nationalised in recognition of their contribution to the society. Consequently, most of these early private higher education institutes became leading national institutes in terms of accommodating large numbers of students and benchmarking quality in higher education from the 1970s until the late 1980s (Kabir, 2010).

Shifting the concept of the private university: demand-driven and a new 'entrepreneurial' space

In the early 1990s, a new form of privatisation emerged following the enactment of the first Private University Act 1992 (Kabir, 2010). This move helped in establishing a new kind of university system in Bangladesh which saw private higher education become the fastest growing sector in Bangladesh during the

1990s and up until the present. The first private university – North South University – was approved by the government on 5 November 1992, just three months after the promulgation of the Private University Act 1992 (Ahmad, 2004). As mentioned in Chapter 1, from 1992 to the present date, permission has been given to 105 private universities, of which nine universities conduct programmes through unapproved campuses and four universities offer courses yet to be approved by the UGC (University Grants Commission, 2018b).

In order to understand the specific form neoliberalism has assumed in Bangladesh it is helpful to trace the inherent ideologies and agenda leading to the development of private higher education in Bangladesh. In addition to quality issues (discussed in Chapter 6), through the early Act 1992 the government identified that the existing public higher education institutes in Bangladesh had failed to accommodate a large number of students. The early Act 1992 identified three key areas where private universities could contribute:

> Whereas it is necessary to set up universities at the private sector to meet the growing demand for higher education in the country and for its wide dissemination, to make available higher education to the general public and to create skilled manpower through it.
>
> (Government of Bangladesh, 1992, p. 7581)

This demand-driven rationale for private universities bears the quintessential hallmarks of neoliberalism. Under a neoliberal state, the state emphasises the need to shape an individual's potential as an enterpriser and competitive entrepreneur, and the higher education sector is seen as needing to foster such entrepreneurism (Olssen & Peters, 2005). Therefore, in many countries, providing opportunities for the development of private universities is synonymous with providing opportunities for the higher education sector to be influenced by individual public figures, benevolent philanthropists and sponsor agencies with permission from the government (Altbach, 1999). In line with the global trend, the government of Bangladesh wanted to create opportunities for local entrepreneurs to be involved in the higher education sector, and of course in doing so, establish a steady and solid source of income for the state. The first Act 1992 stated that the government was formulating the Private University Act because "certain public welfare oriented persons, assemblage of persons, charitable trusts and institutions of the country are desirous of setting up and administering university at the private level" (Government of Bangladesh, 1992, p. 7581).

The early Act 1992 defined the private university as "any private university established under this act" by a person or a group of persons (Government of Bangladesh, 1992, p. 7582). Although the early Act 1992 identified a person or a group of persons as the recognised body for the purpose of establishing any private university, it did not provide a straightforward definition of private university. In fact, the Act 1998 recognised foreign universities and their campuses as private universities too. As exemplified in the Act 1998 (amended), "Private University means any private university established under this act and any institution conducting graduate and postgraduate degrees, diploma or certificate courses in Bangladesh under any foreign university in conformity with the provisions of the act" (Government of Bangladesh, 1998, p. 5607).

In the post-1998 Acts, the government finally stepped up to regulate foreign universities' campuses operating in Bangladesh. Consequently, both the Ordinance 2008 and the Act 2010 imposed additional restrictions on the operation of foreign universities' campuses in Bangladesh. As stated in the Ordinance 2008, "Without the prior approval from the government no one or no organisation can establish a university or institution in the name of a foreign campus anywhere in Bangladesh nor can they take students in any program or course" (Government of Bangladesh, 1998, p. 17585). The Ordinance 2008 and the Act 2010 also specified that the government will formulate rules and regulations for the operation of foreign universities' campuses in Bangladesh. Eventually the government formulated the Guiding Rules for Foreign University 2014 under Act 2010 (Ministry of Education, 2014). By formulating the guiding rules for foreign universities under this Act, the government specified the types of entrepreneurs who could run a university in the private sector in Bangladesh.

Marginson (2011) discusses the implications of the growth of higher education institutions that could be 'public' or 'private' and argues that public purposes could be accomplished in privately owned institutions, just as in public ones. As shown earlier, the pre-1998 Acts allowed both local and international entrepreneurs to be engaged in the private higher education sector. However, these Acts did not delineate a straightforward definition of whether these private universities should be 'not for-profit' or 'for-profit' institutions. Instead, the key focuses of the pre-1998 Acts were growth and the creation of easy access to higher education for all. In the post-1998 period concerns about the excessively profit-led activities of private universities became conspicuous. As a result, the following was included in the Ordinance, "What it has been in other law, without the government's prior approval no private university can operate any distance program or course" (Government of Bangladesh, 2008, p. 17585). The government thus attempted to shape the private university into a form of 'not for-profit' institution to confine the operation of private universities to academic activities only. As is stated in Subsection 2 of Section 3 in the Ordinance 2008, "Each private university under this ordinance will be established in a form of 'not for profit' organisation" (Government of Bangladesh, 2008, p. 17571).

Although the pre-1998 Acts in Bangladesh allowed both local and international entrepreneurs to be involved in the private universities to expand higher education, the government also wanted to shift higher education costs away from the state. Therefore, the pre-1998 Acts show the ways in which the government gradually pushed higher education costs onto the institutions, although in the post-1998 period the government did not want to push the institutions so far that they became purely private, for-profit businesses. Subsequently, through the Ordinance 2008, the government wanted to shape private universities as 'not for-profit' institutions. However, in the latest Act 2010, the government omitted the provision of private university as 'not for-profit' and the Act became silent about whether private universities would be 'not for-profit' or 'for-profit' institutions.

As discussed in Chapter 3, many governments in Asia and the Global South – for example, China, India, Malaysia, Vietnam and Sri Lanka – have developed a distinctive hybrid-form of private university through a blending of a neoliberal model and the typical state-owned public university model. Similar to a hybrid-form of private university, the above analysis shows that over the last three decades, the Bangladesh government too has developed its own form of the private university model. The analysis also shows that by the idea of the 'private university', the government of Bangladesh refers to a type of academic institution that is structured as a charitable trust organisation to provide higher education, parallel to public higher education. A further defining feature of these private universities is that they have not been established by the government, but by individuals, a group of people or a charity organisation who are education-oriented (Government of Bangladesh, 1992, 2010b). Furthermore, by not defining whether a private university would be a 'for-profit' or 'not for-profit' academic institution, the government of Bangladesh has developed their own kind of private university model that could be designed for *both* purposes.

However, shifts in the explicit definitions provided in the aforementioned policy texts indicate that there are ongoing political debates over the issue that needs to be explored further. The following two sections focus on how socio-political and economic contexts influence both the government and owners in shaping the private university in Bangladesh as neither 'for-profit' nor 'not for-profit' academic institutions or both, and the politics of shaping the private university in a way that helps them to preserve their personal and political interests in and through the private university system.

Private universities as sites of political struggle over 'not for-profit'/ 'for-profit'

As we have shown, many private universities became involved in making profit through unlawful activities in the period after 1998. Several journalists from national newspapers published series of reports about the business-led activities of the private universities that often led to practices that either ignored or took advantage of regulations that were in many cases obscure. For example, a journalist of a national daily newspaper, Plabon, stated, "After getting approval some founders (of private universities) became involved in the business of selling certificates.... So I attempted to produce investigative reports as much as I could about their business-led activities".

Other reports published in national newspapers revealed that some owners had become involved in corruption and had even transferred ownership on exchange of money. For instance, Professor Alimul, an academic who later became the Chairman of the UGC, said, "There was widespread news in the media about high irregularities, corruption and cheating with the students.... Some universities were 'flown' [exposed]". Some of these extensive newspaper reports constructed what Lingard and Rawolle (2004) call the 'mediatisation' of the discourses of assumption in the private universities which eventually pressurised the government in the post-1998 period to rethink the roles the private universities should play in the society. Professor Alimul also explained how such reports pushed successive governments in taking the initiative to formulate a new Act in the post-1998 period: "The market-led activities of the private universities concerned the society. We saw the reports in the newspapers, and here and there ... so the government became concerned about the unlawful activities of these universities".

As previously stated (Chapter 4), the previous Act 1992 did not define whether private universities could be operated on the basis of a profit venture or not. Following the reports about the massive market-led activities in the post-1998 period, people from all segments of society debated whether the private universities should be classified based on the idea of 'for-profit' or 'not for-profit'. In the Ordinance 2008, the Army-backed Caretaker government defined the private universities as 'not for-profit' organisations. When interviewed, most of the participants argued that the government should clearly specify the private universities as 'not for-profit' organisations in the latest Act 2010. Some of the private sector representatives, who had involvement in the APUB, talked off the record and rephrased their comments for the record stating that though many of their colleagues believed private universities should be 'for-profit' institutes, they personally believed that private universities should be there for the public good. For example, the former President of the Association of Private Universities, Zafar, stated, "I agree to some extent that higher education should not be used as a commodity in the Bangladeshi social context".

Journalists had mostly presumed that the government deliberately remained silent about whether the private universities should be 'for profit' or 'not for-profit' because of the influence and lobbying of some founders. As one of the journalists Nasir, argued, "These people [the founders] are richer and powerful ... so they've got strong connection with the government. They influenced the government through their connection, and through their money to relax the Act 2010". However, some founders under the APUB argued that the private universities could be run as *both* 'for profit' and 'not for-profit' institutes, after all. For example, Anzus, a private sector representative who established a private university and played a leading role in the APUB, explained that "We advised the government to have both options – 'for profit' and 'not for-profit' – so that universities would have a choice". Other founders, who were involved in private universities after their retirement, wanted to run universities based on the idea of 'not for-profit'. For example, the former President of the Association of Private Universities, Zafar, commented how some of other founders under the Association disagreed with his view: "Some of us showed their disagreement.... I had a strong feeling on this.... I wanted to see the wording, 'private university as non-profit organisation', in the beginning of the latest Act 2010 ... but that didn't happen".

Although perceptions differed among founders under the APUB about whether private universities should be operated as 'not for-profit' institutions, all founders believed that the government remained silent for the obvious reason that it was using this sector to generate significant revenue. They argued that the government proposed to impose taxes on the private universities' income for the financial year of 2009–2010. In the fiscal year 2010–2011, the government also imposed a value added tax (VAT) on fees in the private universities for collecting revenue. They further argued that according to a government regulation of 1988 the income from the universities had been exempted from income tax. All founders under the APUB argued that if the Act 2010 had clearly defined the private universities as 'not for-profit', the government would not be able to impose taxes on the income of private universities according to the Income Tax Act of 1988.

They also believed that the government struggled to finance the public universities. Thus, the government intended to use this private sector as an alternative source of income to mitigate the financial burden of higher education. For example, according to Mohosin, a private sector representative who played the role of the Chairman of the board of trustees of a private university, "The private universities earned a huge amount of money from fees.... However, the government struggled to finance the public universities. The government wanted to subsidise the public universities by earning money through imposing tax on the private universities".

As the government remained largely silent on this issue, two founders voiced their scepticism towards the government's intention to see higher education as a 'public good'. Rather, they argued that the government had shaped the private universities as 'for-profit' organisations by adding certain provisions in the latest Act 2010. As Zafor explained, "Some rules, for example, imposing taxes on private university's income, ensured private universities' status as 'for-profit' organisations". He viewed the incorporation of these rules as an act of duplicity on part of the policy makers.

However, several academics who had moved from public universities into the position of the VCs of private universities indicated that the government did want to shape private higher education as a 'public good'. However, they felt that imposing taxes on the income of this sector could encourage many founders to use universities for profit. As stated by Professor Kowsar, an academic who had moved in 2002 from a public university into the position of the VC of a private university, "What we have been experiencing, nobody calls it a 'social service' but a student-exploitive, profit-making venture". Other private sector representatives, who became involved in private universities after their retirement, echoed similar concerns. Zafar, a private sector representative, explained, "By not declaring private universities as 'non-profit' organisations, you are giving an opportunity to a person to abuse the facilities to make it a profitable organisation".

In the following section we look at the micro-politics inherent in the shaping of the private university as neither 'not for-profit' nor 'for-profit', or both.

Ruling party-founder nexus: private universities as socio-political and personal gain

The debate over whether private university is 'for-profit' or 'not for-profit' or both indicates that the process of the establishment of the private university did not simply originate from an altruistic educational cause. Rather, there were certain factors beyond the scope of a purely educational agenda that pursued both government and private sector players in establishing private universities in

Bangladesh. Among others, one strong factor was that both government and private sector people identified the private university as way of ensuring their own socio-political and personal interests. In so doing, the nexus between the ruling-party and founders developed and reconfigured over the decades to shape the private university in ways that would help them to carry both their political and personal interests. As we have seen in previous chapters, this meant that numerous negotiations occurred between the government and the owners and founders in relation to what should be adopted and what should not be adopted in the Acts.

In its early stages in the early 1990s, private sector people – including academics, private sector representatives and politicians – directly influenced the development of the private universities in a number of ways. In the post-1998 period there was a gradual shift in the discourse, when owners of the private universities began to organise themselves through a consolidated APUB and started to identify themselves as 'founders' rather than 'owners' of the private universities. They saw the term 'founder' as a more neutral designation because it sounded more generous and philanthropic. As former president of the APUB Zafor argued, "Some people would say, 'the owners of private universities'. They were not like owners. They [the owners] provided the facilities and established infrastructure. Some of them are still contributing to the foundation of the universities".

Analysis of interview transcripts done as part of this study show that, in the post-1998 period, the formation of the APUB helped the founders of the private universities to act, in effect, as a pressure group. Through persistent lobbying and through the platform of the APUB the founders influenced successive governments not to modify or develop any new Acts in this sector. To influence the government, the founders would typically select someone who had kept good terms with the ruling party as the leader of the Association of Private Universities. As stated by Anzus, a private sector representative who had also been the Vice-President of the APUB, "We used tactics to select someone as the President of our association who had secured a good connection with the ruling parties. Otherwise, the government felt uncomfortable to discuss any confidential matter with us".

In 2004, the government took an initiative to repeal the earlier Act 1992 but stopped the process because of pressure from some founders represented through the APUB which was led by people affiliated with the ruling party. A policy administrator of the Ministry of Education, Azam, who was involved in that formation process, admitted the founders' influence on the then government:

> The BNP [Bangladesh Nationalist Party] government (2002–2006) started to enact a new Act. The government had almost finalised the draft of the Act but retreated from this process because the General Election was due in 2007. The ruling party presumed that the introduction of a new Act could infuriate some influential people [founders] and they could withdraw their support from the ruling party in the National Election.

The journalists were generally in agreement with the policy administrators of the Ministry of Education. They argued that the Ministry of Education drafted the new

Act in 2005, but it had failed to convince the Prime Minister into finalising it. As one of the journalists Rason, stated, "The then Education Minister and the UGC chairman wanted to introduce a new private university Act, but they failed because of the influence of the owners [founders] in the government". The journalists perceived that the Prime Minister had asked the Education Minister not to proceed further with the new Act until after the General Election. Several journalists in this study also argued that the founders under the APUB had forced the Education Minister not to include certain points in that new Act, although this Minister voiced his disagreement on these points. As stated by Plabon, a journalist who claimed that he had first-hand witnessed the conversation between the Education Minister and some influential founders under the APUB in 2005 at that time:

> One day some owners – some influential businessmen and former bureaucrats met the Education Minister.... They handed over a list to the Minister and asked the Minister not to include these points into the new Act. Once the Minister showed his disagreement, they just shouted at the Minister.

The founders' direct influence on the government in 2005 was also acknowledged by the then Education Minister, who had also served the World Bank, in another study conducted in 2011 (see Kabir, 2011). In that study, the Education Minister conceded that he had faced considerable and persistent pressure from the APUB when he took the initiative to introduce a new Act. As he explained, "Unfortunately, I allowed pressure groups to stop the initiative. That is why we could not do more in the higher education sector.... These are realities like pressure groups; these are big industrialists, businessmen who are investing in private universities" (Kabir, 2011, p. 90).

To stop the formulation of a new Act in 2005, the founders under the APUB ran a strong lobby group with the ruling party. For instance, private sector representative Anzus, who led the APUB at that time, explained, "We brought Mr Hashem [an influential businessman who was a ruling party MP and the Chairman of the Board of Trustees of North South University at that time] to the Ministry. ... We tried to convince the Education Minister not to frame that law but failed". When the founders were unable to convince the Education Minister, they met the Prime Minister herself to stop the initiative the Education Minister had taken. Anzus, continued, "We went to the Prime Minister and finally we convinced her not to formulate a new Act".

Despite the countless efforts of the founders under the APUB to influence the BNP government (2002–2007) not to introduce a new law in 2005, they failed to influence the Army-backed Caretaker Government (2007–2008) not to promulgate the Ordinance 2008. Professor Nasim, an academic who played the role of the Secretary of the APUB at that time, said, "We met the then Law and Education advisor [name] to tell him not to do that. Then (we met) Hossain Zillur Rahman, who became the Education Advisor, to convince not to initiate the Ordinance". When the founders failed to influence the Caretaker Government, they met the head of the state, the President of Bangladesh to persuade him not to sign the Ordinance 2008. Professor Nasim continued, "we even appealed to the Chancellor [the President of the country] not to sign the Ordinance 2008".

Towards the end of their tenure in 2008, the Army-backed Caretaker Government promulgated the Ordinance 2008. However, when the Bangladesh Awami League formed government in 2009 after the General Election, the founders under the APUB once again began to influence the ruling party not to pass the Ordinance 2008 in the National Parliament. Private sector representative Anzus noted, "When the Awami League came to power in early 2009, we met the Law Minister and requested him not to ratify the Ordinance 2008 in the Parliament.... They accepted our proposal, and we stopped it again".

Although the APUB succeeded in persuading the Ministry of Education and the UGC to abandon the initiative to introduce a new Act during 2002–2007, a group of journalists continued to report on the illegal activities of private universities across the country. However, an analysis of interview with journalists has shown that the media did not take a stand against the growth of private universities; rather, they presented a line of argument quite similar to that of the government, because their concern was to limit the marketisation of private university. For example, one of the journalists, Rason, contended,

> From the very beginning some private universities were involved in the education business and they had failed to provide higher education in a true sense. One of my goals was to highlight this aspect of universities to make the people and the government more aware.

An analysis of both policy administrators' and journalists' statements has shown that there was no conflict of interests between the government and the media in terms of introducing a new Act to ensure the public accountability of the private universities. Instead, the analysis has shown that the government actually encouraged the media to publish reports on the unscrupulous activities of the private universities to create pressure on the APUB and sway public opinion in favour of the government's position. As journalist Plabon stated, "The then UGC chairman encouraged us to report on private universities' irregularities. He described these reports as media trial". Some of the journalists also claimed that because of the stance they took in their publications against the education business of the private universities, they were threatened by the powerful business elite who were leading members of the Association of Private Universities of Bangladesh. Plabon continued:

> The owners conveyed a meeting in Hotel Sonargaon to discuss the news published in the daily newspapers. In a meeting of the Association some of the owners made allegations against the UGC Chairman over provoking journalists to publish baseless news against private universities. They decided to file a defamation case against the UGC Chairman and some journalists – including me – to destroy their good will and reputation among the general public through publishing baseless news in the newspapers. One owner, who

> happened to be a source of mine, was in the meeting and informed me about that decision through a text message. Soon I informed the UGC Chairman about their decision and he told me not to be worried about it.

Following such political pressure from the APUB backing the private university owners, the counter-resistance from the alliance of the media and the UGC enabled the Awami League government to formulate a new Act in 2009, instead of ratifying the Ordinance 2008 promulgated by the Army-backed Caretaker Government in 2008. To finalise the draft, policy administrators of the Ministry of Education and the UGC organised several meetings with different groups, such as academics and leaders of the APUB. The Association tried to influence the UGC and the Ministry of Education in shaping the Act, but they failed to achieve their agenda. As Anzus, the Vice President of APUB at that time stated in his interview:

> We fought, but we failed to bring changes in the draft Act 2009 framed by the UGC and the Ministry of Education. The basic things that we identified in the Ordinance 2008 as obstacles that kept this sector from flourishing were retained in the draft.

Consequently, the founders under the APUB started to use their ties with the ruling party, the Awami League, to shape the Cabinet Approved Act 2010 to ensure the interest of the founders in the private universities. They met with the Parliamentary Standing Committee on Education where the Cabinet Approved Act 2010 was sent for review. The founders identified that some members of the Standing Committee on Education might be interested in the private universities. For example, Anzus explained, "We found some of them were interested in setting up private universities in future. We communicated with them and let them know they could also be affected if they let the Act be approved without bringing changes into it".

Through the influence of the founders under the APUB, the Parliamentary Standing Committee on Education organised discussion meetings with different stakeholders in the higher education sector. At these discussion meetings the APUB emphasised the need to ensure the founders had power over the universities to enable the sector to flourish. They argued that the founders were committed to the universities because they created them in the first place. For example, a private sector representative Zafor, who had been the President of the APUB, explained, "They [founders] created all facilities.... They were committed to helping this sector flourish. A paid employer [the VC] would not have the same commitment.... The board of trustees needs to play an important role in financial management". The founders brought some changes into the Cabinet Approved Act of 2010 by influencing the Parliamentary Standing Committee on Education. Zafor added, "So, instead of VC, we made a board of trustee member the chairman of the finance committee.... We were less successful in gaining consensus at the Ministerial meetings, but we became successful at the parliamentary level meetings".

As we have argued, the Parliamentary Standing Committee on Education eventually reviewed the Cabinet Approved Act 2010 and brought significant changes into it. As a policy administrator of the UGC, Nayan noted that "We included the VC as the chairman of the finance committee, but the Parliamentary Committee changed it.... They also increased the number of the board of trustees in the finance committee". Three academics who had moved from public to private universities, argued that the changes the Parliamentary Standing Committee on Education brought into the Cabinet Approved Act 2010 would help the founders not only control finances, but also to influence the entire administration of private universities. For example, Professor Kowsar, an academic who had moved from a public university into the position of the VC of a private university in 2002, said,

> Why did founders pressure the government to make a board of trustees' member to be the chairman of the finance committee? Because the notion was if you control financial matters you can control the entire decision-making processes of the universities.

Although the founders under the APUB influenced the ruling politicians in bringing changes into the different Acts to serve their own personal and community interests between 1992 and 2010, ruling politicians often intended to protect their own socio-political and personal gains from these changes. Several journalists argued that the approval of any private university often relied on political persuasion. For example, journalist Rason explained, "Although there were some conditions to be fulfilled to get the permission ... the ultimate decision came from the top level of the ruling parties.... The political affiliation of the applicants was considered as key criteria to get permission".

Politicians of the ruling party who were involved in the Parliamentary Standing Committee on Education to review the Cabinet Approved Act 2010 argued that the previous government, led by the BNP, had approved most of the private universities. They also identified that most of the founders of these universities were linked with BNP. Consequently, in reviewing Cabinet Approved Act 2010, the ruling politicians recognised Act 2010 as a political instrument to serve individuals' own political agenda. A politician admitted in an interview the veracity in the argument of several journalists. This politician, Obaidul, who was an MP of the ruling party and who had worked as a member of Parliamentary Standing Committee on Education, described why they were relaxed in the Cabinet Approved Act 2010,

> About 54 universities were established until 2010 and most of the founders of these universities inclined towards BNP and Jamaat [political parties] politics. ... I brought some changes into the Cabinet approved Act, so that new initiators would be encouraged to invest in this sector.

The changes the ruling party politicians brought into the Acts also helped the politicians to serve their own personal interests from this process. For example, as a politician of the ruling party Obaidul described what he wanted to ensure through the changes in the Cabinet Approved Act 2010 – "I've been involved in national politics since 1980s. I had already set up some academic institutions in my locality. I had a plan to establish a medical college and a private university in my locality". Consequently, this ruling politician showed interest in looking at the Cabinet Approved Private University Act 2010. When he went through the Act, he found no power for owners, so, he said he tried to "empower the owners in the private universities".

Who really controls the private university sector?

As discussed above, and in previous chapters, approval of the establishment of a private university largely depends on some sort of political affiliation with the government of the day. Around 105 universities have been approved by different governments over the last 40 years and these are not merely numbers; rather it is highly significant to the ruling party and it shapes how politics work in the private university sector. As indicated in Chapter 1, for example, during the tenures of the BNP government (1991–1996 and 2001–2006), 50 private universities were given permission to start their academic programmes. In 2003 alone, a total of 16 private universities obtained permission. Four private universities were added during the first tenure of the Awami League government (1996–2001). During the second and third tenures (2009 onwards) of the Awami League government, 51 private universities were given permission, of which 16 were given permission in 2013 alone (Kabir, 2020a).

In the early stages of its establishment, influential academics from public universities, former bureaucrats and businessmen exploited their informal networks and ties to influence the then government to formulate an Act to open private universities (Kabir & Webb, 2018). Although the new Act 2010 now shapes the running of private university, private interests and the influence of the founders are still evident according to a report (Transparency International Bangladesh, 2014). This report noted that the majority of the founders in the private universities command significant social and political influence in the society. For example, the founder(s) of the private universities include around 30% businessmen, 23% academics and 9% career politicians.

Because of the political affiliation and the commercial practices of private universities, the founder(s) or the 'board of trustees' often recommended and selected like-minded people or relatives for the positions of the VC or the Pro-VC of the university (TIB, 2014). The mere fact that until the latest enactment of 2010 most of the private universities did not have a career academic as a VC is astounding. In most of the cases, the founder(s) themselves or their relatives were appointed as VC to operate the university (University Grants Commission, 2006). Once the latest enactment came into effect in 2010, specific requirements were made for appointing a professional academic as the top official of a private university. However, until the end of 2019, out of 105 private universities, 28 had no legally appointed VC, 82 no Pro-VC and 55 no treasurer respectively (*The Bangladesh Post*, 2019). More interestingly, 20 private universities have been operating without having any VC, Pro-VC and treasurer; while these three posts have been shown as vacant in only 10 out of 105 universities (*The Bangladesh Post*, 2019).

One might ask: why do top positions in private universities remain vacant for months or even years and why are they not filled in? Two key political factors have been detrimental here. First, as the private university becomes the site of political struggle between the government and the founders, both parties need to achieve political consensus on who will be appointed in the top positions. This means appointing someone as a VC or Pro-VC or Treasurer is becoming a part of an increasingly political process. Also, the VC, Pro-VC or Treasurer needs to develop the capacity to maintain an equal relationship between the government and the founders, and this process has essentially created a crisis of institutional autonomy of the private university (Kabir & Webb, 2018).

Second, keeping these top positions as vacant is used as a strategy by the founders to retain a degree of control over the private university and use it for their own purposes. In many cases, the founders have claimed that they have failed to hire a competent executive as a VC or Pro-VC or Treasurer; however they are not able to provide evidence in support of their claims as to how many times they circulated recruitment advertisements to appoint top officials, whether anyone was interviewed and what the disqualifications of these candidates were. Rather, it is because founders or the board of trustees assigns someone from the university to play an acting role in these top positions to carry out day-to-day administrative and academic activities. This enables the founders and trustees to run the university as 'for-profit' organisations. In an interview with a daily newspaper in 2019 the then Chairman of the UGC claimed that only 20 out of 95 functioning private universities were running 'properly' and the rest had been failing to comply with the rules in various ways – for example, many of them running certificate selling businesses without taking classes. Most alarmingly, Ahmed (2019) notes that only three private universities had met the required criteria set out by the UGC.

Conclusion

This chapter explored the complexities embedded in situating private higher education in Bangladesh as either 'for-profit' nor 'not for-profit' or both by various interest groups and over a long period of time. This chapter first discussed how the idea of private higher education looks like globally and then analysed how it has developed in Bangladesh. This chapter argued that the way in which the idea of private university has developed in Bangladesh can be identified as a 'vernacular' version considering the socio-political factors of the postcolonial setting. The discussion shows that the shaping of the private university as either 'not for-profit' nor 'for-profit', both, or none, created the grey area that has been exploited by both the government and the founders to take advantage of long-term socio-political and economic and personal benefits from this sector.

More importantly, this chapter showed that rather than relying on market fundamentalism in terms of how the private university operates, both the government and founders and owners of the private university negotiated and developed mechanisms to control over the private university's activities.

Labelling the private university as neither 'not for-profit' nor 'for-profit' or both also created deep crises in its operation system. At the current time the large number of private universities that do not have top level full-time appointees to operate the university indicates the ongoing tensions between the government and these stakeholders. Having vacant full-time top positions also indicates that both the government and the founders not only want to exhibit their power in the university settings, but this also helps both parties to create pressure on current teaching and professional staff.

Despite the current Act 2010 ensuring power for the top positions e.g. chair of the Syndicate or Academic Council (Chapter 5), being tentative about the university's status as 'not for-profit' or 'for-profit' or both has created further space for these founders and board of trustees to run them for making money. The ruling party-founder nexus continues to control the operation of private universities and therefore, the question of 'academic freedom' and autonomy of private university remains questionable (Kabir & Webb, 2018).

8 The politics of neoliberal planning in public higher education

The case of Jagannath University

Introduction

This chapter looks into how the adoption of the Strategic Plan for Higher Education (SPHE) resulted in the establishment of Jagannath University (henceforth, JnU) as a *public* university modelled as a *private* university and how, by converting and upgrading a public college into a university, the government attempted to gain political benefits from this process, significantly by passing the JnU Act in 2005 right before a General Election. As discussed in previous chapters, one of the key espoused beliefs in neoliberal policies is that human welfare is best served by the detachment and withdrawal of the state from welfare policies. While such motives are based on notions of economic freedom and choice, various socio-political groups, and often loosely constructed entities, organise resistance against neoliberalist moves in higher education. These groups are concerned that under the market-oriented discourses of neoliberalism individuals are seen as a commodity of the market (Lipman, 2007) and higher education is primarily shaped by money-driven priorities such increased tuition fees and the preference for market-oriented subjects, as we see in the case of a public university in this chapter.

As further discussed, the marketisation of higher education in Bangladesh has been achieved in several ways – through commercially profitable evening courses offered by public universities (Chapter 4), the continued growth and expansion of private universities, and in the case of JnU, shifting it to a private university model while retaining the public university badge. Indeed, among the public universities, the case of Jagannath University is a curious one for several reasons and is the result of mechanisms such as the Public University Acts of 2005 and 2006 which espoused a conspicuous neoliberal policy agenda.

In this chapter, by looking into the salient characteristics of the Jagannath University Act 2005 and how this evolved over time – sometimes in response to violent student protests or change of governments – we discuss the government's *dual* role in retaining control over this public university's administration while at the same time gradually withdrawing from providing funds. Through the case study of this public university, this chapter looks at journalistic, media and scholarly discourses that have shaped various issues in the higher education sector as a whole and explores how the government has succeeded in pulling various neoliberal ideas together into the operationalisation of public higher education in Bangladesh.

To explore the dominant trends in neoliberal planning in the public higher education, this chapter identifies the (re-)establishment of the Jagannath University during the time of the formation of the SPHE as a typical, but also in some ways a unique, case. As we will see, the SPHE created the socio-political context which legitimised the formation of a new kind of general public university. We take the SPHE as a departure point to analyse the micro-politics of neoliberal planning in public higher education sector and pay attention to the relationship between local and global policy actors. By looking at related policies and government directives, the chapter also considers the various ways in which the principles of the neoliberal agenda were gradually incorporated in shaping JnU into a classic neoliberal university.

The chapter starts with a brief overview of the formation and evolution of the Strategic Plan for Higher Education (SPHE) in Bangladesh, which sits at the centre of the policy level rationalisation for the developments of JnU; it then presents a brief chronology of the history and formation of Jagannath University, focussing in particular on the political and social conditions shaping its establishment.

A new model for public higher education

The SPHE highlighted that through increased tuition fees and student loan interests, a reduction in financial aid and other cost-recovery measures, developed and developing countries worldwide had reduced public expenditure in the public higher education sector. It recommended that in line with this, Bangladesh needed to introduce similar measures in reducing government expenditure in higher education. In doing so, to avoid financial burden, the SPHE suggested a variety of financing schemes for the government including a reduction of financial pressure on the government in the medium and long term, increased tuition fees, partial offloading of costs onto students through increased tuition fees (as we will see in the case of JnU), encouraging increase investment, donation, scholarships and financial aid, offering options for student loan schemes, and fostering greater efficiency in allotting and using public resources among and within institutions (University Grants Commission, 2006, p. 60).

However, Jagannath University was not the only university that followed this pattern of gradual privatisation among public universities. Originally conceived as a 'cultural-based' university – the first of its kind in Bangladesh – the government established the Jatiya Kabi Kazi Nazrul Islam University (JKKNIU) in 2006 as a general university, with focus on liberal and performing arts education. Upon establishment four departments were in operation – Bengali Language & Literature, English Language & Literature, Music and a standalone department of Computer Science and Engineering. Quickly, however, two market-oriented departments – Accounting and Information Systems, and Economics were established in 2009.

Soon after the establishment of JKKNIU, the government established Comilla University with seven departments: Mathematics, English, Economics, Public

Administration, Accounting & Information Systems, Management and Marketing. The following year, and following the same pattern as JKKNIU, Computer Science & Engineering (CSE) was introduced, and later in 2009, Information and Communication Technology (ICT), among a few other subjects. This same pattern can be seen in the case of JnU, as we discuss below.

Other than historically, the case of JnU is somewhat similar to these two more recently established public universities. However, it is noteworthy that unlike these two universities, the much older JnU *already* had its infrastructure and resources in place, therefore the government saved substantial additional costs when it upgraded it to a public university. In fact, Section 56(2, *Chaa*) of Act JnU 2005 (p. 502) allowed and directed the appointments of the current Principal, Vice Principal and all other teachers and officers transferred to the Ministry of Education, and the acquisition of JnU as a public university meant that existing JnU teachers were dispersed into other government colleges throughout the country while their salaries were still partially funded by JnU's own income. This, of course, was a strategically important move for the government, ensuring government control over the university without however the burden of full financial responsibility it had to take up with other public universities.

As we will see in the ensuing discussion, although the Jagannath University movement succeeded in achieving its desired changes, there has been no meaningful change in the overall direction of neoliberal transformation in public higher education sector. Not the least of this is manifested through the way public universities have creatively adopted various measures to offload financial pressure onto students, as we see in the case of Jagannath University. This chapter focuses on how the Strategic Plan's World Bank inspired neoliberal agenda experimented with this university and eventually shaped it as its product, and at the same time how the university embodied the political ambition of the then government in an election year.

The case of Jagannath University

As one of the most prestigious educational establishments in Bangladesh, Jagannath University has a variegated history in terms of its status as a private or public institute and in terms of what its academic programmes have offered – degrees or non-degree qualifications such as certificates and diplomas. As one of the oldest seats of education in the country and widely known as the best-equipped private college in Dhaka as early as 1910, JnU was initially established as a private college in 1858 during the colonial period by a group of elite intellectuals and named after the father of one of the landlords in this group. While a management committee was in charge of its administration in the first 30 years of its operation, a board of trustees was appointed in 1907. As a 'first grade' college, it then started offering degrees until 1921 when the University of Dhaka (DU) was established as the first seat of higher education in the region. The establishment of DU resulted in an immediate downgrade of JnU to a non-degree offering "intermediate college", a status which it retained until after the end of the 1949, when it reopened degree classes. The college was taken over by the government for the first time in 1968. In 1975, after Independence, JnU started offering Bachelors (Honours) and Masters degrees for the first time, having been upgraded to the status of a postgraduate degree college. However, in 1982, all high school level programmes discontinued and in 1992 for the first time, evening shifts were introduced.

The political motive behind the nationalisation of JnU was the idea of using a private model for a public university to reduce government spending. When JnU was nationalised and upgraded from a university college to a fully-fledged university offering degree awarding postgraduate programmes, some of the existing staff, who were government employees, were dispersed into other government institutes. As a government institute, through the existing network of public schools and colleges, JnU not only had an already well-established infrastructure in place, but the salaries of these teachers were partly being sourced by JnU's own income, which meant the government did not have to take the full burden of additional costs. Yet it was able to reduce its contribution and to minimise its massive burden by adopting the private model. Historically this was a well-timed strategic decision for the government.

The Awami League political party, which historically proclaimed to be pro-education, came into power in 2009 and quickly modified the Act 2005 that would allow JnU to receive government funding like all other public universities. However, tuition fees at JnU were already higher than other public universities. Currently JnU has 36 departments under seven faculties. As of August 2019, there were 960 teachers and 17,134 students in Honours, Masters, M.Phil and PhD programmes.

The governance system of Jagannath University

In this section we briefly discuss the current structure of the governance system of JnU to provide an understanding of how government, through built-in mechanisms of power, retains substantial control over the current NPM-based governance system, yet in terms of financing the university, it insists on students, parents and the university itself to take the main responsibility of defraying most costs.

In appointing Vice-Chancellors, the first four public universities in Bangladesh have always had to follow the University Ordinance of 1973. The Senate, comprising of members representing a fairly wide spectrum of the broader community, would first propose a three-person Panel of prospective Vice-Chancellors (see Chapter 5 for more details). As Chancellor of all public universities, the politically appointed President would then select the Vice-Chancellor from the three-member panel. Therefore, despite the government's indirect representation through the Senate, arguably this process followed a fairly democratic approach.

In the absence of a Senate at JnU, however, the Vice-Chancellor is directly appointed by the Chancellor. Act 2005 specified in Section 9(1) (p. 477) that the head of government – the Prime Minister – to be the Chancellor of the University. This was changed in 2012 when the head of state – the President – was designated as the Chancellor (Government of Bangladesh, 2005). Notable too is that there is no position for Pro-Vice Chancellor at JnU. Instead, the Treasurer, who is also appointed directly by the government for a four-year term, performs the dual role of Treasurer and Pro-Vice Chancellor. Both these roles are only accountable to no one other than the Chancellor (the President), who can ask them to step down in case their activities are deemed to be inappropriate. An example of this was in 2008, when Professor Prof Sirajul Islam Khan, affiliated with the BNP, had to resign before completing his term, at the request of the newly appointed Chancellor, the President.

The governance system at JnU, including the formation and composition of the Syndicate, the Academic Council, various committees, structures and processes such as teacher selection, reflects the disproportionately high representation of the government, and the overwhelming power it exerts in the decision-making process in the university's day to day activities. As stated earlier, the top executives, including the Vice-Chancellor and the Treasurer are both directly appointed by the Chancellor (the President). Faculty Executive Committees are headed by Dean, and comprises among others, Chairpersons from all Departments, ten Professors appointed by the Vice-Chancellor, five academics selected by the Academic Council, and three non-faculty academics, again, selected by the Academic Council, all serving a two-year term. Committees for the selection of Registrar and Librarian similarly follow a similar pattern, as does the Planning, Development and Workers Committee, the Selection Committee and the Disciplinary Committee – all based on mechanisms that ensure the direct control of the government in making decisions.

The Syndicate is the highest decision-making body of JnU, which comprises 15 members from different categories – including the VC and Treasurer, teacher representatives and government representatives. In analysing the composition of the Syndicate members, it is overrepresented by government officials – seven out of 15 are directly nominated by either the government or government bodies; whereas only three Deans are nominated by the Syndicate and three professors by the Academic Council in the Syndicate (Government of Bangladesh, 2005).

Although the Syndicate is the highest executive body of JnU, the VC of JnU exerts power over the Syndicate. In trying to make the entire range of decision making more explicit, Sections 36(3) and (4) state that all proposals made by the Syndicate will require approval from the Vice-Chancellor, who has the right to reject any proposal without room for reconsideration. Section 10(2) makes it clear that regardless of the law, the Vice-Chancellor, appointed for four years, will remain in position only to the satisfaction of the Chancellor, is fully responsible to the Chancellor (11(2)), and that the Treasurer will step in as Acting VC in case the VC is unable to operate due to any reason (10(3)). In addition, Section 53 states in no uncertain terms that in case of any dispute of whatsoever nature, the Chancellor will have the final say in all matters related to the university (Government of Bangladesh, 2005).

The inherent power structures facilitated by such form of new public management in which the government, either through selected representatives, or the UGC of Bangladesh, exert influences that have implications in the overall direction of JnU. NPM's heavy reliance on such a bureaucratic system may enhance the deciding power of university administrators, but it often does so at the cost of compromising the voice of academics (Altbach, 2005). For example, although Departmental Curriculum Committees are comprised of all academics from the faculty, two academics from other universities are also directly appointed by the Dean of the concerned faculty, upon approval of the Vice-Chancellor. In the case of Promotion Committees for different levels – where external members are required – all selections are made by Vice-Chancellor. It could be said that most academic decisions are therefore linked to the interests of the government through officials in the UGC and the Ministry of Education.

The first Vice-Chancellor of JnU was appointed by the then BNP government in 2006. He served for two terms until he resigned in July 2008, 19 months before the expiry of his second term (*The BD News 24*, 2008). This happened quickly as the military-led Caretaker government seized power in 2008. At this point, the Treasurer took up position as acting VC and later the government appointed him to serve as VC for just one year. After the General Election when Awami League returned to power in early 2009, the Awami League government appointed a ruling-party affiliated academic from the University of Dhaka as JnU VC. This coincidence was not surprising, given the governance structure where the Vice-Chancellor is a direct political appointment through the government appointed President. In his farewell speech the first VC of JnU stated that "Vice-Chancellors of some universities have tarnished the honour of the post. We are no longer respected as VC" (*The BD News 24*, 2008).

All Vice-Chancellors had explicit political affiliations – for example, the first Vice-Chancellor was a member of the BNP-aligned teachers' 'White Panel' while he was an academic and later Treasurer at Dhaka University; the current VC of JnU, from the Awami League-aligned 'Blue Panel' was also a leader of Jubo League, the youth wing of Awami League. His continued strong affiliation with the student wing of the government's party is reflected in news media reports in which he had once claimed in an interview that students from Bangladesh Chhatra League (BCL), the student wing of the Awami League, should get first priority when it comes to jobs. It is alleged that the VC of JnU recruited a large number of leaders from ruling party affiliated student organisations and when he was asked about this recruitment he made comment in the newspaper that he is 'obliged' to give jobs to BCL leaders (Jamil, 2019).

The 2005 JnU Act which stated that the government would discontinue financing the university after 10 years of its establishment was changed in 2012. Amendment Act. Law no. 31 of 2012 amended the Jagannath University Act, 2005 Law no. 28 through the Amendment Act passed in the national Parliament on September 24, 2012 on approval from the President. Two significant changes included a) Section 26 of Law No. 28 of the 2005 Act, Law no. 28 was amended to "Contribution or funding from the Government or University Grants Commission"; and Law 28, Section 27 of 2005 amended to "Upon establishment of the university, it will rely on income from the university's own assets and university treasury as well as funds from the Government and University Grants Commission" (Government of Bangladesh, 2012). Section 27

(3) states that during the transition of upgrading to a university, JnU will bear up to 16% for infrastructural development while the remainder will be paid by the government (Section 27(4)). Upon establishment of the university, the government will incrementally decrease spending, and after five years, all costs will be borne by the university. Yet the rest of the governance system remained intact, which included the direct appointment of the Vice-Chancellor and the Treasurer by the Chancellor – the President. This meant that even though the government continued funding JnU, administrative power remained in the hands of government-appointed officials.

A new financial structure

While public universities in Bangladesh receive significant funding from the government, private universities do not. In the private sector, where tuition fees instead are the main source of income, universities adopt the cost sharing, user-pays approach. Increasingly, however, the government has encouraged public universities to adopt a 'costsharing' or even user-pays approach (Kabir, 2020a). On paper, as analysed in Chapter 5, the Strategic Plan emphasised the importance of ensuring a 'de-politicisation' of public universities partly through the abolishment of the existing system of appointing the VCs and deans of the faculties through political means. However, as discussed in Chapter 7, the SPHE still espoused the idea of a 'cost-sharing' model for financing public universities, which includes "formula-based funding linked to categories of students or measurement of performance and competitive funding that reward the best institutional bids for new programmes or projects" (UGC, 2006, p. 27).

Due to such changing funding structures, although tuition fees at public universities still remain significantly lower than their private counterparts, those established after 2006 have had higher tuition fees than older ones. In fact, in order to reduce the financial burden of the government a number of public universities, including University of Dhaka, University of Rajshahi, University of Chittagong, Islamic University, Jahangirnagar University, Professional University, the aforementioned Jatiyo Kabi Kaji Nazrul Islam University, Khulna University and Khulna University of Engineering and Technology introduced fee-driven for-profit evening courses on market-oriented subjects such as business administration, IT and finance and banking. Kabir (2010, 2011) reports that in these courses, students typically pay for the entire cost of their studies.

On paper, the Jagannath University aimed at facilitating the expansion and improvement of teaching and research in producing modern knowledge in line with global standards of higher education (Kabir, 2010). The Act allowed the university to open new departments with the permission of the UGC in response to global demands and the socio-economic condition of the country (Government of Bangladesh, 2005). Section 26 of the Act specifically mentions that the university will generate funds through five strategies: government grant, tuition and other fees levied on students, income from other legal sources, loans and profit from investing in the university's assets. The university was to meet its entire financial demands from these sources.

Crucially, the university had the right to settle tuition fees and other costs on the basis of the yearly expenses of the university. Students would have to pay their tuition fees and other costs before starting a new semester. At least 16% of the project cost of establishing the university was to be mitigated by the university's own sources, while government contribution was to be reduced year by year and to zero within 10 years of the university being set up (Government of Bangladesh, 2005).

Significantly, Sections 26 and 27 of the Jagannath University Act 2005, which describe the financial structure of the university, was changed in the 2012 Amendment where it is stated that after the completion of the JnU project, university funding will be generated by the university's own income and grants or money allocated from the government and the UGC. In terms of the internal income generation however, the strategies remained unchanged in the 2012 Amendment. In particular, Section 27(1) restated the exclusive right of the university to determine tuition and other fees, stating that these fees will be determined by the annual administrative costs of the university. The financial committee is composed of, among others, the Treasurer (who heads the committee), the Registrar, one Dean – based on seniority but selected by the VC, a Syndicate member not working in the university – selected by the Syndicate, a government selected financial planner or expert and a UGC representative – allowing the government full control in making financial decisions.

Following the 2012 Amendment into the original Act of 2005, although the government still continues to provide funding to JnU, government allocation for per student is significantly lower compared to other public universities in Dhaka (See Table 8.1).

Table 8.1 Government expenditure per student in four public universities located in Dhaka in 2017

Name of university	*Year of establishment*	*Nature of university*	*2017*	
			Student numbers	*Government expenditure per student (BD Tk.)*
University of Dhaka	1921	General	33,360	194,390.00
Bangladesh University of Engineering and Technology	1962	Specialised in Engineering and Technology	8,856	195,110.66
Sher-e-Bangla Agricultural University	2001	Specialised in Agricultural	3,436	203,000.00
Jagannath University	2005	General	17,414	49,534.79

Source: University Grants Comission of Bangladesh, 2018b

As we can see, of the four public universities in Dhaka, the capital city of Bangladesh, two – University of Dhaka and JnU – are general universities and other two – Bangladesh University of Engineering and Technology and the Sher-e-Bangla Agricultural University – are specialised in engineering and agriculture respectively. In analysing government allocation between the two general universities, it can be seen that the country's premium and largest university – University of Dhaka – houses about 33,360 students in 2017 and government's costs for per student was about BD TK. 194,390.00 [US$2,315] in the financial year of 2017–2018, which was four-times higher than that of JnU.

The 2011–2012 Jagannath University student movement and amendment of Act in 2012

Despite a prolonged movement, the declaration of cancelling Section 27(4)7 of the Jagannath University Act, 2005 had not been implemented yet. When students became aware of the specifics of the Law, they got involved in a massive student movement in 2011 through 2012 which was heavily reported in mass media. The protesters argued that by placing too much emphasis on neoliberal interests, the formulation of Strategic Plan for Higher Education had ignored the country's historical, social and cultural contexts. Arguments from different student organisations were also recognised by the authority of the JnU. As the JnU First Convocation booklet states:

> The BNP government wanted to rebuild the Jagannath College following a private university model. Five years after its establishment, bearing its own costs was in the manner of a private organisation. From this view, its Act was faulty and against the principles of a public university. In 2011, our current Prime Minister Sheikh Hasina's decisions made it fully a public university.

On 3 January 2012, the university's student political party the Progotisheel Chhatra Jote [Progressive Students' Alliance] activated a pre-planned protest march in the JnU campus, Dhaka to demand the reduction of the elevated undergraduate admission fees for the 2011–2012 session. In response, activists of Chattra League, the student wing of the then government's political party attacked the procession. The Odhikar fact-finding mission into the incident reported that this incident, which happened in the presence of the police, resulted in 15 Progotisheel Chhatra Jote students being injured with several seeking treatment in the hospital. The Odhikar reported that:

> The activists of *Chattra League* attacked the protest march three times that day. Shariful Islam Chowdhury [President, *Samajtantrik Chattra Front*, Jagannath University branch] was beaten badly by them. He was kicked in different parts of body and beaten more severely when he tried to escape. As a result, his left hand was fractured, and he was admitted to the emergency unit of Dhaka Medical College Hospital by his classmates.

The President of Samajtantrik Chattra Front, Jagannath University branch, who was also injured in the incident, claimed that in the name of "campus development", the Jagannath University authority had charged undergraduate students an additional 5,000 Tk. as part of their admission fees for the 2011–2012 session, which abused Section 27/31 of the Jagannath University Act, 2005. According to Section 27/3 of the Jagannath University Act 2005, the University would provide up to 16% from its own fund towards setting up the University while the rest would be provided by the government.

According to the Odhikar report, the Vice-Chancellor of JnU explained that as per Section 27/3 of the Jagannath University Act 2005, the government had paid 84% for campus development while the remaining 16% was indeed provided by the University's own funds. He further explained that an additional Tk. 5,000 per student was charged for the current session and that the new students had not complained about it. He was concerned that a few "irrational" students led the student movement to force the JnU administration to cancel the fee.

Eventually, although the university compromised and settled to reduce the additional fees to Tk. 2000 for that session, the neoliberal mechanism persisted until the government changed the law through a major reform in 2012 – Jagannath University Amendment Act 31 of 2012.

The year 2005 is significant, as it forwarded the BNP government's political ambition in an election year, a year which also saw the launch of the 20-year Strategic Plan for Higher Education (2006–2026). As argued in Chapter 4, public universities in Bangladesh assumed greater political power over the last decades and this empowerment helped Jagannath University to restore its *public* university character. Through the approval of the Jagannath University Act 2005, the National Parliament declared JnU as a full-fledged public university for the first time. In doing so, the government stated that its aim was to expand and improve teaching and research, produce modern knowledge at the national level and maintain a global standard of higher education. Under this model, as stated above, after an initial period of its establishment, the government would incrementally reduce its financial support, forcing public universities to explore ways of mitigating their increasing expenditures. In some cases, however, certain government grants remain, especially in promoting market-related subjects, while pushing public universities towards a private model through residual control of these universities.

In the case of JnU, on completion of the JnU project government financial contributions were to be reduced gradually for the next five years, but after this JnU would be required to be self-sufficient with no further financial contribution from the government. Governance, however, was to remain fully government controlled. The Act came into force immediately in September 2005 with the President of the People's Republic of Bangladesh as Chancellor given the power to appoint the Vice-Chancellor.

Although evening shifts at JnU were introduced as early as in 1992, they were not 'commercial' in nature, at least in the manner of the evening shift offerings of other public universities in more recent times. Rather these 'double' shifts met the demands of local overflow, especially from the political elite living in Dhaka, including government officials lucky enough to get posted in Dhaka as well as members of ruling parties. A lot of these beneficiaries were women who wanted to keep their families in Dhaka and the JnU evening shifts became an opportunity to cater for the educational needs of their children.

The establishment of new market-driven departments at JnU are a more recent phenomenon, with the establishment of the Department of Finance and Marketing (2006–2007); Accounting (later renamed to Accounting and Information Systems) (2010); Department of Computer Science and Engineering (2009–2010); Department of Microbiology and Biotechnology (later 'Biotechnology' was dropped in 2012), and the Department of Pharmacy (2010). In 2015–2016 the establishment of the Institute of Education and Research, and in 2017–18 the abolishment of Centre for English Language and the establishment of the Institute of Modern Languages (IML) are two other ways in which JnU expanded on financially lucrative programmes.

The 2012 Amendment left the governance system entirely untouched, ensuring the continuation of government control in the university's administration. Although the government pledged to continue funding, the reality is that most of the cost was offloaded onto students. While officially remaining fully 'public' in terms of financing, currently the government spends far less per student at JnU, compared to other public universities (see Table 8.1). Yet JnU students do not enjoy the full range of facilities like other public universities, such as on-campus accommodation, subsidised meals and other amenities. In fact, the university's halls of residence were usurped by political parties over the years and only recently some of it has been recovered. This leaves JnU students with greater out-of-pocket costs for their studies compared to students from other public universities, who enjoy a whole lot of resources that are not available to them.

Conclusion

In this chapter we have considered the embedded mechanisms and power structures through which, despite many changes over the years, heavy government intervention and control continue to shape the operation of Jagannath University, even as the government gradually distances itself in terms of financial responsibilities. We have seen how its unique Vice-Chancellor selection process involving direct selection from a politically appointed President, as well as the lack of a Senate that would otherwise be composed of people representing a broad spectrum of the society, make it possible for the leaders of the university to exert full government control.

It is curious that for a university that is so heavily politicised by the government through its governance system, Section 44(4) prohibits any university academic or staff to become a member of any political organisation. This is different from the other autonomous public universities where teachers enjoy open political affiliations and elections of committee are always politically organised.

9 Conclusion

> What matters now is not a question of profitability, not a question of increased productivity, not a question of production rates.... It is the very basic question of not dragging man in directions which mutilate him, of not imposing on his brain tempos that rapidly obliterate and unhinge it. The notion of catching up must not be used as a pretext to brutalize man, to tear him from himself and his inner consciousness, to break him, to kill him.
>
> (Fanon, 2004, p. 238)

As we draw the book into its conclusion, we look back at the complex set of histories, ideologies, politics and interests that have shaped the current landscape of the privatisation of higher education in Bangladesh. In doing so, as we briefly revisit each of the chapters, we will first look at the main underlying analytic – postcolonialism – and how this has framed and informed our understanding of the broad range of phenomena we have attempted to understand in this book. We will then look at emerging trends as a way to locate the trajectory of future *épistémès* (Foucault, 1977) that are likely to take shape in the next decade in the ongoing metamorphosis of the privatisation of higher education in Bangladesh. While registering our concerns, however, we remain optimistic in our anticipation of a more transparently operationalised, if an even more complex, system of the provision of private education in Bangladesh in the coming years.

Postcoloniality and neoliberalism

This book has considered the case of the privatisation of higher education in Bangladesh within the macro context of current day power dynamics – between local, national and international institutes and corporations, nation states and global markets, as well as the instruments and mechanisms of international trade and policy. To that extent, it is difficult to ignore the persistence of networks of power and hegemony distributed across these various actors, and the power hierarchies normatively espoused within such understandings. A colonial mindset and the networks of power dispersed through such established structure, vis-à-vis the agentive role of individuals as education consumers – and in this case, students seeking education in both public and private universities – allow neoliberal structures and mechanisms to be seen as ideological artefacts. While this analytic has been discussed in the Preface and in Chapter 2, here we revisit it in a reflective and retrospective manner, to inform our understanding of what lies ahead.

When analysing the education policy effects of globalisation, we based our critical premise on Beech and Artopoulos' (2016) argument that the postcolonial consideration can facilitate an understanding of the growing complexity of new geographies of power and knowledge in the policy borrowing process and, especially, in shaping current day higher education policies in significant ways. A consideration of contextual variables of the postcolonial space, for example, can provide us with new ways of looking into the politics of power. We have therefore employed Lingard's (2009) argument about the importance of the colonial political and historical processes of adopting the British Education system in Bangladesh and identified how these processes have been discursively reconfigured and repositioned in the last three decades in privatising higher education in ways specific to Bangladesh.

But as we outlined in the Preface, such a consideration goes beyond the historical implications of *imperial* colonialism. We have seen how power relations between the coloniser and the colonised can and do morph and reconfigure into new networks of influences of residual power and their effect on current day policy climate within the postcolonial space. We have seen how elite groups, much in the same way as the colonisers, create a form of cultural hegemony (Gramsci, 1971) to normalise and reinforce policy priorities representing the same structural arrangement between the historically antecedent coloniser and colonised. As an inevitable consequence of the forces of globalisation, these continuing colonial (or *neo*-colonial) discourses help produce the subordinate (the colonised) which becomes part of the power structure and *re*produces colonial habits, attitudes and values. Such myopic vision prevents us from realising how subjects become complacent to the imposition of power by the coloniser.

It is precisely in this sense that we argue that the 'postcolonial' dimension in this book is not so much contingent on the imperial colonial period which ended in 1947 but the subsequent residual colonial discourses that have seeped into contemporary ways of thinking when it comes modern day constructions of policies, laws and bodies of control. In the Preface we have also explained that the term "postcolonial" itself is inherently problematic, and that an understanding of it will vary depending on whose perspectives we are looking from. For example, for the indigenous minority community in current day Bangladesh, the country is not – yet – '*post*colonial'; it continues to be colonised by the majority Bengali Muslims. The power configurations in society that continue to marginalise them have not, after all, changed in centuries in any tangible way.

However, this acknowledgement is also a reminder that problematising the notion of 'postcolonialism' in a purely political manner lies beyond the scope of the book. We have therefore aligned more with Mignolo's (2007) notions of 'coloniality' and 'decolonial thinking' in understanding the postcolonial backdrop against which the case of this study is firmly located. In doing so, we have discussed the inherent power structures within public and private higher education institutes and government bodies – most commonly manifested through policy documents, and those created through instruments such as monetary and financial structures (Chapter 4). Historically speaking, the residue of the colonial mindset continues to persist through such top-down administrative and centralised structures of operation and control, legitimised through legal machineries such as Laws, Acts, Statues and the Constitution.

The subservient and 'obedient' mindset established in the colonial times continues to exert its influence when people understand and exercise power and authority through a two-way relationship. On one hand, vested interest groups such as the politically elite founders of universities need to keep themselves in the good book with the government; and on the other hand, in the name of privatisation the government can retain control through bodies such as the UGC and the Ministry of Education. The University Grants Commission (UGC) as the apex statutory body in the higher education sector, and the Ministry of Education play significant roles in all policy formation processes. Previously, the role of the UGC was merely to deal with the Ministry of Education on behalf the universities of Bangladesh to ensure grants for public universities and maintain the autonomous character of the universities (University Grants Commission, 2009a). However, as we have seen, the role of the UGC has gradually expanded from that of a granting agency to that of coordinating the entire higher education sector.

The UGC and the Ministry of Education thus became directly involved in the governing bodies of both private and public universities to oversee their day to day activities. In addition, on the one hand the key concern is about the state-level agencies' involvement in the universities as controlling agencies, and on the other hand, in many cases the UGC itself is influenced by the Ministry of Education and other international organisations to shape higher education policies towards a particular direction.

Such power play then is a *re*configuration of the historical power structures that where typical in the British colonial times in the Subcontinent. This is clearly reflected when we compare (such as in Chapter 3) the case of Bangladesh with the behaviours and features of privatisation in other countries, for example the community-based universities that have been established in China. In our case, the ready and often uncritical adoption of Western ideas within policy frameworks, such as we have seen not just in Bangladesh, but in Vietnam, Sri Lanka and Malaysia (see Chapter 3) are instances of the "material realities" Nandi (2016) talked about in the context of the current postcolonial scenario and in the age of a conspicuously neoliberalist globalisation of education.

Freedom and control: the duality in government positioning

As we have seen, privatisation is a quintessentially neoliberal concept, which promotes the idea of resisting or reducing state intervention. In the case of Bangladesh, however, we have seen a different *modus operandi*, given its 'postcolonial' history and the epistemic traces it has left in the current day context. This combination gives Bangladeshi neoliberalism a paradoxical dual character with the push towards privatisation on one hand, and intervention and control originating from the colonial mindset on the other hand, both accommodated in this system. We have understood that the colonial history of the nation has created the conditions for such a juxtaposition and coexistence to be possible. We have argued that the politicised nature of such control has its roots in the nation's colonial history. We have seen, how, for example, even the establishment of the University of Dhaka in 1921 was possible through only a political process.

However, the desire for state machineries to operate for their own interests also puts them in the precarious state of being nervous to stay in power as the political resistance we have seen in the last one hundred years has almost always originated from higher education institutes. Both the symbolic and enacted power which higher education institutes of Bangladesh embody have placed them somewhat antagonistically with government politics. Such a sensitive and precarious relationship pushes governments to control universities through legally and structurally established mechanisms to resist challenges through financial and leadership structures, academic appointments and teacher politics.

The symbolic power (Bourdieu, 1979) of higher education, such as that manifested in university-led historical movements, such as in the Language Movement of 1952 and, in more recent times, the overthrowing of a decade-long dictatorship regime in 1990, have been significant turning points in the nation's political history. These spontaneously formed movements have been seen as fearsome for the regimes since the colonial times, and it is in the best interests of the government to keep their control over universities through laws and regulations, strategically placed appointees in leadership positions as well as in student wings of major political parties.

Despite its shifting positions, which have often accompanied changes of regimes, the Bangladeshi government remains non-committed to taking greater financial responsibility with the private universities, while in terms of governance it continues to exert as much power and control as it can. This book has problematised the – in many ways – unique model of privatisation adopted in Bangladesh to uncover the complexities inherent in these two opposing positions by focussing on the micropolitics and microprocesses that have quite often been normatively accepted over the last three decades. In fact, as we have seen, in a developing country like Bangladesh the features of privatisation of higher education has evolved to include *both* private and public sectors to function as a machinery of ensuring and consolidating state control. While enjoying the benefits that can only come through privatisation, the government retains and ensures the legal and structural framework to intervene at will. With the financial interest as the primary concern, student as customers will pay while the state will continue to benefit and claim its share in the profit.

Future trends

This leaves us with the inevitable question – what is the likely trajectory of the privatisation of higher education in Bangladesh in the next decade? Along with the general growth of the sector, both in terms of quantity and quality, we anticipate new financial structures, a more decentralised but firmer government control, a consolidation of the role of the UGC and the Ministry of Education and other governing bodies, as well as alternative means for universities to generate funding to defray increasing costs in providing their services.

While the autonomy of universities, and within them, that of academics, will continue to feel the pressure of external controlling mechanisms, partisan politics intervening on the broader concept of the university as a provider of higher education as a public good will likely be constrained. The quintessential democratic and autonomous character of an educational institute whose primary purpose, at least theoretically, is the development of critical understanding and critical thinking, and offering a platform that allows and facilitates criticism of authoritarian attitudes of governments and regimes, will face resistance from powerful external bodies of vested interest groups. Teachers might continue to suffer from a sense of insecurity which would position them as reluctant agents in the reform process.

As long as the self-interests tied to political power of students and teachers continue to prevail, only a major cultural change can enable progress and a true decolonisation of the mind. In Fanon's (2004) view, the colonial struggle is defined and sustained by violence and therefore decolonisation can only occur through the suppression, in our case, of the symbolic violence exerted by state and institutional machineries. As Fanon points out, the process of decolonisation is never complete with formal independence (such as in 1947 and then in 1971, in the case of Bangladesh) but renouncing forms of *neo*-colonialism, such as capitalist notions of progress, as we see in the government's role in private sector higher education.

One of the ways in which private universities have distinguished themselves is by highlighting their 'apolitical' nature – in the sense of the absence of student politics. In doing so, these universities have espoused the underlying position that student politics and student political involvement are 'bad' or 'non-conducive' for quality education. We see this position frequently featured in their promotional discourses, thereby framing it as a clear marker of how they are able to offer 'better' academic environments compared to public universities. Curiously, the government has been a beneficiary of such narrative and has actively promoted the student politics-free nature of private universities. In doing so, however, they have taken ideologically oppositional roles, for example in saying that student politics is good – such as during the anti-Ershad movement of the 90s – when it clearly suited their purpose, however condemning it as 'violence' as we see in the case of the Jagannath University student movement of 2011 (Chapter 8). Such opposing positions represent the government's ideological usurpation of profit-driven stances for overtly commercial purposes.

However, education is and will always remain political (Freire, 2005). While the government has profited from student politics of public universities for its own purposes, it has also strategically and opportunistically instilled into the minds of the people the notion that politics is bad for education. On the other hand, private universities too have exploited the so-called politics-free environment to their advantage in selling their courses while taking political advantages out of the so-called apolitical feature of their campuses.

It is a given that power and politics will remain; we do not expect a completely apolitical private higher education sector in the country, which is not just futile, logistically impossible, but also undesirable. Instead, it is important to question the hidden agendas that are perpetuated and activated through a system that accommodates such ambivalent views towards student politics in higher education. When politics is framed in a pejorative way, we question – who are the interest groups here? Why such contradictory positions? Is it possible that such views are transferred onto the university classrooms? Are we producing a generation of academics and learners whose sense of criticality is slowly diminishing? Does this mean that opportunities for exercising democratic practices in the public sphere are slowly being compromised? And, is higher education, in the end, becoming not just a business tool but a political tool for the elite few rendering universities to become less autonomous?

Enduring themes: revisiting the chapters

Chapter 2 problematises the central concept of this book – neoliberalism, as a philosophical, financial, ideological, political and administrative paradigm. In tracing the epistemological origins across these multidisciplinary interfaces, the chapter discusses how neoliberalism became the principal logic through which higher education has been shaped in the last 30 years. Within that, the most conspicuous role was that of a number of international financial institutes who promoted ideas based on neoliberal agendas in the name of national development, especially in developing countries. We argue that a distinct dimension of neoliberalism has played out in Bangladesh because of the epistemic residues left by its colonial history. In trying to understand how the global has influenced the local, we draw on a postcolonial analytic showing how current day manifestations of neoliberalism can be explained through the historically contingent coloniser-colonised power relations. This chapter also identifies the key trends of global higher education across the world today.

To understand the broader geographic canvas in which these political and ideological forces are taking place, we have brought into the discussion a consideration of five countries in the region (Chapter 3), highlighting both common and unique or, in Appadurai's (2004) terms, "vernacular" ways in which the privatisation of higher education has evolved in these countries. We have seen that neoliberalist principles have manifested in both distinct and similar ways in the local contexts in the last few decades. These varieties are the consequence of a broad range of ideologies, traditions and beliefs in relation to the sociopolitical and socioeconomic, historical and cultural histories of these countries. We have seen that while the colonial histories of some of these countries left an indelible mark on their higher education systems, once they achieved independence and sovereignty, there was always a reform agenda to transition beyond their colonial legacy.

In some ways as a counter-discourse to the overt and unbridled pressures from globalisation, nationalistic ideologies have seeped into their higher education policies aiming to decolonise systems and imbibe the spirit of greater unity into the next generations. Despite this, the overall nature of changes within policies have been characterised by a careful adoption of neoliberal policy doctrines that have been sensitive to the national politics of the day. In the complex configuration of vested interests and ideologies, this seemed, after all, to be the most prudent way for governments to respond to the inevitable demands of both local and international markets.

The characteristic withdrawal of the state from funding responsibilities and transferring that to the market under neoliberalism seem to have followed a variety of patterns across contexts and time periods. Universities have resorted to adopting a range of strategies to defray additional costs when the state has reduced funding. In Chapter 4 we see how a diverse form of financial strategies adopted in universities helped mitigate the financial burden of higher education in Bangladesh. This chapter also showed how the different financial policies have integrated into political processes and exercises of power, control and governance.

In Chapter 5 we have seen how a distinct Bangladeshi form of new public management (NPM) developed to ensure public accountability of state-run universities during 1992 to 2010 when the governance system of private universities saw an increase of state involvement. In its attempt to reduce the state's responsibility and financial burden and yet still exert power in the management of private sector organisations, various models of NPM were rolled out to ensure public sector accountability without overt government involvement. By ensuring government control and legitimising it through firmly established legal structures, it exerted an illusion of freedom and autonomy in both public and private universities. We see the success of this model of governance apparent in its eventual expansion from the private management model to the public sector, such as in the case of Jagannath University (Chapter 8). Under this system, the government, through the Ministry of Education and the UGC, could oversee the operations of universities in both sectors thereby limiting the roles of academics in the governing bodies.

Chapter 6 explored the unique ways in which various internal and external quality control mechanisms have evolved in the Bangladeshi private sector higher education setting. While primarily responding to a market-driven global economy, these were also shaped by the political and economic priorities of local vested interest groups, seeing an ideological synthesis of external and independent auditing blended with state involvement through the political and financial agenda set by the UGC. In the late 2000s state evaluation was enforced through institutional performance evaluation mechanisms and benchmarks like the Accreditation Council to ensure external accountability of the private universities, giving both the UGC and the Council central roles in the auditing process.

The adoption of the first Strategic Plan for Higher Education (SPHE) in 2006 saw the consolidation of this process through the need for criterion-specific demonstration of institutional performance of quality. The SPHE transferred the responsibility of quality assurance away from faculties and the university to external performance standards for the first time. Through a combination of internal and external evaluation processes, performance of student and academic staff were to be evaluated by standards beyond the control of university administration. We have seen how these changes resulted in private universities coming under intense government and public pressure in responding to markets.

The continuing tentativeness and non-committal policy statements in the global debate about positioning higher education as either for-profit or not for-profit indicates the complex and shifting political and economic agenda of neoliberalist governments. This debate has also created crises in the operation of Bangladeshi private sector higher education, as discussed in Chapter 7. We have seen that even though governments might continue to retain control through regulations and state-sanctioned power through, for example the UGC, they are historically positioned, involving forces far beyond the global market. Founder businessmen as well as governments led by partisan politics have exploited the intermediate grey area between these two positions to take advantage of personal as well as socio-political and economic gain.

In many ways unique, the history and eventual establishment of Jagannath University (JnU) as a public university – however modelled as a private one – exemplifies how it is possible to operationally blend the two models. In Chapter 8 we discussed how the government was able to reap political benefits through the adoption of the 2005 JnU Act following on from the SPHE. We explored how heavy government control was retained in a public university, even as the government gradually withdrew from financial responsibilities by offloading costs to the university and its students. Although neoliberalist practices are characterised by the distancing and/or withdrawal of the state, thereby allowing more economic freedom and choice, resistance from groups and entities in the society at large is often an attendant scenario. In the case of JnU we have seen how student movements have protested against the market-oriented mechanisms that have turned JnU into an institute whose priorities were gradually shaped by an overtly money-driven agenda. This was achieved through its push for increased tuition fees and the prioritisation of promoting market-oriented subjects.

Looking towards the future

As we write this book, the global pandemic triggered by Covid-19 has taken its grip on world economies and no country has been spared from its effects. Governments in welfare economies are taking various initiatives to minimise the impact of this out-of-control catastrophe on their national economies. Although classical liberal theories do not typically rationalise the role of state intervention in such scenarios, the unprecedented nature of this global phenomenon has made neoliberal governments in developed economies get involved in various ways in the personal lives of people.

In Australia, for example, the government has nervously extended a range of welfare initiatives to counter the long-lasting damages to the economy the pandemic is likely to inflict. As Australia enters into a recession for the first time in nearly 30 years and GDP shrinks by 7%, social security schemes and payments like the JobKeeper and income support payments such as the JobSeeker have been offered to assist employers, self-employed individuals and those affected by the pandemic. The JobKeeper, for example, as of now, gives employers a six-month period to plan, while the JobSeeker assists them into get people back into employment. Billions of dollars from government coffers are being spent to prevent the once unthinkable scenario where national economies collapse under the pressure of an out of control pandemic.

However, in Australia and as much elsewhere, such welfare measures have not been extended to higher education. Indeed, massive job cuts, hold on research activities, freeze on capital expenditure and recruitment have characterised the enormous challenges facing universities in the developed world as we write this book. In Australia as widespread job losses have been reported across the nation's universities, it is estimated that about AU$16 billion in revenue will be lost between June 2020 and 2023 (Ferguson & Love, 2020). This is not surprising, given that government figures show that in 2018 (latest available year), overseas or international student enrolments accounted for 26% (AU$8.8 billion) of total university revenue (DESE, 2020).

Current travel restrictions in place mean that in the foreseeable future there is no guarantee that these overseas students, whose tuition fees have fuelled higher education in the last two decades, will be able to come to Australia. While such is the case in an English-speaking country whose economy relies heavily on income from international students, it is important to keep in mind that in Australia only three universities out of 42 are private. The full effects of the current pandemic are yet to be known in countries with more private universities, and those that are more reliant on domestic students, such as in Bangladesh.

Conclusion

Historically, higher education was widely perceived as an elite privilege. Although initially based on the commercial interests of the elite few, the massification of higher education that has been achieved in the last three decades because of globalisation and neoliberal demands, has now opened up opportunities to create skilled workforces through diversified, accessible and largely equitable provision of higher education. This expansion has also led to debates about whom higher education is for, and the even more philosophical question as to whether everyone *needs* higher education. The persistent conundrum around the function of higher education as public or private good (Filippakou & Williams, 2014; Pusser, 2006) continues to take shape through shifting *épistémès* (Foucault, 1977) in successive periods. On the positive side, state interventions through the government's controlling mechanisms have promoted a narrative of higher education as a public good, which has allowed greater academic and administrative freedom for universities. While the government retains control through a complex configuration of micropolitics, this position is optimistic in the way it retains its position as the strongest stakeholder through control; after all it is through the government's imposition of such check-and-balance mechanism that these universities can operate. This position allows the government to control the business element while also focussing on student interest showcasing higher education as public good.

Despite exerting increasing degrees of control, the government continues to heavily fund public universities. If the government has genuine intention in promoting higher education as public good through the system it has developed, there is room for hope and optimism in the private sector too. In this case we will see a future where instead of emphasising on the control mechanism, the government will decentralise and relax the system and allow true autonomy to flourish in both public and private sector higher education. After all, despite the general expansion of higher education globally, the rate higher education receivers in Bangladesh remains low compared to other countries in the world, considering the size of the population (University Grants Commission, 2006).

The uncontrolled mushroom growth of private universities in the 90s has now seen a more controlled environment in which new higher education providers need to comply with government regulations in establishing their campuses and offering services. This comes from not just greater government control but through in-house accountability measures that these institutes have adopted. Such cultural changes are increasingly common and pave the way to a more regulated system.

Our optimism lies more in the changes we are seeing in the private sector rather than in higher education generally. While private higher education is now more equitable, diversified and accessible, achieved through decades long changes and reforms and greater reforms, such control mechanisms have also consolidated the role of the government in its interference and control from afar through securing crucial positions and direct control through state-appointed university officials. Our hope lies in that such power sharing between the state and the founders of private universities would be useful if both parties consider the private education as public good rather than private good.

Within that, because of changing culture, we look to a future where universities can take more prudent steps in trying to find ways in which they can play with the rules of the game to their advantage, affording greater freedom within the imposed restrictions than they did in the past.

References

Aggarwal, J. (2007). *Development of education system in India*. Delhi: Shipra Publications.

Ahmed, M. (2019). Private universities defy rules. Retrieved from https://en.prothomalo.com/bangladesh/Private-universities-defy-rules.

Alavi, H. (1972). The state in post-colonial societies Pakistan and Bangladesh. *New Left Review* (74), 59.

Alam, M., Haque, M. S., & Siddique, S. F. (2007). Private higher education in Bangladesh. Retrieved from https://unesdoc.unesco.org/ark:/48223/pf0000150151.

Alcántara, A., Llomovatte, S., & Romão, J. E. (2013). Resisting neoliberal common sense in higher education: Experiences from Latin America. *International Studies in Sociology of Education* 23(2), 127–151. doi:10.1080/09620214.2013.790661.

Altbach, P. G. (1989). Twisted roots: The western impact on Asian higher education. *Higher Education*, 18(1), 9–29. doi:10.2307/3447441.

Altbach, P. G. (1999). Comparative perspectives on private higher education. In P. G. Altbach (Ed.), *Private Prometheus: Private higher education and development in the 21st century* (pp. 1–14). Westport, Connecticut, & London: Greenwood Press.

Altbach, P. G. (2004). The past and future of Asian Universities: Twenty-first century challenges. In P. G. Altbach, & T. Umakoshi (Eds.), *Asian universities: Historical perspectives and contemporary challenges* (pp. 13–32). Baltimore & London: The Johns Hopkins University Press.

Altbach, P. G. (2005). Patterns in higher education development. In P. G. Altbach, R. O. Berdahl, & P. J. Gumport (Eds.), *American higher education in the twenty-first century: Social, political, and economic challenges* (pp. 15–37). Baltimore & London: The Johns Hopkins University Press.

Altbach, P. G. (2007). Academic freedom: International realities and challenges. In *Tradition and transition: The international imperative in higher education*. Leiden, The Netherlands: Brill Sense. doi:10.1163/9789087903596_004.

Altbach, P. G., Reisberg, L., & Rumbley, L. E. (2010). *Trends in global higher education: Tracking an academic revolution*. Rotterdam, Boston, & Taipei: Sense Publishers.

Amaral, A., Meek, V. L., & Larsen, I. M. (2003). A managerial revolution. In A. Amaral, V. L. Meek, & I. M. Larsen (Eds.) *The higher education managerial revolution?* (Vol. 3, pp. 275–296). Dordrecht, Boston, & London: Kluwer Academic Publishers.

Andreotti, V. O. (2006). *A postcolonial reading of contemporary discourses related to the global dimension in education in England*. PhD Thesis. University of Nottingham, England.

Anis, A., Islam, R., & Abdullah, N. A. (2018). Challenges faced by Malaysian private HLIs in providing quality education: A thematic analysis. *Quality Assurance in Education*, 26 (3), 349–373. doi:10.1108/QAE-10-2015-0039.

Appadurai, A. (1996). *Modernity at large: Cultural dimensions of globalization* (Vol. 1). Minneapolis & London: University of Minnesota Press.

Appadurai, A. (2000). Grassroots globalization and the research imagination. *Public Culture*, 12(1), 1–19.

Asian University of Women (2020). History. Retrieved from www.auw.edu.bd/about/history/.

Ball, S. J. (2008). New philanthropy, new networks and new governance in education. *Political Studies*, 56(4), 747–765. doi:10.1111/j.1467-9248.2008.00722.x.

Bangladesh Bank (2019). *Financial system*. Retrieved from www.bb.org.bd/fnansys/banknkfi.php.

Bangladesh University of Professional (BUP) (2018). BUP newsletter (19). Accessed March 13, 2019. Retrieved from http://bup.edu.bd/assets/uploads/newsletter/154261329119%20th%20issue.pdf.

Basu, A. (1974). *The growth of education and political development in India, 1898–1920*. Delhi: Oxford University Press.

Battiste, M. (2008). The struggle and renaissance of indigenous knowledge in Eurocentric education. In M. Villegas, S. R. Neugebauer, & K. R. Venegas (Eds.), *Indigenous knowledge and education: Sites of struggle, strength, and survivance* (pp. 85–92). Cambridge, MA: Harvard Educational Review Reprint Series No. 44.

Becker, G. S. (1993). *Human capital: A theoretical and empirical analysis, with special reference to education*. Chicago & London: The University of Chicago Press.

Beech, J., & Artopoulos, A. (2016). Interpreting the circulation of educational discourse across space: Searching for new vocabularies. *Globalisation, Societies and Education*, 14 (2), 251–271. doi:10.1080/14767724.2015.1025713.

Bensimon, E., & Ordorika, I. (2006). Mexico's Estímulos: Faculty compensation based on piece-work. In R. A. Rhoads, & C. A. Torres (Eds.), *The university, state, and market: The political economy of globalization in the Americas* (pp. 250–274). Stanford & California: Stanford University Press.

Bhabha, H. (1994). *The location of culture*. London: Routledge.

Biesta, Gert J. J. (2010). *Good education in an age of measurement: Ethics, politics, democracy*. London & New York, NY: Routledge.

Bockman, J. (2013). Neoliberalism. *Contexts*, 12(3), 14–15. doi:10.1177/1536504213499873.

Boron, A. A. (2006). Reforming the reforms: Transformation and crisis in Latin American and Caribbean universities. In R. A. Rhoads, & C. A. Torres (Eds.), *The university, state, and market: The political economy of globalization in the Americas* (pp. 141–163). Stanford & California: Stanford University Press.

Bourdieu, P. (1979). Symbolic power. *Critique of anthropology*, 4(13–14), 77–85. Retrieved from https://doi.org/10.1177/0308275X7900401307.

Bourdieu, P. (2003). *Firing back: Against the tyranny of the market* (Vol. 2). London: Verso.

Braedley, S., & Luxton, M. (Eds.). (2010). *Neoliberalism and everyday life*. Montreal & Kingston: McGill-Queen's University Press.

British Council (2012). The shape of things to come: Higher education global trends and emerging opportunities to 2020. Retrieved from www.britishcouncil.org/sites/default/files/the_shape_of_things_to_come_-_higher_education_global_trends_and_emerging_opportunities_to_2020.pdf.

Buchanan, J. M. (1993). Public choice after socialism. *Public Choice*, 77(1), 67–74.

Byron, R. K., & Rahman, M, F. (2020). State enterprises hand government TK 16, 746 cr of their surplus funds. *The Daily Star*. Retrieved from www.thedailystar.net/business/news/state-enterprises-hand-govt-tk-16746cr-their-surplus-funds-1959413.

Cai, Y. (2020). China's 2020 target: Reshaping global mobility flows. Retrieved from www.eaie.org/blog/china-2020-target-reshaping-global-mobility-flows.html.

Carney, S. (2009). Negotiating policy in an age of globalization: Exploring educational "policyscapes" in Denmark, Nepal, and China. *Comparative Education Review*, 53(1), 63–88.

Chowdhury, R., & Le Ha, P. (2014). *Desiring TESOL and International Education: Market Abuse and Exploitation*. Bristol: Multilingual Matters.

Chowdhury, R., & Kabir, A. H. (2014). Language wars: English education policy and practice in Bangladesh. *Multilingual Education*, 4(1), 16. doi:10.1186/s13616-014-0021-2.

Connell, R. (2010). Understanding neoliberalism. In B. Susan, & L. Meg (Eds.), *Neoliberalism and everyday life* (pp. 22–36). Montreal & Kingston: McGill-Queen's University Press.

Connell, R. (2013). The neoliberal cascade and education: An essay on the market agenda and its consequences. *Critical Studies in Education*, 54(2), 99–112. doi:10.1080/17508487.2013.776990.

Dasen, P., & Akkari, A. (2009). Ethnocentrism in education and how to overcome it. In P. Dasen, & A. Akkari (Eds.), *Educational theories and practices from the majority world* (pp. 7–22). New Delhi: Sage Publications.

de Boer, H., Enders, J., & Schimank, U. (2007). On the way towards new public management? The governance of university systems in England, the Netherlands, Austria, and Germany. In D. Jansen (Ed.), *New forms of governance in research organizations* (pp. 137–152). Rotterdam: Springer.

Delgado-Ramos, G. C., & Saxe-Fernández, J. (2009). World Bank and the Privatization of Public Education. In D. Hill, & E. Rosskam (Eds.), *The developing world and state education: Neoliberal depredation and egalitarian alternatives* (pp. 34–52). New York: Routledge.

Deem, R. (2001). Globalisation, new managerialism, academic capitalism and entrepreneurialism in Universities: Is the local dimension still important? *Comparative Education*, 37(1), 7–20. doi:10.1080/03050060020020408.

Department of Education and Training (2018). Vietnam higher education: Policy and system update. Retrieved from https://internationaleducation.gov.au/International-network/vietnam/publications/Documents/Vietnam%20High%20Education%20Policy%20and%20Systems%20Update.pdf.

Department of Education, Employment and Workplace Relations (DEEWR) (2019). International students' data: Monthly summary. Retrieved from https://internationaleducation.gov.au/research/International-Student-Data/Documents/MONTHLY%20SUMMARIES/2019/Aug%202019%20MonthlyInfographic.pdf.

Department of Education, Skills and Employment (2020a). Approval processes for Sino-foreign joint institutions and joint programs. Retrieved from https://internationaleducation.gov.au/News/Latest-News/Pages/CHINA%E2%80%93Approvals-processes-for-Sino-Foreign-Joint-institutions-and-Joint-programs.aspx.

Department of Education, Skills and Employment (2020b). Approval processes for Sino-foreign joint institutions and joint programs. Chinese universities establishing programs and campuses in foreign countries. Retrieved from https://internationaleducation.gov.au/News/Latest-News/Pages/Chinese-universities-establishing.aspx.

Deraniyagala, S. (2005). Neoliberalism in international trade: Sound economics or a question of faith? In A. Saad-Filho, & D. Johnston (Eds.), *Neoliberalism: A critical reader* (pp. 99–105). London: Pluto Press.

Devault, M. (2006). Introduction: What is institutional ethnography? *Social Problems*, 53 (3), 294–298. doi:10.1525/sp.2006.53.3.294.

Dirlik, A. (1994). The postcolonial aura: Third world criticism in the age of global capitalism. *Critical Inquiry*, 20(2), 328–356.

Education Malaysia (2020). Malaysia higher education: In brief. Retrieved from https://educationmalaysia.gov.my/malaysia-higher-education-in-brief/.

Edwards, K. J. R. (1997). The United Kingdom. In M. F. Green (Ed.), *Transforming higher education: Views from leaders around the world* (pp. 133–149). Arizona: American Council on Education.

El-Khawas, E., DePietro-Jurand, R., & Holm-Nielsen, L. (1998). *Quality assurance in higher education: Recent progress; challenges ahead*. Paper presented at the UNESCO World Conference on Higher Education, Paris.

England, K., & Ward, K. (2011). Introduction: Reading neoliberalism. In K. England, & K. Ward (Eds.), *Neoliberalization: States, networks, peoples* (pp. 1–22). Oxford: Blackwell Publishing.

Esaki-Smith, A. (2020). International student recruitment in a post-China world. *The University World News*. Retrieved from www.universityworldnews.com/post.php?story=20200422154708599.

Fanon, F. (2004). *The wretched of the earth* (Trans. R. Philcox). New York: Grove Press.

Fawcett, P., Manwaring, R., & Marsh, D. (2011). Network governance and the 2020 Summit, *Australian Journal of Political Science*, 46(4), 651–667. doi:10.1080/10361146.2011.623667.

Ferguson, H., & Love, S. (2020). The impact of COVID-19 on Australian higher education and overseas students—what do the numbers say?Parliament of Australia. Retrieved from www.aph.gov.au/About_Parliament/Parliamentary_Departments/Parliamentary_Library/FlagPost/2020/August/Universities_and_COVID.

Filippakou, O., & Williams, G. (2014). *Higher education as a public good: A critical perspective*. New York, NY: Peter Lang Publisher.

Foucault, M. (1977). *Discipline and punish: The birth of the prison* (Trans. A. Sheridan). London: Penguin Books.

Foucault, M. (1982). The subject and power. *Critical Inquiry*, 8(4), 777–795.

Freire, P. (2005). *Pedagogy of the oppressed*. New York, NY: Continuum International Publishing Group.

Friedman, M. (1962). *Capitalism and freedom*. Chicago: University of Chicago Press.

Gamage, D. T. (1983). The struggle for control of higher education in a developing economy: Sri Lanka. *Comparative Education*, 19(3), 325–339.

Giddens, A. (1998). *The third way*. Cambridge: Polity Press.

Giddens, A. (1999). *The third way: The renewal of social democracy*. Malden: Polity Press.

Giroux, H. A. (2002). Neoliberalism, corporate culture, and the promise of higher education: The university as a democratic public sphere. *Harvard Educational Review*, 72(4), 425–464.

Giroux, H. A. (2005). The terror of neoliberalism: Rethinking the significance of cultural politics. *College Literature*, 32(1), 1–19.

Government of Bangladesh (1973a). *The Dhaka University Order 1973*. Dhaka: Ministry of Law, Justice and Parliamentary Affairs.

Government of Bangladesh (1973b). *The Rajshahi University Act 1973*. Dhaka: Ministry of Law, Justice and Parliamentary Affairs.

Government of Bangladesh (1973c). *The Chittagong University Act*. Dhaka: Ministry of Law, Justice and Parliamentary Affairs.

Government of Bangladesh (1973d). *The Jahangirnagar University Order 1973*. Dhaka: Ministry of Law, Justice and Parliamentary Affairs.

Government of Bangladesh (1973e). *The Engineering and Technology University Ordinance, 1961*. Dhaka: Ministry of Law, Justice and Parliamentary Affairs.

Government of Bangladesh (1973f). *The Agricultural University Ordinance 1961*. Dhaka: Ministry of Law, Justice and Parliamentary Affairs.

Government of Bangladesh (1973g). *The University Grants Commission of Bangladesh Order, 1973*. Dhaka: Ministry of Law, Justice and Parliamentary Affairs. Retrieved from www.ugc.gov.bd/sites/default/files/files/ugc.portal.gov.bd/legislative_information/a028ffe7_bd7c_427f_b99e_4d5ff44e2aac/GAZATTE-1%20(1).compressed.pdf.

Government of Bangladesh (1987). *Shahjalal Science and Technology University Act, 1987*. Dhaka: Ministry of Law, Justice and Parliamentary Affairs.

Government of Bangladesh (1990). *Khulna University Act, 1990*. Dhaka: Ministry of Law, Justice and Parliamentary Affairs.

Government of Bangladesh (1992). *Private University Act 1992* (pp. 7581–7586). Dhaka: Ministry of Law, Justice and Parliamentary Affairs.

Government of Bangladesh (1998). *Private University Act 1998* (pp. 5607–5610). Dhaka: Ministry of Law, Justice and Parliamentary Affairs

Government of Bangladesh (2005). *Jagannath University Act 2005*. Dhaka: Ministry of Law, Justice and Parliamentary Affairs.

Government of Bangladesh (2006a). *Comilla University Act 2006*. Dhaka: Ministry of Law, Justice and Parliamentary Affairs.

Government of Bangladesh (2006b). *Jatiyo Kobi Kaji Najrul Islam University Act 2006*. Dhaka: Ministry of Law, Justice and Parliamentary Affairs.

Government of Bangladesh (2008). *Private University Ordinance 2008* (pp. 17569–17588). Dhaka: Ministry of Law, Justice and Parliamentary Affairs.

Government of Bangladesh (2010a). *Cabinet Approved Private University Act 2010* (pp. 1–14). Dhaka: Ministry of Law, Justice and Parliamentary Affairs.

Government of Bangladesh (2010b). *Private University Act 2010* (pp. 7423–7445). Dhaka: Ministry of Law, Justice and Parliamentary Affairs.

Government of Bangladesh (2017). *Bangladesh Accreditation Council Act 2017*. Dhaka: Ministry of Law, Justice and Parliamentary Affairs.

Government of Pakistan (1958). *Report of the commission on national education*. Karachi: Ministry of Education.

Grameen Bank (2019). Monthly report 2019–01 issue. Retrieved from www.grameen.com/monthly-report-2019-01-issue-469-in-bdt/.

Grameen Phone (2018). Grameen Phone, BUP sign MoU to drive collaborative learning, loT adoption and digital learning. Retrieved from https://grameenphone.com/about/media-center/press-release/grameenphone-bup-sign-mou-drive-collaborative-learning-iot-adoption.

Gramsci, A. (1971). *Selections from the prison notebooks* (Ed. and Trans. Q. Hoare, & G. Nowell Smith). New York: International Publishers.

Gürüz, K. (2008). *Higher education and international student mobility in the global knowledge economy*. Albany: State University of New York Press.

Hall, P. A., & Soskice, D. (Eds.). (2001). *Varieties of capitalism: The institutional foundations of comparative advantage*. Oxford: Oxford University Press.

Hall, S. (1996). When was the post-colonial? Thinking at the limit. In L. Chambers, & L. Curti (Eds.) *The postcolonial question*. London: Routledge.

Harman, G., Hayden, M., & Nghi, P. T. (2010). Higher education in Vietnam: Reform, challenges and priorities. In G. Harman et al. (Eds.), *Reforming higher education in Vietnam: Reform, challenges and priorities* (pp. 1–15). doi:10.1007/978-90-481-3694-0_1.

Harvey, D. (2005). *A brief history of neoliberalism*. Oxford: Oxford University Press.

Harvey, D. (2006). *Spaces of global capitalism*. New York: Verso.

Harvey, D. (2007). Neoliberalism as creative destruction. *The Annals of the American Academy of Political and Social Science*, 610(1), 21–44. doi:0.1177/0002716206296780.

Hayden, M., & Khanh, D. V. (2010). Private higher education in Vietnam. In G. Harman et al. (Eds.), *Reforming higher education in Vietnam: Reform, challenges and priorities* (pp. 215–226). doi:10.1007/978-90-481-3694-0_15.

Hayek, F. A. (1944). *The road to serfdom*. London & Henley: Routledge & Kegan Paul.

Hegde, G. A. (2016). Privatization in higher education in India: A reflection of issues. In M. Shah and C. S. Nair *A global perspective on private higher education* (pp. 157–168). Amsterdam, Boston and Cambridge: Chandos Publishing.

Hoang, L. (2019). Twin privatization in Vietnam higher education: The emergence of private higher education and partial privatization of public universities. *Higher Education Policy*, 32(3), 359–380.

Holford, J., & McKenzie, L. (2013). *Conceptual model and questionnaire: LLight'in'Europe: Lifelong learning, innovation, growth, and human capital tracks in Europe*. Unpublished Working Paper. University of Nottingham School of Education. Nottingham.

Hood, C. (1991). A public management for all seasons? *Public Administration*, 69(1), 3–19.

Hood, C. (1995). The "New Public Management" in the 1980s: Variations on a theme. *Accounting, Organizations and Society*, 20(2), 93–109.

Hou, A. Y. C., Hill, C., Chen, K. H. J., & Tsai, S. (2018). A comparative study of international branch campuses in Malaysia, Singapore, China, and South Korea: Regulation, governance, and quality assurance. *Asia Pacific Education Review*, 19(4), 543–555.

ICEF (2016). China now the leading host for international branch campuses. Retrieved from https://monitor.icef.com/2016/11/china-now-leading-host-international-branch-campuses/#:~:text=The%20number%20of%20international%20branch,an%20estimated%20180%2C000%20students%20worldwide.

Indian Legislative Council (1920). *The Dacca University Act, 1920* (XVIII of 1920). Retrieved from https://archive.org/details/in.ernet.dli.2015.85951/page/n3/mode/2up.

Integrated Development Foundation (IDF) (2019). Halda river research laboratory. Retrieved from http://idfbd.org/halda-river-research-laboratory/.

International Education Consultancy (2020). States/cities sending students abroad. Retrieved from www.iecabroad.com/blog/the-2020-trend-for-indian-students-studying-abroad/.

Islamic University of Technology (2020). About IUT. Retrieved from www.iutoic-dhaka.edu/about.

Jamil. S. S. (2019). Is there any difference between vice-chancellors and party leaders? *The New Age*. Retrieved from www.newagebd.net/article/85251/is-there-any-difference-between-vice-chancellors-and-party-leaders.

Jamshidi, L., Arasteh, H., NavehEbrahim, A., Zeinabadi, H., & Rasmussen, P. D. (2012). Developmental patterns of privatization in higher education: a comparative study. *Higher Education*, 64(6), 789–803.

Jayawardena, D. (2017). The 'MacBurger', non-state universities and the changing landscape of higher education in Sri Lanka. *Journal for Critical Education Policy Studies*, 15(3), 213–240.

Johnstone, D. B. (1997). The United States. In M. F. Green (Ed.), *Transforming higher education: Views from leaders around the world* (pp. 223–237). Arizona: American Council on Education.

Johnstone, D. B., & Marcucci, P. N. (2010). *Financing higher education worldwide: Who pays? Who should pay?*Baltimore: The John Hopkins University Press.

Kabir, A. H. (2010). The neoliberal policy in higher education sector in Bangladesh: Autonomy of public universities and the role of the state. *Policy Futures in Education*, 8 (6), 620–632. Retrieved from http://dx.doi.org.ezproxy.lib.monash.edu.au/10.2304/pfie.2010.8.6.619.

Kabir, A. H. (2011). *The politics of neoliberalism in the higher education sector in Bangladesh.* University of Canterbury, College of Education. Retrieved from http://hdl.handle.net/10092/5752.

Kabir, A. H. (2013a). Neoliberalism, international financial institutions and a vision for higher education in Bangladesh. In J. Greenwood, J. Everatt, A. H. Kabir, & S. Alam (Eds.), *Research and educational change in Bangladesh.* Dhaka: University of Dhaka.

Kabir, A. H. (2013b). Neoliberalism, policy reforms and higher education in Bangladesh. *Policy Futures in Education*, 11(2), 154–166. Retrieved from http://dx.doi.org/10.2304/pfie.2013.11.2.154.

Kabir, A. H. (2016). *The micro-politics of neoliberal policy formulation in the higher education sector in Bangladesh.* A PhD thesis, Faculty of Education, Monash University, Australia. Retrieved from http://arrow.monash.edu/vital/access/manager/Repository/monash:173095?query=ariful+haq+kabir.

Kabir, A. H. (2020a), Higher education: Trapped in the neoliberal reform. In M. T. Khan, & M. S. Rahman (Eds.), *Neoliberal development and the Bangladesh state* (pp. 127–152). Dhaka: University Press Limited.

Kabir, A. H. (2020b). 'Network governance' and the formation of the strategic plan in the higher education sector in Bangladesh, *Journal of Education Policy.* doi:10.1080/02680939.2020.1717637.

Kabir, A. H., & Chowdhury, R. (2017). 'Donor logic', NGOs, ruling elite and the decolonisation of education in Bangladesh. In J. Murphy, & N. Jammulamadaka (Eds.), *Governance, resistance and the post-colonial state: Management and state building social movements* (pp. 162–181). London & New York: Routledge.

Kabir, A. H., & Greenwood, J. (2017). Neoliberalism, violence and student resistance in the higher education sector in Bangladesh. *Society and Culture in South Asia*, 3(1), pp. 68–91. doi:10.1177/2393861716674106.

Kabir, A. H., & Webb, S. (2018), Governance of private universities in Bangladesh: The myth of institutional autonomy. In R. Chowdhury, M. Sarkar, F. Mojumder, & M. M. Roshid (Eds.), *Engaging in educational research: Revisiting policy and practice in Bangladesh* (pp. 279–297). Singapore: Springer.

Kamat, S. G. (2011a). Neoliberal globalization and higher education policy in India. In R. King, S. Marginson, & R. Naidoo (Eds.), *Handbook on globalization and higher education* (pp. 273–285). Cheltenham: Edward Elgar Publishing Limited.

Kamat, S. G. (2011b). Neoliberalism, urbanism and the education economy: producing Hyderabad as a 'global city', *Discourse: Studies in the Cultural Politics of Education*, 32 (2), 187–202. doi:10.1080/01596306.2011.565639.

Khandekar, A. (2013). Education abroad: Engineering, privatization, and the new middle class in neoliberalizing India. *Engineering Studies*, 5(3), 179–198.

Klijn. E. H., & Koppenjan, J. F. M. (2000). Public management and policy networks, *Public Management: An International Journal of Research and Theory*, 2(2), 135–158.

Kochanek, S. A. (2000). Governance, patronage politics, and democratic transition in Bangladesh. *Asian Survey*, 40(3), 530–550.

Kohl, B., & Farthing, L. C. (2006). *Impasse in Bolivia: Neoliberal hegemony and popular resistance*. London & New York: Zed Books.

Kumar, R. (2012). The charge of neoliberal brigade and higher education in India. *Journal for Critical Education Policy Studies*, 10(2), 258–281.

Lang, A. (2011). *World trade law after neoliberalism: Reimagining the global economic order*. Oxford: Oxford University Press.

Lee, M., Wan, C. D., & Sirat, M. (2017). Hybrid universities in Malaysia. *Studies in Higher Education*, 42(10), 1870–1886.

Leggett, W. (2014). The politics of behaviour change: Nudge, neoliberalism and the state. *Policy & Politics*, 42(1), 3–19.

Levidow, L. (2007). Marketizing higher education: Neoliberal strategies and counter-strategies. In E. W. Ross, & R. Gibson (Eds.), *Neoliberalism and education reform* (pp. 237–255). New Jersey: Hampton Press Inc.

Levine, A. (2001). Privatization in higher education. In H. M. Levine (Ed.), *Privatizing education: Can the market place deliver choice efficiency, equity and social cohesion* (pp. 133–148). Colorado, CA: Westview Press.

Lingard, B. (2009). Researching education policy in a globalized world: Theoretical and methodological considerations. *Yearbook of the National Society for the Study of Education*, 108(2), 226–246.

Lingard, B., & Rawolle, S. (2004). Mediatizing educational policy: The journalistic field, science policy, and cross-field effects. *Journal of Education Policy*, 19(3), 361–380. doi:10.1080/0268093042000207665.

Lingard, B., & Rawolle, S. (2011). New scalar politics: Implications for education policy. *Comparative Education*, 47(4), 489–502. doi:10.1080/03050068.2011.555941.

Lingard, B., & Sellar, S. (2013). Globalization, edu-business and network governance: The policy sociology of Stephen J. Ball and rethinking education policy analysis. *London Review of Education*, 11(3), 265–280. doi:10.1080/14748460.2013.840986.

Lingard, B., Rawolle, S., & Taylor, S. (2005). Globalizing policy sociology in education: Working with Bourdieu. *Journal of Education Policy*, 20(6), 759–777. doi:10.1080/02680930500238945.

Linh, T. (2019). Outstanding figures of Vietnamese Higher Education. Retrieved from https://giaoduc.net.vn/giao-duc-24h/nhung-con-so-noi-bat-cua-giao-duc-dai-hoc-viet-nam-post201566.gd.

Lipman, P. (2007). "No Child Left Behind": Globalization, privatization and the politics of inequality. In E. W. Ross, & R. Gibson (Eds.), *Neoliberalism and education reform* (pp. 35–58). New Jersey: Hampton Press Inc.

Loomba, A. (2007). *Colonialism/postcolonialism*. Abingdon, Oxon: Routledge.

Lorenz, C. (2012). If you're so smart, why are you under surveillance? Universities, neoliberalism, and new public management. *Critical Inquiry*, 38(3), 599–629.

Lunga, V. B. (2008). Postcolonial theory: A language for a critique of globalization? *Perspectives on Global Development and Technology*, 7(3), 191–199. doi:10.1163/156914908X371349.

Majumdar, C. K., Ghose, P., Chatterjee, E., Bandyopadhyay, S., & Chatterjee, S. (Eds.) (1994). *SN Bose: The man and his work: Life, lectures and addresses, miscellaneous pieces* (Vol. 2). Calcutta: SN Bose National Centre for Basic Sciences.

Marginson, S. (1997). How free is academic freedom? *Higher Education Research & Development*, 16(3), 359–369. doi:10.1080/0729436970160309.

Marginson, S. (2006). Dynamics of national and global competition in higher education. *Higher Education*, 52(1), 1–39. doi:10.1007/sl0734-004-7649-x.

Marginson, S. (2011). Higher education and public good. *Higher Education Quarterly*, 65 (4), 411–433. doi:10.1111/j.1468-2273.2011.00496.x.

Marginson, S., & Considine, M. (2000). *The enterprise university: Power, governance and reinvention in Australia.* Melbourne: Cambridge University Press.

Mathur, N. (2018). The low politics of higher education: Saffron branded neoliberalism and the assault on Indian universities. *Critical Policy Studies*, 12(1), 121–125.

McLeod, J. (2000). *Beginning postcolonialism.* Manchester & New York: Manchester University Press.

McCarthy, J., & Prudham, S. (2004). Neoliberal nature and the nature of neoliberalism. *Geoforum*, 35(3), 275–283. doi:10.1016/j.geoforum.2003.07.003.

Mignolo, W. (2002). The geopolitics of knowledge and the colonial difference. *The South Atlantic Quarterly*, 101(1), 57–96.

Mignolo, W. D. (2007). Coloniality of power and de-colonial thinking. *Cultural Studies*, 21(2,3), 155–167. doi:10.1080/09502380601162498.

Mignolo, W. D. (2012). *Local histories/global Designs: Coloniality, subaltern knowledges, and border thinking.* Princeton, NJ: Princeton University Press.

Milana, M. (2015). Debating global polity, policy crossing, and adult education. *Comparative Education Review*, 59(3), 498–522.

Ministry of Education (1974). *Bangladesh Shikkha Commission Report* [Bangladesh Education Commission Report]. Dhaka: Ministry of Education.

Ministry of Education (2014). *Rules and regulations for foreign universities* (pp. 13967–13974). Dhaka: Ministry of Education.

Ministry of Education of the People's Republic of China (1993). *Provisional provisions on setting up private higher education institutions.* Retrieved from http://old.moe.gov.cn/publicfiles/business/htmlfiles/moe/moe_621/201001/xxgk_81912.html.

Ministry of Education of the People's Republic of China (2004). *Law of the People's Republic of China on the promotion of private education.* Retrieved from http://old.moe.gov.cn/publicfiles/business/htmlfiles/moe/moe_183/200403/2306.html.

Ministry of Education of the People's Republic of China (2020). *2019 Statistical Bulletin of Education Development.* Retrieved from www.moe.gov.cn/jyb_sjzl/sjzl_fztjgb/202005/t20200520_456751.html.

Mishra, R., & Sirguroh, M. (2014). Higher education in India, transition from socialism to capitalism. *European Scientific Journal*, 569–573.

Mollis, M. (2006). Latin American identities in transition: A diagnosis of Argentine and Brazilian universities. In R. A. Rhoads, & C. A. Torres (Eds.), *The university, state, and market: The political economy of globalization in the Americas* (pp. 60–100). Stanford & California: Stanford University Press.

Mok, K. H. (2003). Globalisation and higher education restructuring in Hong Kong, Taiwan and mainland China. *Higher Education Research & Development*, 22(2), 117–129. doi:10.1080/07294360304111.

Mok, K. H. (2005). Riding over socialism and global capitalism: Changing education governance and social policy paradigms in post-Mao China. *Comparative Education*, 41 (2), 217–242. doi:10.1080/03050060500036956.

Mok, K. H. (2008). Varieties of regulatory regimes in Asia: The liberalization of the higher education market and changing governance in Hong Kong, Singapore and Malaysia. *The Pacific Review*, 21(2), 147–170. doi:10.1080/09512740801990220.

Mok, K. H. (2009). The growing importance of the privateness in education: Challenges for higher education governance in China. *Compare: A Journal of Comparative and International Education*, 39(1), 35–49. doi:10.1080/03057920801951851.

Mok, K. H. (2010). When state centralism meets neo-liberalism: managing university governance change in Singapore and Malaysia. *Higher Education*, 60(4), 419–440.

Morley, L. (2003). *Quality and power in higher education.* Berkshire: Society for Research into Higher Education & Open University Press.

Murphy, M. P. A. (2020). COVID-19 and emergency eLearning: Consequences of the securitization of higher education for post-pandemic pedagogy. *Contemporary Security Policy*, 41(3), 492–505. doi:10.1080/13523260.2020.1761749.

Mortuza, S. (2020). A timely decision on higher education. Retrieved from www.thedailystar.net/opinion/education/news/timely-decision-higher-education-1868128.

Munck, R. (2005). Neoliberalism and politics, and the politics of neoliberalism. In A. Saad-Filho, & D. Johnson (Eds.), *Neoliberalism: A critical reader* (pp. 60–69). London: Pluto Press.

Naidoo, R. (2011). Rethinking development: Higher education and the new imperialism. In R. King, S. Marginson, & R. Naidoo (Eds.), *Handbook on globalization and higher education* (pp. 40–58). Cheltenham: Edward Elgar.

Naidoo, R., & Williams, J. (2015). The neoliberal regime in English higher education: Charters, consumers and the erosion of the public good. *Critical Studies in Education*, 56(2), 208–223. doi:10.1080/17508487.2014.939098.

Naidoo, R., Shankar, A., & Veer, E. (2011). The consumerist turn in higher education: Policy aspirations and outcomes. *Journal of Marketing Management*, 27(11–12), 1142–1162. doi:10.1080/0267257X.2011.609135.

Nandi, S. (2016). Neoliberal globalization and the future of postcolonial studies. *Journal of School of Languages, Literature and Culture Studies*, 19. Retrieved from: www.academia.edu/25183070.

Nghi, P. T., & London, J. D. (2010). The higher education reformation agenda: The vision for 2020. In G. Harman et al. (Eds.), *Reforming higher education in Vietnam: Challenges and priorities* (pp. 51–64). doi:10.1007/978-90-481-3694-0_4.

NSBM Green University Town (2020). Story of NSBM. Retrieved from www.nsbm.ac.lk/story-of-nsbm/.

Nuruzzaman, M. (2004). Neoliberal economic reforms, the rich and the poor in Bangladesh. *Journal of Contemporary Asia*, 34(1), 33–54. doi:10.1080/00472330480000291.

Nussbaum, M. C. (2010). *Not for profit: Why democracy needs the humanities.* Princeton & Oxford: Princeton University Press.

Olssen, M. (2002). The restructuring of tertiary education in New Zealand: Governmentality, neo-liberalism, democracy. *McGill Journal of Education/Revue des sciences de l'éducation de McGill*, 37(001).

Olssen, M., & Peters, M. A. (2005). Neoliberalism, higher education and the knowledge economy: From the free market to knowledge capitalism. *Journal of Education Policy*, 20 (3), 313–345. doi:10.1080/02680930500108718.

One Bank (2019). Student loans. Retrieved from www.onebank.com.bd/home/retail-banking/loan-products/student-loan/.

Ong, A. (2006). *Neoliberalism as exception: Mutations in citizenship and sovereignty.* Durham, NC: Duke University Press.

Peck, J. (2008). Remaking laissez-faire. *Progress in Human Geography*, 32(1), 3–43. doi:10.1177/0309132507084816.

Peters, M. A. (2001). *Poststructuralism, Marxism, and neoliberalism: Between theory and politics.* Lanham, Boulder, New York & London: Rowman & Littlefield Publishers.

Prechel, H., & Harms, J. B. (2007). Politics and neoliberalism. In H. Prechel (Ed.), *Politics and neoliberalism: Structure, process and outcome* (pp. 3–17). Oxford: Elsevier.

Pusser, B. (2006). Reconsidering higher education and the public good: The role of public spheres. In W. G. Tierney (Ed.), *Governance and the public good* (pp. 11–28). Albany, NY: State University of New York Press.

Quadir, F. (2000). The political economy of pro-market reforms in Bangladesh: Regime consolidation through economic liberalization? *Contemporary South Asia*, 9(2), 197–212. doi:10.1080/713658731.

Quddus, M., & Rashid, S. (2000). The worldwide movement in private universities: Revolutionary growth in post-secondary higher education. *American Journal of Economics and Sociology*, 59(3), 487–516.

Quijano, A. (2000). Coloniality of power, Eurocentrism and Latin America. *Nepantla*, 1 (3), 533–580.

Rahman, M. (2009). *Improving the relevance of humanities higher education in Bangladesh*. Unpublished PhD thesis, Monash University, Melbourne.

Raina, S. (2019). Academic deprofessionalization: A case study of the effects of privatization on academic profession in private Indian Universities. *International Journal of Sociology*, 49(5–6), 370–388.

Ranson, S. (2003). Public accountability in the age of neo-liberal governance. *Journal of Education Policy*, 18(5), 459–480. doi:10.1080/0268093032000124848.

Rizvi, F. (2014). *Encountering education in the global: The selected works of Fazal Rizvi*. New York: Routledge.

Rizvi, F., & Lingard, B. (2010). *Globalizing education policy*. New York: Routledge.

Roberts, P. (2007). Neoliberalism, performativity and research. *International Review of Education*, 53(4), 349–365. doi:10.1007/s11159-11007-9049-9049.

Roberts, P. (2009). A new patriotism? Neoliberalism, citizenship and tertiary education in New Zealand. *Educational Philosophy and Theory*, 41(4), 410–423. doi:10.1111/j.1469-5812.2008.00437.x.

Roberts, P., & Peters, M. A. (2008). *Neoliberalism, higher education and research*. Rotterdam: Sense Publishers.

Ross, E. W., & Gibson, R. J. (2007). Introduction. In E. W. Ross, & R. Gibson (Eds.), *Neoliberalism and education reform* (pp. 1–14). New Jersey: Hampton Press Inc.

Rosser, A. (2016). Neo-liberalism and the politics of higher education policy in Indonesia. *Comparative Education*, 52(2), 109–135. doi:10.1080/03050068.2015.1112566.

Salmi, J. (2019). Academic governance and leadership in Vietnam: Trends and challenges. *Journal of International and Comparative Education*, 8(2), 103–118.

Saigol, R. (2003). *Becoming a modern nation: Educational discourse in the early years of Ayub Khan*. Islamabad: Council of Social Sciences.

Sanyal, B. C., & Martin, M. (2007). Quality assurance and the role of accreditation: An overview. In J. Tres (Ed.), *Higher education in the world 2007: Accreditation for quality assurance: What is at stake?* (pp. 3–17). New York: Palgrave Macmillan.

Schriewer, J. (2000). World system and interrelationship networks: The internationalization of education and the role of comparative inquiry. In T. S. Popkewitz (Ed.), *Educational knowledge: Changing relationships between the state, civil society, and the educational community* (pp. 305–343). Albany: State University of New York Press.

Schultz, T. W. (1960). Capital formation by education. *The Journal of Political Economy*, 68(6), 571–583.

Schultz, T. W. (1961). Investment in human capital. *The American Economic Review*, 51 (1), 1–17.

Selwyn, N. (2013). Researching the once-powerful in education: The value of retrospective elite interviewing in education policy research. *Journal of Education Policy*, 28(3), 339–352. doi:10.1080/02680939.2012.728630.

Shohat, E. (1992). Notes on the "post-colonial". *Social Text*, 31/32, 99–113.

Sidhu, R. K. (2005). *Universities and globalization: To market, to market*. Mahwah, NJ: Lawrence Erlbaum Associates.

Sidhu, R., Ho, K. C., & Yeoh, B. (2011). Emerging education hubs: The case of Singapore. *Higher Education*, 61(1), 23–40.

Singh, R. P. (1989). *Educating the Indian elite*. Bangalore: Sterling Publishers.

Sivalingam, G. (2006), Privatization of higher education in Malaysia. The Forum of Public Policy. Retrieved from www.forumonpublicpolicy.com.

Slaughter, S., & Rhoades, G. (2004). *Academic capitalism and the new economy: Markets, state, and higher education*. Baltimore & London: The Johns Hopkins University Press.

Smith, D. (1990). *Texts, facts, and femininity: Exploring the relations of ruling*. London: Routledge.

South Asian University (2020). About the university. Retrieved from www.sau.int/about/about-sau.html.

Spivak, G. (1990). *The post-colonial critic: Interviews, strategies, dialogues*. New York & London: Routledge.

Spivak, G. (1999). *A critique of postcolonial reason: Toward a critique of the vanishing present*. Cambridge MA: Harvard University Press.

Stake, R. E. (2008). Qualitative case study. In N. K. Denzin, & Y. S. Lincoln (Eds.), *Strategies of qualitative inquiry* (pp. 119–149). London: Sage Publications.

St. George, E. (2010). Higher education in Vietnam 1986–1998: Education in transition to a new era? In G. Harman et al. (Eds.), *Reforming higher education in Vietnam: Challenges and priorities*. doi:10.1007/978-90-481-3694-0_3.

Steger, M. B., & Roy, R. K. (2010). *Neoliberalism: A very short introduction*. New York: Oxford University Press.

Steiner-Khamsi, G. (2004). Globalization in education: Real or imagined. In G. Steiner-Khamsi (Ed.), *The global politics of educational borrowing and lending* (pp. 1–28). New York & London: Teachers College Press.

Steiner-Khamsi, G. (2006). The economics of policy borrowing and lending: A study of late adopters. *Oxford Review of Education*, 32(5), 665–678.

Swanborn, P. (2010). *Case study research: What, why and how?*Los Angeles, London, New Delhi, Singapore & Washington DC: Sage.

Thanglong University (2020). History of the Thanglong University. Retrieved from https://en.thanglong.edu.vn/about-tlu/2014-03-17-06-58-58/history-of-the-thang-long-university/148-about-tlu/profile/history.

Transparency International Bangladesh (TIB) (2014). Besorkary bisshobiddaloy: Sushoner jonno challenge abong uttoroner upai [Private Universities: Challenges for good governance, and a way forward]. Retrieved from www.ti-bangladesh.org/beta3/images/2014/es_ds_private-univ_14_bn.pd.

The Bangla News (2020). Evening Course: 75 kotite acatta banijjo onusheder shikkhok ra. Retrieved from www.banglanews24.com/education/news/bd/773285.details.

The BD News 24 (2008). Teachers, students farewell Jagannath University VC. Retrieved from https://bdnews24.com/bangladesh/2008/07/26/teachers-students-farewell-jagannath-university-vc.

The BD News 24 (2020). Sandho course niye jothajotho bebostha neya hobe: prodhan montri. Retrieved from https://bangla.bdnews24.com/bangladesh/article1723324.bdnews.

The Bonik Barta (2020). Shandho course niye bipake dhaka bisshobiddoloy. Retrieved from https://bonikbarta.net/home/news_description/221503/.

The Daily Star (2009). Student loans, not so. Retrieved from www.thedailystar.net/news-detail-73210.

The Daily Star (2017). Halda River Research Lab launched. Retrieved from www.thedailystar.net/city/halda-river-research-lab-launched-cu-1451623.

The Daily Star (2019). UGC orders closure of evening courses at all public universities. Retrieved from www.thedailystar.net/country/ugc-orders-closure-evening-courses-all-public-universities-1838896.

Tilak, J. B. (1991). The privatization of higher education. *Prospects*, 21(2), 227–239.

Tilak, J. B. (2006). *Private higher education: Philanthropy to profits. Report on higher education in the world 2006: The financing of the universities* (pp. 113–121). Barcelona: GUNI.

Tilak, J. B. (2014). Private higher education in India. *Economic and Political Weekly*, 49 (40), 1–11.

Tilak, J. B. (2020). Dilemmas in reforming higher education in India. *Higher Education for the Future*, 7(1), 54–66.

Torres, C. A. (2009). *Education and neoliberal globalization*. New York: Routledge.

Trow, M. (1973). *Problems in the transition from elite to mass higher education*. Paper presented to the Conference on Higher Education held by the Organisation for Economic Cooperation and Development in Paris

University of Dhaka (1996). The second statutes of the University: The statute regarding the Institute of Education and Research. Retrieved from www.du.ac.bd/download/statutes/DU-2nd-Statutes.pdf.

University of Dhaka (2020). Dhaka University at a glance. Retrieved from www.du.ac.bd/main_menu/the_university/du_at_a_glance.

University Grants Commission of Bangladesh (2006). *Strategic Plan for Higher Education*. Dhaka: University Grants Commission.

University Grants Commission (2009a). *Handbook: Universities of Bangladesh*. Dhaka: University Grants Commission.

University Grants Commission (2009b). *Higher education quality enhancement project: Operational manual for academic innovation fund* (pp. 1–246). Dhaka: University Grants Commission.

University Grants Commission of Bangladesh (2017). *Strategic Plan for Higher Education*. Dhaka: University Grants Commission.

University Grants Commission of Bangladesh (2018a). *Bangladeshe ucchoshikkhai orjon* [Achievement of Higher Education in Bangladesh]. Dhaka: University Grants Commission.

University Grants Commission of Bangladesh (2018b). *Chuallishtomo barshik protibedon 2017* [44th Annual Report 2017]. Dhaka: University Grants Commission.

University Grants Commission of Bangladesh (2019). Names of public universities and approval dates. Retrieved from http://ugc.portal.gov.bd/sites/default/files/files/ugc.portal.gov.bd/legislative_information/a50e2260_72ca_4084_9e04_bbfafd4473ca/Public_University_10_09_2018.pdf.

University Grants Commission of Sri Lanka (2020). Universities and higher education institutions established under the purview of the University Grants Commission. Retrieved from www.ugc.ac.lk/en/universities-and-institutes/universities.html.

University of Nottingham Ningbo China (n.d.). About the university. Retrieved from www.nottingham.edu.cn/en/About/Who-we-are.aspx.

Vats, A. (2008). *Development of education in India*. Delhi: Saurabh Publishing House.

Ward, S. C. (2012). *Neoliberalism and the global restructuring of knowledge and education*. New York: Routledge.

Webster, R. S., & Ryan, A. (2019). *Understanding curriculum: The Australian context*. Melbourne: Cambridge University Press.

Webster, R. S., & Whelen, J. (2019). The importance of rethinking reflection and ethics for education. In R. S. Webster, & J. Whelen (Eds.), *Rethinking Reflection And Ethics for teachers* (pp. 1–12). Singapore: Springer.

Westerheijden, D. F., Stensaker, B., & Rosa, M. J. (2007). *Quality assurance in higher education: Trends in regulation, translation and transformation* (Vol. 20). Dordrecht: Springer.

World Bank (2009). *Bangladesh higher education quality enhancement project: Project appraisal document*. Washington DC: World Bank.

Wickramasinghe, V. (2018). Higher education in state universities in Sri Lanka: Review of higher education since colonial past through international funding for development. *International Journal of Educational Management*, 32(3), 463–478.

Wright, U. T., & Rocco, T. S. (2016). Institutional ethnography: A holistic approach to understanding systems. *International Journal of Adult Vocational Education and Technology (IJAVET)*, 7(3), 27–41. doi:10.4018/IJAVET.2016070103.

Yin, R. K. (2009). *Case study research: Design and methods*. Thousand Oaks & London: Sage Publications.

Zastoupil, L., & Moir, M. (1999). *The great Indian education debate: Documents relating to the Orientalist-Anglicist controversy, 1781–1843*. Surrey: Curzon Press.

Index

Page numbers in **bold** refer to tables.